EMANCIPATION STILL COMIN'

EMANCIPATION STILL COMIN'

Explorations in Caribbean
Emancipatory Theology

Kortright Davis

ORBIS BOOKS

Maryknoll, New York 10545

*Dedicated in grateful and loving memory
of my mother
Florence Edna Clarke*

Second Printing, July 1990

The Catholic Foreign Mission Society of America (Maryknoll) recruits and trains people for overseas missionary service. Through Orbis Books, Maryknoll aims to foster the international dialogue that is essential to mission. The books published, however, reflect the opinions of their authors and are not meant to represent the official position of the society.

Published in the United States of America by Orbis Books, Maryknoll, New York 10545
©1990, Orbis Books, Maryknoll, New York 10545
All rights reserved.

Library of Congress Cataloging-in Publication Data

Davis, Kortright.
    Emancipation still comin' : explorations in Caribbean emancipatory theology / Kortright Davis.
        p.   cm.
    Includes bibliographical references.
    ISBN 0-88344-672-3
    1. Liberation theology.   2. Theology, Doctrinal—Caribbean Area.
3. Caribbean Area—Church history—20th century.   I. Title.
BT83.57.D38   1990
230'.09729—dc20   89-77601
                                                                    CIP

CONTENTS

PREFACE

This book has been in preparation for the last ten years. It represents the culmination of many stages of exploration, reflection, research, and dialogue. At one stage, the manuscript that I submitted to Orbis Books covered a much wider spectrum of action for emancipation in the Third World. That earlier effort did not afford my own region, the Caribbean, the intense study it deserved, especially since very little has been published in this area to date. I am therefore grateful to Orbis for encouraging me to shift the focus.

Yet, in shifting the focus, I have not lessened my conviction that peoples across the world who acknowledge their need for greater freedom from all forms of oppression must pick up on each other's story and own it as best they can. The feelings of suspicion and distrust among the oppressed peoples of the world continue to linger cancerously; and whatever lines of communication, or links of solidarity, can be forged should be effectuated with urgency and commitment. The common solidarity against South African apartheid, which is globally shared by people of African descent in particular, must equally be matched by a common solidarity against the internal apartheid of our own making.

Accidents of birth, variations in accent or language, and differences in cultural heritage should not hinder the vision of radical change for the better, or the rights of all our people to be free. The exploration of the contextual connections has therefore been of utmost importance to me, as I have sought to interpret some of the inner realities of Caribbean existence to a wider audience. Chapters Four and Eight are particularly concerned with these connections, while the first three chapters examine the Caribbean context in its changing manifestations. Chapters Five, Six, and Seven offer some specific historical and theological reflections on the Caribbean religious enterprise.

Most of the material in Chapters Six and Seven has appeared in previous articles in the *Journal of Religious Thought*, and I am grateful for the editor's permission to modify them for this book. Chapter Four is essentially the text of the public lecture I delivered in Bridgetown, Barbados, in October 1988, when my former university (the University of the West Indies) invited me to speak at the ceremony marking its fortieth anniversary and the twenty-fifth anniversary of the Cave Hill Campus. I extend to the university's faculty my abiding gratitude, not only for this honor but also for the intellectual formation that accompanied my period of research and study toward a master's degree in Caribbean history.

Finally, so many persons gave invaluable assistance in the final stages of preparation of this work that by naming some I run the risk of neglecting to mention others. I have therefore chosen simply to say to my wife, my children, my close friends and associates, the members of the Holy Comforter congregation (in Washington, D.C.), my colleagues, students at the Howard University School of Divinity, and the courteous and helpful editorial staff at Orbis—thank you all for your support and encouragement. Throughout this work, I have come to know more truly what St. Paul must have meant when he thundered to the Christians in Galatia: "For freedom Christ has set us free; stand fast therefore" (Galatians 5:1).

INTRODUCTION

Caribbean existence is full of many mysteries, in the most basic sense of that word. A mystery is essentially something hidden—not so hidden that it cannot evoke wonder and amazement, but hidden in the sense that we do not understand too much about it. No one can ever satisfactorily explain how Caribbean people have managed to survive in the way that they have. No one can ever assume full knowledge of Caribbean realities, even if one was born and raised in the region; for there is still so much around, or beneath, or beyond (particularly one's own shores) that exceeds one's grasp. The Caribbean context is so elusive that nothing short of divine wisdom could enable one to put all its pieces together.

Somewhere in the midst of that strange context there exists a fertile tension between human paradox and divine possibility. When people on the outside confidently assert that Caribbean people just cannot thrive, a deep, yet sharply persistent, voice counters that they can. Caribbean people are not quite sure whose voice it is, or why it persists in the face of apparently overwhelming circumstances to the contrary, but they settle for the conviction that it must be the voice of God. It must be the voice of God, they say, lingering in the harsh realities of their context; for the realities have always been harsh anyway, and yet the people have somehow managed to keep their faith alive and their humanity intact; and they cannot explain how.

So God moves in a mysterious way throughout the Caribbean, performing wonders of every kind and returning to the sons and daughters of its soil the hope that springs eternal in the face of threatened hopelessness. Caribbean people do not seem to give up; they do not even like to give in. They stubbornly refuse to be intimidated by anyone or anything—even by forces beyond their control. Natural resources may be limited; technical skills may be lured away to greener pastures; external powers may induce patterns of alienation and dependence, which assault and hurt the Caribbean soul; weaker minds may be won over to imitating the ways and wishes of the stranger. Yet there lies within the Caribbean heart a common love of that freedom to which the persistent voice beckons them all. Emancipation rises out of its own context. The people live out their freedom in their own way.

Emancipation is the major thrust of Caribbean existence, however much the signs of its authenticity may be obscured. Emancipation is the common project of those whose lives have been constantly encumbered by structures of poverty, dependence, alienation, and imitation. Emancipation has been the common bond that has welded together Caribbean struggles for the better life—whether through education, emigration, or plain perspiration. Emancipation has been the vision of God in the context of Caribbean history; for every time the Caribbean was written off as a sure and certain Gehenna, God seemed to answer with a greater certainty of survival and meaning for the region. One writer after another gives in to cynical disdain and despair about the region and its people: "They will never create." "They are the Third World's Third World." "They are the children of Sisyphus." "They are the wretched of the earth." The seeds of divine emancipation still germinate, however, and the people maintain their determination to survive and to surge forward toward a greater experience of freedom.

That is the underlying theme of the current study. It is an attempt to interpret contextually the meaning of human freedom in the light of a popular faith in the God of Jesus Christ, whose Gospel of liberation and whose life of historical confrontation have constantly inspired and strengthened such faith. All the realities of the Caribbean context have been brought into the process of reflection: history, culture, economics, politics, social relationships, demography, external relations, and religion. There are no statistical analyses or technical computations about the people and their efforts to assert their humanity and reconstruct their society. The present emphasis is on the English-speaking Caribbean, but many features of the discussion would find ample currency in any of the four language areas of the region.

The study is primarily based on my own research, reflections, and actual acquaintance with the region. I was born on the island of Antigua, trained for the Anglican priesthood in Barbados, and employed extensively throughout the region for nearly twenty years. I consider myself a Caribbean person, and therefore write intensely about what such a consciousness should mean for all who love the region and would treasure it as God's happy acre. Readers familiar with the region will find many general assertions that might seem to demand some qualification. The more they find, the better it is for engaging in an ongoing dialogue, for there has been very little dialogue about many of the issues raised in this work.

The Caribbean is clearly experiencing a traumatic period of transition— politically, culturally, economically, and religiously. Several attempts are being made to define the nature of the trauma and the extent of the transition. It is the theologian's task to offer a framework whereby the Caribbean experience can be presented in the light of Caribbean faith. That historical faith has brought Caribbean people from a "mighty long way"; without it, the future might be ominous indeed.

The future of Caribbean emancipation is guaranteed by the unmistakable experiences of God's emancipation in the past. That future will be a shared experience with other peoples, who, in other corners of the globe, also struggle for the concrete meaning of freedom in the light of their own historical faith. Contextual connections are both viable and valuable; the bridges of understanding between oppressed and estranged people on the underside of modern history must be built and kept strong; and all those who have sown in tears for so long must bind themselves together in full assurance of their harvest of freedom and joy.

Here, then, are the possible foundations of a new and dynamic emancipatory theology for the Caribbean. They set the stage for further exploration of the Christian profession of faith through the use of sources indigenous to the region—most notably, the common folk wisdom that has sustained God's people in the Caribbean for over 350 years. Such an exploration will require the renewed patience and insight that would inspire another book. That work will come in time, if circumstances so permit. In the meantime, I offer this present work as the fruit of a prolonged and sustained process of interaction and reflection. I trust that it will serve as a useful contribution to the creative imagination of all those who share the vision of God's basic design—namely, that all oppressed peoples should be set free.

CHAPTER ONE

SUN AND PEOPLE, LAND AND SEA

The Caribbean sun is the world's best friend. It is warm, bright, regular, strong, dependable, functional, friendly, funny, and liberating. You can play games with it. You can predict its "movements" and its changes of hue. You can wink with it, talk to it, hide from it, curse it, and even harness it. It gives you a green flash as it disappears under the horizon of the blue ocean, and it gives you a yellow beam as it makes its way up over the opposite horizon the next morning. It is ever faithful, ever sure. It conveys a most powerful and concrete idea of what God must be like.

No wonder people of old worshiped the sun as a deity. This was what I often thought to myself as I stood on the edge of the lawn of my seminary campus, high over the Atlantic, and looked out toward the East, facing the rising sun. I often stood alone, in silent meditation, breathing in the fresh breezes from the ocean below. No land came between the shores beneath me and the shores of Africa. If only I could get into a boat, I thought — not one as small as the fishing boats just leaving port to make the day's catch but a boat capable of taking me across the sea — I could reach the shores of the mother country, Africa, over which the sun had already risen that morning.

My seminary, Codrington College, was located on the island of Barbados in the parish of St. John. It had been built some two centuries before on lands bequeathed by Christopher Codrington, an Englishman born in Barbados. He had stipulated that two sugar estates on the island of Barbados should be maintained by a labor force of some three hundred slaves and that the college should be supported from the profits of that enterprise. The college was to train persons in physic, chirurgery, and divinity. I was being trained in divinity, but not in physic or chirurgery. The only link I had with the slave labor he bequeathed was that I was being awakened each morning by the large bell which had most likely summoned the slaves to work on the plantations. At least, that was what I thought.

The Anglican church in the Caribbean had been struggling to maintain the seminary with a large inflow of resources from outside the region. During my period of training, 1961 to 1966, I was trained by a religious order from Britain, the Community of the Resurrection. The regimen of training was obviously patterned along monastic lines, to which the mem-

1

bers of the order had already committed their lives. Although as students we had no intention of becoming monks, but only priests of the church, we still found ourselves being rigidly disciplined along monastic-like rules. The rule of silence was one such rule, and that was why I stood in silence on the edge of the lawn looking at the rising sun. I was not expected to speak to my fellow students until the silence ended after the celebration of the Mass.

I therefore formed a spiritual community of my own on the edge of that lawn. It was comprised of person, land, sea, and sun. However much I would have wished to speak to others, I was conscious that the land on which the slaves had once labored, the sea which had brought my ancestors from the motherland on the other shore, and the sun which linked me with all those on the other side proffered a major discourse of their own. Further, the chirping of the birds and the noise of the waves breaking on the rocks below tended to make human speech superfluous. Perhaps, then, my tutors were right in insisting on such silence at the start of the day. It was a double-edged silence. It both liberated and domesticated me at the same time. It liberated me to share in that discourse between sun, sea, land, and people, without unnecessary interruptions. It made me feel bound to a particular form of discipline in the church and its institutions, which created a distance between me and the way in which my Caribbean people generally operated. We are a noisy people. Silence is sometimes a serious form of bondage for us; but silence is also golden at times. In silence, then, I mused at the golden sun, which was totally free to roam over the whole blue heaven each day and to radiate some sense of order, light, and freedom on the sea, the land, and the people. That was why I regarded the Caribbean sun as the world's best friend.

The Caribbean sun spells freedom, but freedom is still an elusive quality in the Caribbean. The same sun that guided the Europeans across the Atlantic from economic bondage to prosperity on Caribbean plantations also guided the slave ships with my ancestors from freedom to bondage on the same plantations. Such was the paradox until the early nineteenth century, when emancipation from enforced servitude was decreed. The paradox continues in another form; for, although the people have been freed, they are still oddly enchained. The people of the land have yet to become the owners of the land. The power of the sun and the riches of the sea are still to be harnessed in their favor. The project of emancipation is not yet fully on the way. It is therefore a fundamental theme of this book that the major force which Caribbean people have to call their own, religion, must become the primary instrument for their active engagement in the reconstruction and historical emancipation of their society. A new force of emancipation must emerge out of the realities of their sociocultural and historical context.

THE CARIBBEAN CONDITION

Every Caribbean plantation was fundamentally an extension of a metropolitan manor or estate, rather than a segment of an islandic community.

Thus, there were not only many Caribbean islands within the region but also, practically speaking, many islands within each island. The systems of slavery and indentureship, undergirded by a unique and rigid policy of colonial domination, provided the groundwork for a mosaic of racism and social contempt. The only point on which consensus and common principle could be expected was the importance of the crop for all people everywhere—both near and far.

Plantation economy, ideology, sociology, politics, ethics, and theology are all based on one cardinal truth: The land is divine. The land is that from which all life and livelihood spring. It produces sustenance and profit. It creates hope and fulfills it. It certifies power and exercises it. It withstands the demons of disaster and restores the wealth of foreparents to generations and generations. It determines being and nothingness, as it separates the "haves" from the "have-mores" and the poor from the full knowledge of their own poverty. Land means permanence. It generates the spirit of rootage and gives to its owners a sense of place. It dispels the rootlessness of living and defies the human search for peace in detachment or escape. It is the sign of security and freedom. It is the germ of prosperity.

Land is power, and they who own the land possess the means of defining and controlling the fate of those who do not. To live on land that is owned and controlled by another is essentially a hazardous and problem-filled form of existence. Most of the Caribbean people have had to exist on lands belonging to others, lands in which they could plant no seeds of prosperity, or power, or pride. They could not love the land when the land did not belong to them. They could not respond to a "God" who had not called them to "inherit" or "possess" the land. They had no Canaan.

The importance of the ownership of land cannot be overemphasized in any analysis of the social, historical, political, or economic realities of a people. Even today, land disputes of every sort abound, from Guyana (and Venezuela and Suriname) in the southeast to Belize (and Guatemala and Britain) in the northwest. But the Caribbean story is unlike many other stories because, historically, there has been a great deal of absenteeism among the landowners. Most of the plantation owners hardly ever set foot on their plantations, and chose rather to luxuriate in the metropole. Absenteeism has been a curse in Caribbean history. It has produced so many ill effects in the entire social, political, and economic fabric of these societies that the task of social reconstruction is retarded and threatened by the unresolved question of who really owns what. Questions such as these are still to be answered: How much of the Caribbean is still mortgaged to external sources? How much of the power exercised in the Caribbean is actually controlled by higher powers outside? Why is the gap between formal authority and actual power widening rather than narrowing? The Caribbean today has become a proving ground for various experiments in neocolonialism—transnational corporations, transistors, Japanese vehicles, tracking stations, satellite dishes, foreign television, military exercises, millions of tourists, and off-shore banking schemes.

It is in the light of all these considerations that the realities of the Caribbean condition have to be understood. They explain why the current structures of poverty continue to be overlaid with a veneer of progress instead of being dismantled altogether; why the prospects for the sharing of power among the broad masses of landless people are neither nearer nor clearer; why formal political independence has essentially ushered in new forms of structured economic dependence; and why the ideals of racial, cultural, and regional integration are ignored more often than they are pursued. The process of underdevelopment, which began in 1492, has never been substantially challenged. The only major shifts in the region have been from one form of dependence to another.

The Caribbean is an open space, with no exits or entrances. There are no curtains to be drawn to shut off the outside world. Indeed, the Caribbean's *raison d'être* lies in its umbilical connections with the outside world, to such a degree that global consciousness often takes precedence over local consciousness. Caribbean people are thus a migrant people, moving "forward" and leaving nothing behind to which they need return. To move up often means to move out. They carry their belongings and their sense of belonging with them. Their creative energies fructify their existence, and they measure their growth in terms of lessening discomfort and augmenting security. Their chief resources are their wits and their spirit. But where is their God?

THE ABSENTEE GOD

Caribbean plantations and institutions were generally managed over the years by a level of leadership that lacked absolute power or high quality. The real owners of the Caribbean lived away from the Caribbean, and they left the care and control of their property—both human and material—to generally inferior mortals. Thus, the people heard of distant owners but managed only to see their subordinates in the flesh. The overlordship of the Caribbean was executed by remote mechanisms, while the on-the-spot authority wielded limited power and manipulated naked privilege. Mediocrity never surpassed itself. Human excellence never gained admittance. The structures of Truth and Beauty and Goodness assumed an inimitable creolized flavor. Within this Caribbean incubator of human depravity, the Europeans set their "God" to work.

That "God" was to sanction and protect everything that the Europeans had designed and implemented. That "God" was to vacillate between right and wrong, justice and injustice, humanity and inhumanity, according to the circumstances. That "God" was to ensure that the plantation ethic flourished in the hearts and minds of all who had to depend on the crop. That "God" was to transform and reorient all factors—whether physical or metaphysical—toward the attainment of an ever bountiful profit. That "God" was to be a trader of goods and services of all kinds. Under so heavy a burden, that "God" could not survive. That "God" died from suffocation.

The God who met with Moses at the burning bush in Africa met with the Africans in the Caribbean at the burning bush of slavery. God stayed in the wilderness of their hearts and bluntly refused to be enshrined anywhere. So the people worshiped one deity with their lips, and another—their real God—in their hearts. This was the absentee God, the *deus absconditus*, whose absolute power and overlordship enabled men and women to be burned by slavery without being consumed. They worshiped God secretly and quietly in their own way. Sometimes they worshiped together in the ceremonies which they knew best; at other times they worshiped alone in the fields or in the huts. Their masters kept them apart from one another as much as they could, but they could not intercept the flow of that cultural and spiritual substream in their lives through which one day the *deus absconditus* would become the *deus revelatus*.

THE CARIBBEAN PEOPLE

Most of the people who now live in the region are not the descendants of its original inhabitants. The original inhabitants were Amerindians, the Arawaks and Caribs. The Caribs populated the eastern Caribbean (notice the derivation of the region's name from these people), while the Arawaks lived in the northern parts, mainly the Bahamas and the Greater Antilles. The Caribs were said to be more aggressive than the Arawaks. Christopher Columbus found them to be widely cannibalistic. He spoke of them as a "wild people fit for any work, well proportioned, and very intelligent, and who, when they have got rid of their cruel habits to which they have been accustomed, will be better than any other kind of slaves."[1] Eric Williams, the late Trinidadian historian, aptly notes that the slave trade really began as an outward movement from the region; for in 1498, on his third voyage, Columbus shipped six hundred Indians back to Spain.[2]

Although the Arawaks were eventually eliminated by the Spaniards, the French and the British colonizers had a more difficult time with the Caribs. Attempts by the British to settle in St. Lucia in 1605, and in Grenada in 1609, were repelled by the Caribs. The Caribs also frequently attacked the British when they attempted to settle in Antigua, St. Kitts, and Montserrat. In the end, the French prevailed over the Caribs in Grenada; and the Caribs then hurled themselves into the sea rather than be captured by the French. Caribs survived in the mountainous terrains of St. Vincent and Dominica. Today, descendants of Caribs still thrive in those countries with faint vestiges of their cultural and ethnic heritage.

The Caribbean is therefore peopled by those who have originated elsewhere, and who have brought with them the roots of conflicting cultures. Europeans have always thought of themselves as being extensions of their motherland, while Africans and Indians have struggled to cope with the realities of being displaced persons. Although the sun and the sea have been common denominators in the consciousness of the people, and have created something of a melting pot for the creolization of the societies, the land and the people have tended to retain such distinctions as have perpetuated structures of power, class, race, and freedom. The Europeans and their descendants have held the ascendancy, while the Africans and their descendants have been struggling to gain it. Caribbean peoples have thus been constantly engaged in a struggle for the ascendancy of power, control, and emancipation. Domination and dependence have been incessantly at work in a historical dialectic of social conflict, and colonialism has renewed itself in a pattern of neocolonialism, under the guise of formal independence. As the twentieth century draws to its close, then, the Caribbean population, made up largely of African and Indian stock, is still encumbered with poverty, dependence, alienation, and grave uncertainties. The struggle for emancipation is not from slavery on the plantations; it is rather from the slavery of neocolonialism and inertia.

Caribbean institutions have developed mainly along the patterns bequeathed to them from their European pioneers. The school, the church, the public service, and the judiciary have all sustained a close allegiance to the historical antecedents through which they were nurtured in former times. The people of the Caribbean have not yet taken hold of the basic roots of their own institutions, and therefore have been unable to transform their existence toward an emancipatory and affirmative dynamic. Initiatives in the region are still circumscribed by external reactions and implications, and efforts at indigenization are never advanced far beyond the sphere of the approval of extraregional powers. Part of the Caribbean bondage therefore subsists in the spectacle of people who, instead of governing their institutions, are governed and controlled by those institutions.

Nevertheless, there exists in the region a vast wealth of cultural resources that cannot be measured in terms of economic or political value. These resources lie deep in the hearts and lives of the people, and they sustain these people even in their darkest moments. The cultural substreams have been strengthened because the people have had to rely on them to counter oppressive systems of social control and estrangement from institutional benefits. For Caribbean people, religion has had to play a major role in the art of survival.

It must also be borne in mind that there are many Caribbeans in the region. The traditional distinction between the Greater Antilles and the Lesser Antilles can be further expanded by the distribution of the four major language areas—French, Spanish, Dutch, and English. Communication among these four areas is not as easy or active as their geography might suggest. Because each of the European colonial powers held its territories in a strong grasp, the various inhabitants lived in mutual suspicion and ignorance of each other's circumstances within the region. Thus, it is very rare that any writer on the Caribbean attempts to write with equal emphasis and interest on each language area. This book will therefore be mainly focused on the Commonwealth Caribbean—that is, the English-speaking areas, or the former British territories. We shall have occasion to refer to some non-English-speaking countries, such as Haiti and Cuba; but the study will draw largely on the realities of the Anglo-Caribbean and the dominant sector of that grouping, the Afro-Caribbeans—although the issues we will address are not peculiar to this group of Caribbean countries. One country is much like another in its demographic components and socio-economic conditions. Differences lie mainly in self-perception or in histor-ical linkages to European, or North American, centers of power. My own background, experience, and expertise happen to be Afro-Caribbean, and I have therefore confined the study to the area with which I am most familiar.

Caribbean existence is unparalleled anywhere else in the whole wide world. It cannot be surpassed for its widely ranging contrasts in human livelihood, social experimentation, political adventure, religious expression, and cultural activity. The region consists of various contexts in which dif-ferent groups of people possess varying opportunities and resources, many of whom experience diminishing returns while they nurture rising expec-tations. It is a heterogeneous region. Such is the range of differences that even the term "Caribbean" itself often means different things to different people. For example, some Guyanese citizens prefer to regard themselves as South American rather than as Caribbean, simply because their country is situated on the South American mainland, or because there is greater prestige in claiming such a designation. Some Bahamians are not always sure whether they should identify themselves as Caribbean persons, chiefly because they live close to the North American mainland and many of their cultural preferences and economic activities are conditioned by what hap-pens in the United States. Puerto Ricans regard themselves as Puerto Ricans first; then as Hispanic Caribbeans; and, finally, as United States citizens.

Even on the international scene there is often some ambivalence about how the Caribbean should be identified. The general tendency of linking the Caribbean with Latin America has not always found wholehearted sup-port from Latin Americans or from the Caribbean representatives. Tensions are sometimes in evidence in the affairs of the Organization of American States (OAS), where some Caribbean countries attempt to assert their non-Latin historical and political outlook, or where some Latins accentuate their sociopolitical differences from Anglo-Caribbean cultures. In United Nations debates, most Caribbean countries usually identify more with their African counterparts than with their Latin American neighbors. The failure of the Barbados representative to be elected president of the United Nations General Assembly was partly attributed to the lack of support from the Latin Americans. We shall deal with the problem of Caribbean frag-mentation in Chapter Three.

THE CARIBBEAN SEARCH FOR FREEDOM

Among the least contentious aspects of Christian theological discourse is the assertion that God is sovereign. God as the First Cause, or the Omnipotent Creator, has been beyond contention and substitution in the minds of most Christian thinkers. This sovereignty has been traditionally expressed in terms of a God who is answerable to no higher level of being. Hence, we refer to God as Ultimate Reality. Oddly enough, the sovereignty of God has not always denoted the inherent freedom of God. Ultimate Reality has not always been translated into terms of ultimate and unconditional freedom for God.

At times in the history of the West, the sovereign God has been made to look less than sovereign through an apparent reluctance to exercise impartial and unconditional sovereignty over divine choice, divine favor, divine selection and privilege, or even over the availability of divine grace. Under such circumstances, the nature of God becomes subject to the predilections of those who would seem to determine, or control, the definition of such a nature; moreover, the very fact of God has sometimes been rendered highly questionable and suspect. In the final analysis, Christians either behave as if they believe that humanity is created in the image of God, or else they practice an ideology which affirms that God is merely an image of human creativity.

Divine sovereignty spells divine freedom. Human freedom subsists in the continuing affirmation of divine freedom, and in the human response to the perceived call from God to be free. Freedom, then, is not merely the nature of God; it is also the will of God. God wills that all human beings should be free, and the absence of that freedom raises questions about the nature of God's sovereignty in accomplishing God's will, and about the capacity of the human response to overcome conditions of bondage. It is the fundamental theme of this book that the only freedom deep enough to offer and inspire emancipation, and authentic enough to be concretely functional, is essentially that which actively acknowledges its origins in the sovereign free God.

Freedom has historically been taken to mean many things, or to be associated with several different causes. Plato, for example, associated freedom with intelligent and educated judgment; Thomas Hobbes regarded the law as the guarantor of freedom, and Jean-Jacques Rousseau regarded freedom as deliverance from the bondage of the artificial network of legal conventions.[3] More recently, Howard Thurman has defined freedom as a sense of alternatives; without an alternative, there is no freedom.[4] Others have equated freedom with the assertion of oneself and one's will against strong obstacles, or with disengagement or commitment in the light of prevailing circumstances. Robert Neville makes a distinction between personal, social, and religious dimensions of freedom:

Personal freedom has to do with the structures or capacities or ways of life that can be considered in relative abstraction from the person's social and religious context. Social freedom has to do with the dimensions of freedom individuals have particularly because they participate in social groups. Religious freedom has to do with the experience of transcending the ordinary world of experience and returning to it without being bound by it; this experience is religious insofar as it is possible because of some particular connection with God.[5]

Neville further outlines what he considers to be four basic dimensions of personal freedom: "external liberty, freedom of intentional action, freedom of choice, and creativity."[6] He describes creative activity as "prehensive, deliberative, and a matter of agency."[7] With respect to social freedom, he suggests four parallel dimensions: freedom of opportunity, social pluralism, freedom of integral social life, and participatory democracy. Under the rubric of opportunity, Neville outlines three opportunities of culture which he considers most important for social freedom: freedom to have a historical heritage, freedom to enjoy a high culture, and freedom to use one's cultural experience in social interactions.[8]

It seems to me, however, that freedom itself must transcend categories and dimensions; it must integrate every aspect of human experience and aspiration, and it must be so transparently appropriate to all sorts and conditions of humanity that no sector should be bound by the dictates and definitions of another. The human condition should always convey the concrete demands of freedom as the goal of human striving and social interaction. Intentionality, opportunity, creativity and sociality are involved here, but the value placed on each aspect of the human endeavor will always be determined by the context of that endeavor, as well as by the commitment to spiritual transformation and cultural enrichment at the highest possible level. There are, therefore, priorities for freedom rather than dimensions or categories of freedom, and these priorities are directly related to the context in which the human person has to exist. Who determines those priorities, and who presides over their configuration, is the question that lies at the root of human conflict and social discomfort. It is also the question that germinates seeds of revolution and social change. More significantly, however, it is the question that energizes the spiritual quest for religious meaning and self-fulfillment. Thus, because freedom has different emphases with different people, different cultures, and different contexts, the reconstruction of social and religious reality will itself differ quite significantly in different contexts. Theological initiatives therefore respond appropriately to the contextual priorities for freedom.

Theology is a science for freedom. Its initiatives are therefore related to the search for understanding the relationship between faith and freedom. Faith is human, but freedom is not generated by human beings. Theologically understood, freedom is the gift of God because it is the nature of

God. Theology has its own rules, which are not exchangeable with other methods. Theology must possess an integrity of its own; and in their search for theological integrity, many Christians recently have been forced to question the presumed alliance between Western culture and Christian theology.

Given the realities of the Caribbean condition, Caribbean institutions, and the complexities of Caribbean populations, what are the fundamental bases on which the meaning of freedom in the Caribbean can seriously be addressed? If life in the region is typified by the game of cricket (known by its admirers as the "game of glorious uncertainties"), and if poverty and dependence continue unabated in spite of gallant efforts to redress such conditions, what are the real prospects for identifying a sphere of genuine freedom among Caribbean people?

Christians who have begun to renounce their received historical structures of domination and dependence, alienation and poverty, have also begun to reject the theological and ideological structures of thought, belief, and practice with which their lives have been so long encumbered. They have begun to take the initiative in raising political, historical, economic, and cultural questions about truth—questions about salvation in all its ramifications; and questions about the relationship between salvific truth and human freedom. The key word has been neither "salvation" nor "freedom," for these have borne the burden and heat of the Western political and ideological sun. The key word has been either "liberation" or "emancipation." The word has served to bring together the meaning of political and historical action for change and the new understanding of the theological priorities for change.

This book is an attempt to demonstrate theologically that, in spite of the prevailing conditions, many features of Caribbean existence already spell freedom and hope. There is sufficient ground for a theology of liberation that is already on the way in the Caribbean. Much of what the people have been engaged in has had some emancipatory dimensions. The principal forces have been their cultural and religious strengths. Whenever organized religion has attempted to make full use of the religious wellspring of Caribbean people, without any further forms of domestication and suppression, signs of emancipation have been in evidence. Wherever the people as a body have been able to give full expression to what they believe, and to establish priorities for their faith in action, the taste of emancipation has been unmistakable. Wherever they have been able to recognize the possibilities for solidarity with other oppressed peoples, and have attempted to link their struggle for full humanity with the struggles of similar contexts elsewhere, the sounds of genuine hope have filled the air.

We shall therefore have cause to examine the creative energies and celebrative styles of the people, in the context of their many crises. We shall look at the efforts to organize indigenous projects for community building and ecumenical cooperation. We shall explore the broad meaning of emancipatory theology in the context of Caribbean struggles for freedom, and we shall seek to establish some linkages and prospects with which the people of the Caribbean in general, and Afro-Caribbeans in particular, might go forward into a more practical and liberating future. It is a major theme of this book that emancipation for the Caribbean is an integral part of God's design and that, when God emancipates our people, no other source of validation, however intimidating or pretentious, is in any way required.

The Caribbean is thus a region of contrasts and paradoxes; it boasts of many countries and contexts, many linkages and leaders. The possibilities for a consensus of what exactly the "Caribbean" means to those who know it well are as shifting as the sands with which the region abounds. The environment provides for innumerable forms of personal discourse between the sun, the people, the land, and the sea. Between the land and the sea, however, there is an abundance of sand; and this has substantial significance for our present study. We shall therefore turn immediately to a discussion of the "Caribbean Sandscape."

CHAPTER TWO

THE CARIBBEAN SANDSCAPE

In a real sense, it is easier to describe the "sandscape" of the Caribbean than the "landscape," for there is relatively little land in the region. Many of the islands vary considerably in size and formation, and the factor of natural cohesion is the Caribbean Sea, which washes the sand onto almost all the shores of the region. Some people believe that the trouble with the Caribbean is not that there is too little land but, rather, that there is too much sea. The Caribbean sand is chiefly symbolic of the region itself, for the Caribbean is a place of shifting sands and changing circumstances. Three typical experiences of changed circumstances will serve to illustrate this condition: hurricane "Gilbert" (Jamaica, 1988), economic catastrophe (Trinidad and Tobago), and political upheaval (Haiti).

THE WINDS OF CHANGE

The first experience was a severe hurricane. Hurricanes are a normal fact of Caribbean life. Many of the older folk on the islands are accustomed to dating historical events by referring to devastating hurricanes in their experience. Long before meteorologists were able to track storms and predict their likely courses, local island folk knew what to look for and how to govern themselves accordingly. They sense the change in the atmosphere, they watch for the unusual flight of birds, and they detect the movement of clouds. They know how to make their plans with the hurricane season in mind, for they are aware that hurricanes are very unpredictable. They have a clear understanding of the devastating effect of such natural disasters, and they are normally prepared to face the storms with as much determination as their circumstances can generate.

They also know that, after a severe hurricane has struck, they will have to begin all over again and try to put their lives together in anticipation of another storm, perhaps in the same year. The island of Jamaica was devastated by hurricane Gilbert, in September 1988, with extensive loss of life and destruction of property and crops, and with the fortunes of thousands substantially ruined. Just at the very time when Jamaica was preparing for national elections, and just when there was every confidence that the economic fortunes of the country could be held up for popular scrutiny and political debate, the hurricane struck. The political focus has shifted from economic growth to the rehabilitation and reconstruction of an entire country; national priorities have changed radically as the stark realities of dependence on the beneficence of external sources have once again become painfully obvious. In February 1989, national elections were held in Jamaica, and the government of Edward Seaga was swept from power as if by yet another hurricane. Michael Manley and his People's National Party have regained control of public affairs, and only time will tell whether every wind that blows in Jamaica is actually filled with far-reaching omens.

Yet, in spite of the natural calamity of "Gilbert," Jamaicans have largely weathered the storm in typical Caribbean style, with tough spirits and calm determination to survive. Local folklore has already turned the disaster into a source for creative artistry. Just a few days after the hurricane, the Jamaican National Dance Theater Company was still able to travel to Washington, D.C., to give a sterling performance at the famous Kennedy Center. They danced and sang before a large and appreciative audience as if nothing had happened in their homeland. Many of the performers had suffered losses in the catastrophe, but still they danced and danced as if nothing had happened at all. Gilbert has been renamed "Kilbert," because it took many lives; it "killed" many people. It has also been called "Roofus" (Rufus), because it has leveled many roofs. Jamaicans have been heard to declare: "Gilbert was rough, but we are tougher."

Such is the nature of the Caribbean sandscape. The capacity to survive in the face of oppressive conditions is not peculiar to the Caribbean, for other parts of the Third World are constantly struggling against the effects of widespread natural disasters. Bangladesh is a case in point. What is significant here, however, is that the realities of shifting circumstances and the cataclysmic change in national fortunes often generate new surges of resilience and survival techniques, as well as a fresh impetus for mutual collaboration.

Another aspect of the Gilbert catastrophe depicts the nature of Caribbean society as a whole. All Caribbean countries are familiar with the ravages of hurricanes, for all have suffered at some time or other from them. In September 1989, hurricane Hugo caused widespread destruction and death in the Caribbean and the Carolinas. Hurricanes normally originate off the African coast, pick up speed over the Atlantic, and then travel across the Caribbean chain with changing course and fluctuating intensity. Hurricanes are a common threat to the region, so that every country remains on the alert for any eventuality. The people who lived on islands in the southern Caribbean breathed a sigh of relief when they experienced merely strong winds and heavy rainfall from Gilbert, but they were genuinely distressed when Jamaica was itself struck by the strongest hurricane ever recorded in the Western Hemisphere. They each knew that it could have been any of them, for hurricanes have struck in the south and bypassed Jamaica in the north. The mobilization of relief efforts, out of the store of

meager resources in the smaller islands, constituted a most significant demonstration of the Caribbean sandscape. For, even though the islands are
completely separate, there still exists in the region some degree of common
neighborliness and solidarity, which disasters tend to evoke instantly. The
common sea and sands are more powerful than the separate lands. It is a
paradox of the Caribbean sandscape that the winds of change often produce
stronger character and more durable spirit.

The second experience relates to the recent economic story of the oil-
rich nation of Trinidad and Tobago. While economic fortunes declined
rapidly in the Caribbean as a result of the oil crisis in the early 1970s,
Trinidad and Tobago experienced a phenomenal rise in industrial growth
and economic power. During these years of prosperity, the nation—an agricultural society with comparatively little industrial capability—had to
decide how to make the most prudent use of its massive revenues. Trinidad
and Tobago opted to expand its industrial sector with numerous projects
based on the production of natural gas. Although some groups regarded
some of these projects as too grandiose, there was general euphoria
throughout the country as consumer patterns took on a Madison Avenue
style. Imports mushroomed, and wages, prices, and profits soared. At the
same time, other productive sectors of the economy, particularly agricultural exports and food production, experienced decline or stagnation. The
popular folklore gave full voice to the expression "Money is no problem;
but money is the problem." For things changed suddenly as the price of oil
slumped and the level of inflation continued to rise.

At the beginning of the 1980s, Trinidad and Tobago enjoyed a healthy
balance-of-payments surplus; but by 1983 balance-of-payment deficits had
already become entrenched, and by 1986 the local dollar had been devalued
by 50 percent. Fortunes have steadily declined since then, and the once
rich Caribbean country now faces grave economic difficulties, of almost
unbelievable proportions. At the end of 1988, some workers in the public
sector were notified that there were insufficient funds to pay them their
salaries. Private North American organizations have been providing medical supplies for government-run hospitals, while local businesses have been
releasing other supplies to the government, although many of its bills
remain unpaid. The government has made feverish efforts to reschedule
international debts or to refinance current loan arrangements, and the
International Monetary Fund has been approached for help in balance-of-
payment support. All government employees had their remuneration cut
by 10 percent in the 1989 budget.

Private-sector activities have been severely affected, and the general
feeling among most of the citizens is not far from despondency, as they
have witnessed further decline in the value of their currency. Oil-rich Trinidad and Tobago is now faced with real poverty. An economic hurricane
has swept over the nation, and gestures of rescue from Caribbean neighbors
are hardly forthcoming because of the widespread poverty already being

experienced in those islands. This is another manifestation of the Caribbean sandscape, the regional drift of changing circumstances and mixed fortunes. It points us to a very important facet of Caribbean poverty—namely, that huge inflows of money do not necessarily make poor countries rich. The Caribbean experience has constantly attested to the truth that emancipation from poverty and oppression does not consist only in the acquisition of wealth, since wealth itself can become a new form of bondage.

An illustration of the third experience is offered in the history of Haiti. At the close of the eighteenth century, revolution had become an effective way to assert popular rights and freedoms. The American Revolution of 1776 was followed by the French Revolution in 1789. Under the leadership of Toussaint L'Ouverture, the slaves in Haiti revolted against the French, and they gained their independence in 1804. But this revolution has never been fully successful. Apart from gaining the distinction of being the first independent black country in the Western Hemisphere, Haiti has historically acquired another distinction—that of being the poorest and most repressive black country in the same area.

The Haitian people as a whole have at no time in their history ever come near to assuming the commanding heights of their country's economic, political, or military power. Powerful landowning interests and military might have often combined with external forces to maintain repressive and rigid control of the people and the country's meager resources. During successive Duvalier regimes between 1957 and 1986, killings, tortures, disappearances, and unjust imprisonments have been compounded by the abject poverty and deprivation of the majority of the Haitian people.

Within the past two decades, the churches in Haiti have largely been in the vanguard of promoting the struggle for equal rights and justice for the people of Haiti. Other groups within and outside the country have also been engaged in the struggle. In a letter published in Mexico in 1984, a group of Haitians spoke out on behalf of their people, who they claimed were without security, defense, support, or protection. They protested against the repressive practices of the army and made the following affirmation:

> We do not ask for money nor do we demand contributions of food and used clothing; that is humiliating. We only demand that which money cannot provide: freedom, equality, democracy, justice for everyone, work, access to the land, and the means with which to cultivate the land.[1]

That letter was signed by at least two thousand persons. As a 1987 statement by the Caribbean Conference of Churches (CCC) indicates, Caribbean persons outside the country have constantly been impressed by the determination of most Haitians to improve their conditions:

From time to time we have been encouraged by the people's obvious
resolve to participate fully in the determination of the future direction
of Haiti towards justice and peace for all; we have been heartened by
signs of growing consciousness of the need to assert, respect and
protect basic human rights; we are overjoyed at the people's insistence
upon parliamentary democracy as the appropriate constitutional
framework within which to work for a meaningful and productive
existence.[2]

It had been generally believed that the Duvalier regime in Haiti had the
blessing of powerful interests within and outside the country, and that the
military might of the local army held enough sway to keep the country
under steady control. But in 1986 there came yet another hurricane of a
different nature. Duvalier was overthrown and, with his wife and family,
left the country for exile in France. The army took over the leadership of
the country and promised to restore democracy to the people by free and
fair elections. But, so far, efforts at elections have been frustrated by circumstances and forces opposed to democratic processes. Several changes
of leadership have taken place in the country since Duvalier's departure,
yet the brutality and torture have hardly abated.

Hopes for a new Haiti had begun to be planted in the hearts of many
of its people, but these hopes were to be dashed when the military fired
on people queued up to vote for their representatives, when worshipers in
churches were assaulted by gangs, and when religious ministers were
attacked by soldiers with machine guns and hand grenades. A prominent
Haitian Methodist minister, Allain Rocourt, writes thus:

Christian people in [the U.S.] who have visited Haiti and have seen
the suffering under which the majority of the people have lived, who
also have come to admire the extraordinary resilience of those people
and their gentle nature, must have asked themselves this question:
couldn't our government have intervened in a positive way and early
enough to prevent the massacre? Did it condone the action of the
military people who protected or helped the murderers? Is there anything we could and should have done to help the Haitian people
realize their dream of establishing democratic structures, the rule of
law, equal justice for all, the protection of the legitimate rights of
each citizen?[3]

The story of Haiti is not just about the Haitians; it is a Caribbean story.
The hurricane that has hit Haiti, especially within the past four years, is
indeed a political hurricane, since efforts to move toward the full participation of the people in the determination of their own affairs have been
brutally assaulted by repressive forces in the country. The poverty of Haiti
has been compounded by the impotence of the Caribbean as a whole to

bring about any form of liberation from the historically entrenched structures of bondage. It is instructive to take careful note of the following words of the Trinidadian scholar Anthony Maingot, who has visited Haiti on many occasions:

> The irony of Haitian underdevelopment is that while the peasant has developed a stoic realism in the face of deteriorating structural conditions, that stoicism can change to active hostility quite unpredictably. Peasant anger comes to a boil only slowly everywhere, and nowhere is this more true than in Haiti.[4]

Such is the nature of the Caribbean sandscape. The three experiences described—hurricane Gilbert, economic collapse, and political upheaval—portray the realities endemic in the region. The rapid shifts of promise and regression have been frequent in much of Caribbean life. Circumstances hardly hold out much hope for long; but in the context of such changing conditions, the people have managed to survive with rigor and determination. It is perhaps this determination, which breeds hardiness and creative survival, that has marked out Caribbean people as being rooted in the sands, but rooted nevertheless. The winds of change may cause the raging seas to wash against the sands, but the people have largely been conditioned to seek their emancipation in the face of natural devastation, economic collapse, or social repression. How such a search is possible can best be understood as we turn to a closer examination of contemporary Caribbean society.

CARIBBEAN SOCIETY: STILL IN THE MAKING

The historical antecedents of Caribbean society continue to be the crucial factors through which a realistic assessment of the region can be properly developed. For the principal fact of Caribbean social history is colonialism. Europeans conquered these islands for their own mercantilist expansion and drove out the original inhabitants as best they could. The islands were then resettled with Europeans first, for the original intention was not to establish new societies but to run profitable plantations. New crops and slave labor (whether by force or indentureship) were introduced mainly for industrial and commercial purposes. The Caribbean was therefore organized for production and not for social life, and most of the meaning of its existence is still directly attributable to the lingering fact that it subsists mainly in the shadow of the plantation.

There is considerable debate among Caribbean sociologists and economists about the most appropriate theory to use in conceptualizing Caribbean societies. In an essay published in 1982, Susan Craig, the Caribbean sociologist, provides a comprehensive analysis of that debate. She begins with the notion that there is an absence of "society," as suggested by

Orlando Patterson, who also regards all efforts to bring about Caribbean social transformation as futile. Next she deals with the "plantation society" theory, as promoted by R. T. Smith, George Beckford, Lloyd Best, and Kari Levitt. She calls for substantial modification of this theory if it is to be applicable to the wide range of Caribbean societies, since "the appealing attempt to derive social structure from the plantation experience is too simple and too reductionist."[5] Another theory is the "plural society" theory made famous by M. G. Smith, following the pioneering work of J. S. Furnivall on plural societies and colonial policies. Although Smith's theory has been repeatedly challenged by other social scientists, Craig acknowledges that it still enjoys wide appeal. This is perhaps because it highlights the cultural complexity of the Caribbean and its racial antagonisms. In any event, it attempts to deal with the Caribbean on its own terms.

Craig also looks at the "creole society" theory, which has appealed to historians such as Edward Brathwaite, Elsa Goveia, and Douglas Hall. Finally, she looks at the notions of class and classlessness as they emerge in the literature about Caribbean society, including the attempts to apply Marxian concepts to sociological analysis in the region. Craig describes the various theories as a "rich blend of description, prediction, and prescription," but she regards them as "necessarily partial and . . . unable to explain the variations between Caribbean societies, and the race/class/cultural conflicts."[6]

Although Caribbean societies are admittedly very complex and therefore difficult to assess, the centrifugal fact of the plantation seems to stand out as the salient historical characteristic in Caribbean existence. C. L. R. James has poignantly stated:

> Nobody knows what the Caribbean population is capable of. Nobody has ever attempted to find out. The only history that there is is the accumulation of facts and fantasies of intellectuals physically, mentally and psychologically products of the colonial plantation system, telling the people what they ought to do to accommodate themselves to the very system which in all its brutalities is stifling and strangling them.[7]

The plantation has been referred to as a "total institution," since it enveloped every aspect of the social lives of the people. Although the Guyanese scholar Clive Thomas prefers to describe the old socioeconomic order as "the colonial slave mode of production," he himself concedes that the "plantation structure of the Caribbean has worked against the development of cultural traditions of democratic or representative rule, and of political participation in social life."[8] At the present time, the structures of plantation power are being remolded under the guise of being removed.

Colonization went hand in hand with the plantation, for two pivotal factors were operative in both systems—exploitation and domination, or control. Colonies had to be exploited for the benefit and prosperity of the European overlords, who could achieve prosperity only by getting the most out of the land and those who worked on it. Prosperity could not be assured without social order and control, for all the productive energies had to be channeled in the direction of the crop. Thus, every social institution, every form of organization and management, every principle of order and mobility had to be related to the reinforcement of the plantation system.

As the twentieth century draws to its close, almost all the Caribbean territories have been granted political autonomy in one form or other. Britain and France still remain as colonial powers over a few islands, but this lingering arrangement is not without its present difficulty, for even the small island of Montserrat (population 12,000) is contemplating a break with imperial Britain. Other colonies, such as Anguilla and the British Virgin Islands, remain comfortably situated under the shade of the Union Jack. The major question, however, is not about the remaining colonies but about the nature of the independence of the former colonies. In the context of the Caribbean sandscape, patterns of leadership may have changed, and the locus of authority may have been relocated from Europe to the region, but the power of the plantation has remained intact. The real centers of power still remain outside the region, as far as economic control and industrial viability are concerned. This has two implications.

First, there is the question of political sovereignty as it relates to the real ownership of the Caribbean. With the decline in the economic fortunes of Europe and the increase in the wealth of North America, both the United States and Canada have become more actively engaged in Caribbean affairs. The Caribbean has historically been regarded as a geopolitical sphere of the United States, apart from the presence of Puerto Rico and the Virgin Islands as United States territories. There have been widespread fears that certain threats—communist alignments, drug trafficking, and illegal immigration—will arise if the United States fails to pay particular attention to the region. But Caribbean people find it demeaning to have their countries regarded as American problems. One Caribbean writer, Rickey Singh, puts it this way: "The struggles of the Caribbean people, in all four major language areas of the region, for cultural and political sovereignty in the very shadow of the world's most powerful nation, are being seriously undermined by the menacing claws of the American Eagle!"[9]

When the former prime minister of Barbados, the late Errol Barrow, addressed a conference in Miami in November 1986 on Caribbean-American relations, he made it clear that the Caribbean is indeed a civilization with its own resource potential necessary for continued development, and with a "heritage of exquisite natural beauty." Barrow acknowledged that there are strong ties between the Caribbean and American peoples in history, culture, and shared values. Nevertheless, he was disturbed by the excessive reliance by the Caribbean on the United States. He regarded it as the "patronage mendicancy syndrome." Barrow continued:

The Caribbean is not the responsibility of the US, and it is totally unfair and unkind to Americans to ask them to shoulder all our burden. However poor we may be, however severe the economic difficulties we face, it must be clearly understood that the well-being and security of our peoples are our own responsibility. Let us face it, with all the money, all the technology and all the will in the world, the US cannot solve the problems of the Caribbean.[10]

Barrow called instead for a collective self-reliance through Caribbean multilateralism. But such collective self-reliance would be realized only with extreme difficulty, since the heavy reliance on the plantation owner (the United States) as the fount of power and wealth was now assuming new proportions. Plantation economies have never encouraged self-reliance; for this virtue would weaken the concentration of power at the center, which is vital for the success of the system. How the leadership in the Caribbean presides over the transition from the plantation to an industrial society is a fundamental challenge within the Caribbean sandscape, but this challenge is compounded by a second implication.

Immediately after the Cuban revolution in 1959, the rest of the Caribbean realized that a new industrial sector would be opened up to them—namely, tourism. The tourists would no longer be vacationing in Havana, and they would need to find alternative destinations in search of sun, sea, sand, and other pleasurable experiences. The previous attempts to foster industrial investment, along the lines of Operation Bootstrap in Puerto Rico, had not been successful; and, in any event, there was stiff competition among the Caribbean countries to woo North American investors to their shores. Many of the countries were still colonies of Britain, and therefore had to consult with the imperial power when negotiating with non-British parties. Tourism offered an instant revolution in the concept of quick returns on investments, both in capital and labor.

For the past three decades, the Caribbean has witnessed a phenomenal growth in the tourist industry and a steady collapse of the agricultural sectors and local food production. The agricultural worker has become the servant of tourists in many related fields. In addition, the tourists have brought with them their own tastes and styles, which are now emulated by the host communities. A heavier reliance on North American food production has been created; massive increases in importation of goods and services have exacerbated severe foreign exchange problems; patterns of skill training have been geared toward the comforts of the foreign visitors; and the hotel has actually become the new plantation. The political directorate now finds itself trying to protect a fragile and volatile industry while presiding over a constant strategy of damage control, whether in response to natural disasters such as hurricanes, or to local unrest by the citizenry because of depressing conditions. Nothing must be done to drive the tourists away, they say, for tourism has now become the chief dollar industry in the region. The patient waiting for the sale of crops has been replaced by the eager welcoming of foreign tourists with their ready cash. Thus, the shift from agriculture to tourism has not washed away the reality of the plantation from the Caribbean sandscape.

In spite of the centrality of the plantation in our assessment of Caribbean society, however, there is nothing that comes close to homogeneity in the region. The four basic language areas—English, French, Spanish, and Dutch—have all been subjected to the Caribbean process of creolization; that is, each language area has been transformed by the local mixtures of various cultural and artistic forms. So, for example, there is a viable language and culture in Haiti called Creole, which differs significantly from the Patois in St. Lucia or Dominica. Yet Creole and Patois are both related to the French language. In the Netherlands Antilles, there is a language called Papiamento, which is a combination of linguistic forms and vocabularies from Dutch, French, Spanish, English, and Portuguese. Those islands had a peculiar arrangement whereby the official language was Dutch, the local vernacular was Papiamento, and the commercial language was English. Local Antilleans who could not communicate efficiently in Dutch and English were therefore severely handicapped, and an effective class distinction—based on these language distinctions—was created in those communities.

CARIBBEAN SOCIAL PLURALISM

The absence of homogeneity points to the realities of social pluralism in the Caribbean sandscape. Pluralism exists at several levels, such as language, race, cultural allegiances, ideologies, economic organization, and religious heritage. Because the region is made up of islands, the Caribbean is an open society. There are no curtains to be drawn, no borders to patrol, no means of keeping residents in or visitors out. External linkages are just as crucial to its nature as they are to its survival. The migratory habits of Caribbean people account for their presence all over the globe, particularly in the metropolitan North. This Caribbean diaspora performs a very important function, since successful emigrants help to sustain some of the human welfare at home, through substantial financial remittances and material support. Further, many Caribbean activities are motivated by external initiatives or modes of operation; and with the rapid expansion of instant communication throughout the region, television culture contributes significantly to the pluralistic nature of Caribbean social existence. Pluralism in creativity is often conjoined with pluralism in imitation. It is perhaps this pervasive spirit of openness in the Caribbean sandscape that renders its social pluralism both a strength and a weakness in the struggle for emancipation.

Social pluralism is a strength for the Caribbean to the extent that it engenders a spirit of tolerance for the differences between its various groupings. Such tolerance has its darker side in the sense that an accommodating attitude to mediocrity, and to low levels of performance or productivity, tends to reinforce the mistaken belief that in the Caribbean anything goes. There is often an atmosphere of laissez-faire, which non-Caribbean people categorize as a "calypso mentality." Standards of public behavior, styles of social leadership, and levels of expectation in human achievement are often conditioned less by notions of excellence and more by the overriding need to live and let live. It will be difficult to generate effective strategies of development for the region if these attitudes persist unchecked.

Yet there is a brighter side to this spirit of social tolerance. A strong sense of mutual understanding is often in evidence, especially in small communities in the region, and with it have come assurances of solidarity and support, a readiness to share the scarce resources available to the community, and a determination to be identified on the side of those who are struggling together for the better. It is a remarkable characteristic of the typical Caribbean community that the business of sharing is not confined to matters of wealth and resources. The sharing of poverty and needs is a common practice, for Caribbean people live by the dictum that "Only those who know it feel it" or by the belief that "Today belongs to you, but tomorrow may belong to me; so if I share your pain now, you will be more disposed to sharing my pain when my turn comes." This sharing of poverty and needs forms an integral part of the Caribbean people's innate capacity to develop patterns that enable them to resist the shifting sands of time and circumstance. Such residual patterns of Caribbean communalism have to be given credit for the remarkable way in which thousands of Caribbean families have managed to survive.

With the rise in social sophistication, and with the gradual growth in patterns of rabid materialism, individualism is likely to wage a major assault on such fundamental patterns of Caribbean social existence; and the sense of belonging to a community, or even to an extended family, will be replaced by one's sole identity with a nuclear family. The dynamics of survival in the region will gradually be transformed as the patterns of social tolerance and mutual support are overtaken by social competitiveness and individualistic enterprise. Whether this battle between traditional communalism and modern individualism will advance the basic cause of Caribbean emancipation and development is very much a matter of debate at the present time. The fact is that increasing levels of individualism are often accompanied by decreasing levels of social tolerance, for the "dog-eat-dog mentality" gives rise to a social Darwinism that extols the "survival of the fittest." Up to this point in its history, the Caribbean has resolutely defied the experts by managing to survive where it was not expected to.

The greatest threat to Caribbean survival may, in the future, lie not in the lack of external largess or support but, rather, in a radical shift away from the social and human qualities that have so far ensured at least a modest quality of survival. The seeds of authentic emancipation have already been sown by divine Providence, and the conditions for germination can be determined only by the Caribbean people themselves. This thesis will be further explored later in this book.

Caribbean people believe strongly that "It takes all sorts to make a world" and that "All horses cannot run alike." Such sayings encapsulate their working understanding of what social pluralism means to the region. They have found much strength in this approach, for they affirm in human terms the dictum that Paul attributed to the process of general resurrection in 1 Corinthians 15:23: "Every man in his own order" (Authorized Version). They shift the meaning slightly by preferring to say, "Every man *to* his own order." Whenever this social pluralism breeds further mutual solidarity and fruitful communalism, therein lies its brighter side. But where declining standards become crystallized, or where the weak and the poor are further marginalized by the materialistic greed and individualism of the strong and the nonpoor, the values of social pluralism are in grave danger.

Another significant dimension of the strength of social pluralism lies in the historical processes by which the Caribbean communities came to be established. In the Caribbean there was a coming together of Africa and Europe for the establishment of plantation communities. We shall have occasion to examine what this meant for the religious history of the region later on. But Africans had to mix with Europeans; and, even if one culture was dominated by the other, the process of creolization enabled most of the people in the region to exist in several different worlds at the same time, and to make as many adjustments as would ensure their survival and progress. This social pluralism has always worked to the advantage of Caribbean people, for it has enabled them to master the arts of other cultures, to adjust comfortably in any cultural setting, and to make social strides forward in differing contexts.

West Indians now sit in the British Parliament and in the United States Congress. They are the world champions of cricket. They hold prominent positions in international organizations such as the World Council of Churches and the Commonwealth Secretariat. They have always combined a variety of cultural and artistic forms in their patterns of dress, music, and social style. Thus, in many different spheres of their social existence, the Caribbean people are driven by a principle of participatory praxis, which often pays considerable dividends in their relentless struggle for freedom and social progress. The constraints of social pluralism have impelled Caribbean people toward this participatory praxis. It has stimulated them to share in the spread of ideas and customs and enabled them to derive benefits from the varieties of cultural interaction that tourism, communications, international opportunities, and other common experiences make possible. Therefore, for the Caribbean people, cultural liberation will depend largely on their management of the strengths of their social pluralism. But social pluralism also has some major weaknesses.

When we turn to look at the weaker side of Caribbean social pluralism, we are confronted with the realities of racism, classism, social contempt, populism, and the politics of personalism. We shall deal with each of these in turn.

Racism

Unquestionably, the Caribbean historically has been a persistent incubator of racism in the Western Hemisphere. The institution of slavery was heavily overlaid with racism, in that white Europeans brought black Africans from their homeland to be slaves on plantations, where they were treated as chattel and subhuman property. Plantation society thrived on a system that ensured to white propertied classes the permanence of a black laboring class; and every effort was made through the legal and social systems to guarantee that the structures of racism would remain in place. Colonialism perpetuated the system throughout the region, and even the dawning of formal independence was not enough to ensure that such a social blight would begin to evaporate from the face of the Caribbean. Neocolonialist structures remain in place today; for neocolonialism does not consist only in economic relationships between rich and poor countries. Neocolonialism also consists in a persistent system of internal colonialism in much of the Caribbean, where the rich upper classes (black and white) still exert domination and control over the poor black lower classes.

The problems of racism in the region are compounded by the realities of skin complexion, hair quality, and physical appearance. People with darker skin have traditionally been accorded lower status than people with lighter skin, to such an extent that preferment in jobs and social mobility have often been closely related to the complexion of the persons concerned. The Caribbean has managed to sustain an effective "elite of skinocracy," in that the people of mixed or Negro race who possess Caucasian characteristics are assured of special attention solely on the basis of their physical appearance. Europeans, Asians, and Africans have contributed to the miscegenation that has characterized Caribbean procreation over the past 300 years, but the structures of racism have maintained the dominance of the European superiority in the context of an African majority.

Patterns of institutional, economic, social, and political relationships are still heavily overlaid with racist considerations. Although there has been a significant rise among the black middle class in the hierarchies of power and authority, in other respects racism is still very much in evidence throughout the region. The economic significance of white tourists from Europe and North America to the industrial welfare of the Caribbean has also contributed to the survival of structured racism in the area; for many are the instances in which black waiters, waitresses, taxi drivers, entertainers, and other local personnel have had their rights and dignity assaulted so that they might not scare away the tourists from Caribbean shores. White sandy beaches have sometimes functioned as bastions of white racism against the black inhabitants of Caribbean islands, as hotel owners have been known to close off "windows to the sea" from the access of those who were born so close to it. Foreign ownership of beach property in the Caribbean continues to be associated with a continuing vestige of white racism in the region; for Caribbean blacks cannot always build sand castles out of their most common resource, or exult in the natural beauty of their natural heritage. Such is the paradox and pain of the Caribbean sandscape.

Classism

The reality of classism in the region continues to be a complex phenomenon, chiefly because it is difficult to define and yet is painfully obvious in many aspects of Caribbean social relationships. An analysis of classism must take into account a great many elements: the pluralism over which the European colonial powers presided, the inherent racism in the social system, the modes of production and patterns of family life, the levels of education and shades of skin color, patterns of speech and places of abode, religious affiliations and social connections, political activities and economic potential (rather than power), circumstances of birth and external credentials. Classism resolutely defies any simple analysis, yet Caribbean sociologists and inhabitants are very much aware that notions of class are always operative in any form of social interaction or planning.

In more recent times, however, the rise of the trade union movement and the assumption of power by the popular political parties have added new characteristics to the meaning of social class in the region. Those not previously qualified for social status on the basis of birth, ethnicity, or economic or professional virtues have managed to achieve prominence on the strength of their participation in the political organizations. This does not mean that "class" is gradually giving way to "classlessness" but, rather, that the structures of class are themselves being redefined from below, and that the social hierarchy of the plantation system is being modified mainly by a democratization of values. Yet the skeleton of the plantation remains. Money and power still determine class.

Clive Thomas of Guyana notes that there is far more interaction between what he calls "class-based and non-property-based structures" in the Caribbean than there is in capitalist countries. He goes on to make a very pertinent observation:

The greater interaction of class with ethnic, sex, colour, religious, rural/urban and even language divisions in the region makes the social structure even more difficult to analyse. The coexistence and interaction of non-property and class relations is the product of the particular stage of development of these societies and until class structures, class consciousness and class outlook become more defined, any attempt to understand the social structure of the region must take the nature and character of this interplay into account.[11]

The Antiguan sociologist Paget Henry, in his study of class and race on the island of Antigua, has attempted to identify the continuities and discontinuities in the social structure as the country has moved from a plantation economy to a service economy (tourism). He concludes that the new economic elite is not as powerful as the former plantocracy and that the new laboring class is more powerful than the former laboring class. He notes that a "rank-ordering of class and race" remains intact, that there are continuities between colonialism and neocolonialism as the industrial base has moved from sugar to tourism, and that "the changes in the structures of power, and not the mere transition to tourism, . . . brought about the observed changes in the class structure and in class relations."[12] With tourism fast becoming the major dollar earner in the Caribbean, the realities observed in the Antiguan society are fairly typical in many other Caribbean countries.

Social Contempt

Classism also shows itself in various forms of social contempt. The factors outlined above contribute significantly to the way in which Caribbean people assess themselves and each other. Patterns of contempt often run along lines of color, educational background, and socioeconomic status. In addition, the way people speak is often held in evidence either for or against them. This is of particular importance in a region with many dialects and language patterns, each in some way related to the dominant European language from the colonial past. Thus, language is not only "correlated with social class differences and generally used as the most widely recognized index of social class but also has become associated with backwardness and lack of 'culture,' whereas the use of the standard form of European languages is associated with intelligence, enlightenment, and 'culture.' "[13] It is therefore not surprising to find that Caribbean families lay great stress on the need to "speak properly," since the distinguishing factor between good breeding and the lack of it lies in one's ability to express oneself correctly on the appropriate occasions. In the Anglo-Caribbean, for example, children are brought up to understand that to "have an English tongue in your head" is an important means of upward social mobility. Yet the function of language as a crucial engine of social emancipation should never be underestimated, for Caribbean folklore and dialect ought not to be devalued in any search for authentic freedom.

Populism and Personalism

Yet another manifestation of weakness in the social pluralism of the Caribbean has to do with the politics of personalism, which pervades the entire region. Ever since the general enfranchisement of the masses at the beginning of the 1940s in the Anglo-Caribbean, populist politics has been the order of the day. Popular leaders of trade union movements have risen to assume official leadership, and also to exercise almost unlimited power. Thomas believes that many of these leaders resented their second-class status in colonial society "and expected, with independence, either to be consecrated by the colonial authorities or seen by the masses, or both, as the logical inheritors of the Colonial Office's 'right-to-rule.' "[14] In his view, independence merely meant that the masses were excluded from participating effectively in the exercise of power.

The restoration of political power to the masses, however, is not the only desirable goal for Caribbean emancipation. There is also a need to redress the effects of the politics of personalism; that is, the practice of adopting political positions and making political decisions on the basis of personalities and personal connections, rather than principles, policies, and national priorities. This practice may be a direct corollary of the populist politics in the region, but the fact that so many persons are victimized solely because of their personal affiliations or family connections, or even because they have been known to hold independent or divergent views, militates against the genuine search for freedom and integrity in the political process. The dominant principle that those who do not gather with the powerful are to be regarded as scatterers does not help to usher in a mature participatory democracy. Further, the naming of major airports after political figures such as Grantley Adams, Norman Manley, and Vere Bird continues to be an entrenched form of the politics of personalism, since it sets a precedent for the parties in power to perpetuate the memory of their own heroes (never heroines), whether they are nationally acclaimed or not.

Given the harsh realities of race, class, and social contempt, personalist politics adversely affects those who lack the social characteristics considered necessary to achieve power and prominence in Caribbean societies. Adversarial tactics predominate both inside and outside the formal structures, and those who have no one to speak for them come up against the truth of the Caribbean proverb: "It's not what you know but who you know that counts." This truth reaches far into the ranks of the public service, where ordinary rights of access to civic and official privilege are often aided by personal connections on the inside. Caribbean people have regretfully resigned themselves to this pattern of social function, and generally seek to govern themselves accordingly. Thus, the forces of personalism, when coupled with the forces of populism in Caribbean political life, make social relations in the region even less emancipatory for the poor and the oppressed. Michael Manley, the new prime minister of Jamaica, offers this comment on the matter:

In populist politics the moon is promised by the politicians, and democracy consists of making a choice between competing sets of promises which are dangled temptingly every four or five years. The system is the very antithesis of a process of participation and mobilization. Nowhere is the person enlisted in the service of a national enterprise which is understood and believed to be worth great effort.[15]

The Caribbean sandscape is dominated by the permanence of flux, shifting circumstances and conditionalities, changing fortunes and prospects, realignments and false starts, fresh beginnings and short-lived hopes. The factor of the hurricane experience is never absent from the social or economic fabric of Caribbean existence. Hurricanes of one kind or another are always in season somewhere in the region. Those who build edifices with the dream of prosperity and the hope for progress are always ambivalent about the durability of their endeavors, for loss or frustration is always a distinct possibility.

Caribbean society is still in the building stage; for, if the new Caribbean is to emerge, the continuing realities of plantation structures and a neocolonialist mentality cry out for revolutionary and emancipatory change. Pluralism is mixed with poverty and powerlessness. The very strengths of a mixed society are under constant assault by a complex web of social weaknesses. Racism, classism, social contempt, personalism, and populism all take their heavy toll on the social norms and values of these islandic cultures. They move from one crisis to another, from one set of experiments to another. Even the spectacle of Carnival does not seem to be confined to a short-lived festival before Lent, since the Caribbean conjures up all the marks of a perpetual carnival of crises. What do these crises entail, and how have the Caribbean people sustained their personhood in such a context? The role of Christianity as the dominant religion in the region is of central importance in all this, for it is impossible to understand the nature of Caribbean survival apart from the story of Caribbean Christianity. We therefore proceed to a discussion of the confluence of Caribbean crisis, Carnival, and Christianity.

CHAPTER THREE

CRISIS, CARNIVAL, AND CHURCH

The sandlike nature of Caribbean existence is characterized not only by the features discussed in the previous chapter but also by a complex mixture of crises, celebrations, and creeds. Crises accompany or replace one another with amazing frequency, and yet the celebrative spirits of our people are hardly ever smothered by them; for the people often are sustained by an overwhelming sense that God mercifully protects the Caribbean even from itself. It is true that crisis may provide fertile ground for cynicism; some Caribbean writers and poets occasionally give expression to such attitudes. There is, for example, a strong note of cynicism in Edward Brathwaite's epic poem "Islands." Here is an excerpt:

Islands
islands
stone stripped from stone
pebbles
empty shells
chapels of broken windows
no one calls here on the Sunday sand.

For the Word has been destroyed
and cannot live among us
look how your agates glitter
look what your snakes conceal.

When I was hungry, you fed me books, Daniel's dungeons
now I am thirsty, you would stone me with syllables.

We seek we seek
but find no one to speak

the words to save us;
search

there is no destination;
our prayers reach

no common
sun

no
sum

no good beyond our gods
of righteousness and mammon.[1]

The foregoing passage elicits three brief comments. First, "Sunday sand" points to the place of arrival on the island, which is void of human activity, for Sunday is a day of rest. Although, in fact, the beaches are frequented on Sundays and holidays by the local inhabitants, yet Brathwaite reminds us that the sand reveals something about Caribbean existence. Second, the poet points to snakes that conceal. The hypocrisy of the received religious traditions is always cause for concern; and yet Caribbeans have the capacity to distinguish the true Word from the false prophet. Third, the constancy of crisis in the region could perhaps be taken to mean that God has neglected the people, since their prayers are not answered. Nevertheless, the persistence of deep religious fervor would strongly attest to the power of creed over the threat of crisis.

What, then, is the scenario of the Caribbean crisis? How can the dimensions of this underlying reality be best outlined? It is important for us to examine these in some detail, for they provide a most instructive background for understanding some persistent forms of Caribbean bondage, and they also give us some sense of the direction in which emancipatory changes are moving.

A CARIBBEAN MARKED BY SIX CRISES

The Caribbean did not originally create its own crisis. We must never forget that it was the crisis of poverty in sixteenth-century Europe which created waves of mercantilist expansionism. If the Europeans could have supported themselves entirely on their resources in Europe, perhaps they would not have risked their lives in seeking their fortunes outside and would not have exploited other people's lands for their own survival. European necessity (crisis of need and poverty) was the mother of European expansion (invention). Some would add that greed was a stronger motor force than need, but suffice it to say that there was some crisis in Europe.

Crisis followed crisis for the Europeans. Plantations could not be maintained without a constant labor supply; and when Europeans could not withstand the climate of the region, they imported slaves or indentured servants to deal with their crisis. Plantations would always generate crises, especially where enforced labor was the order of the day, or where brutal policies were adopted toward the production of the crop. Economic pressures would be reinforced by societal and climatological forces; tensions would always run high among all sectors of plantation society; and whenever the crops failed, a persistent crisis of survival was always accentuated. White planters, African and Asian laborers, and an assortment of traders and artisans from various ethnic backgrounds could not all be brought together under the control of external colonial authority without endemic crisis. Thus, it is a historical fact about the Caribbean that the Europeans who stumbled upon it in crisis also built institutions for themselves that could profit from the persistence of crisis. The urgent need in the present crisis is therefore to distinguish clearly between what the Europeans have left behind and what is authentically Caribbean.

Everyone agrees that the Caribbean is always in crisis; but—because of the complex mix of peoples who make up the region, there is little agreement on the nature of the crisis, or set of crises. In other words, not every crisis affects everyone, and Caribbean people often remind themselves of the local proverb: "What is joke for one is death for another." In the contemporary Caribbean, for example, the crisis faced by the white mercantilist classes is largely due to their resentment of the political power exercised by black governments. Caribbean whites have been known to seek refuge in North America, Europe, or New Zealand, in preference to being ruled by the descendants of those whom they and their ancestors once ruled. The historical myth that whites must always rule has been under siege in the Caribbean for several decades now, and patterns of power relationships have changed.

Whatever may be the feeling of crisis among those who are unwilling to accept the changes in the region, especially where the empowerment of the masses is concerned, there is at least no crisis of identity in the Caribbean, even if physical appearances and cultural expressions suggest otherwise. Caribbean people know deep down exactly who they are, and this inner knowledge of their own identity enables them to adapt quite easily in various cultural contexts. Again, there is no crisis of pedigree in the Caribbean; for even if Africa, Europe, and Asia have come together in shaping new people, lines of pedigree are not obscured, however much they may be denied. Also, although there is a need for cultural affirmation and liberation, there is no crisis of culture in the Caribbean. Culture is the sum total of the creative human spirit, and that has always been in evidence as Caribbean people have mastered the art of survival.

Some people say that there is a crisis of indolence in the region. They claim that there are hoards of idle, able-bodied men and women who laze around in the shade of the trees, hiding from the pull of hard work or waiting for the beneficence of those who would take pity on them. Unemployment levels are exceedingly high, and patterns of underemployment are often an assault on human dignity. But when the totality of Caribbean effort is assessed in relation to Caribbean resources and achievement, when the enormous success of the Caribbean diaspora is fully acknowledged, when indigenous entrepreneurship is comprehensively reviewed, and when working conditions or opportunities for work are taken into account, the charge of indolence fades. The truth is that Caribbean pride expresses itself in many different ways, and those who appear to be indolent may actually be manifesting a deeper sense of human pride and dignity, however misplaced and costly it may happen to be.

The psychology of work in the Caribbean has historically been scarred by the elusiveness of reward. Those who have labored the most have not enjoyed most of the fruits of their labor. Thus, there comes a time when people who have been hewers of wood and drawers of water for others call a halt to such an existence, and sometimes even neglect to hew and draw for themselves. The substance of self-reliance must radically displace the appearance of indolence. One of the fundamental victories that emancipatory practice will have scored in the region is the concrete assurance that hard work will be sweetened by just and sustainable reward. Caribbean people are not indolent; they are only resolutely opposed to being exploited again.

Yet the Caribbean continues to be a laboratory of crisis experiences, and there is overwhelming evidence that those who can survive in this laboratory can readily thrive elsewhere, all things being equal. What, then, are these crisis experiences? Six major manifestations require particular attention (although it should be readily admitted that the list could be much longer): (1) persistent and structured poverty, (2) migration, (3) cultural alienation, (4) dependence, (5) fragmentation, (6) narcotics.

Persistent Poverty

Caribbean people are poor. They live in a poor region with extremely limited resources for wealth formation and with increasingly fewer opportunities for economic self-sufficiency. The Caribbean was never meant to be a self-sustaining region; it was conquered and resettled for the sustenance of Europe. Europeans began to discard it systematically in the early nineteenth century, after its prospects for wealth became unprofitable and after new modes of wealth formation nearer home made unprofitable plantations overseas an unwelcome burden. Caribbean poverty today is a direct result of European frustration yesterday. The critical test of history is whether Caribbean people will succeed in dismantling the vestiges of those failures and frustrations.

Many ideological and philosophical approaches to Caribbean poverty have been adopted over the years. One theory advanced to explain the cause of this persistent poverty is that the very nature of the descendants of black plantation slaves makes underdevelopment and poverty inevitable.

What else could normally be expected from such people? Could anything good come out of the Caribbean? Another explanation is that the demographic factors were compounded by the geographical realities, so that there was too large a population for so little land, which in any event was relatively unproductive and devoid of natural mineral resources. Yet another explanation is that the region is not large enough to hold its own in the competition of world trade and therefore is perpetually at a comparative disadvantage.

In direct answer to these approaches, Clive Thomas has this to say:

> These were fundamentally ahistorical theories which explained poverty and powerlessness in terms of the innate characteristics of people and their environments or self-perpetuating cycles of poverty. Given that Europe was initially attracted to the Caribbean because of its wealth, this was indeed an ironic historical development.[2]

Caribbean people should not accept any of these theories about their poverty, and they should renounce any ideology which suggests that this condition is irreversible. It is true that almost every Caribbean country is experiencing serious balance-of-payments problems, that unemployment levels are unacceptably high, that the cost of living in most territories is substantially beyond the economic capacity of the lower classes, and that the pace of trade and industrial development has generally been retarded by a number of external factors. The fact of poverty is not in itself the hallmark of a crisis; it is, rather, the complacent acceptance that poverty in the Caribbean is eternal. To the extent that those who affect the lives of the people in the region function under the rubric of such beliefs, the efforts to achieve economic and social transformation will be gravely jeopardized.

Migration

Life in the Caribbean has always been a migratory form of existence. The original inhabitants, driven out by the marauding Europeans, had to find new homes elsewhere. The Europeans migrated to the region in search of fortune. The various sectors of the Caribbean population arrived, either by force, contract, or adventure, to participate in social and industrial experiments. The very islandic nature of the region made it inevitable that there would be extensive hopping from island to island; and living conditions in the Caribbean territories have never been adequate enough to render emigration an entirely undesirable option for personal betterment.

Dawn Marshall, the Bahamian sociologist, has contended that West Indians have been "moving from limited opportunities, chronic poverty and deprivation to what are perceived as better conditions, both within and without the Caribbean," ever since emancipation.[3] With this in mind, we have only to recall the waves of migration throughout the region to Guyana, Trinidad, Panama, Cuba, and the Netherlands Antilles; followed in this century by emigration to the United Kingdom, Europe, and North America. Opportunities for emigration have been drastically reduced in recent times, especially to the United Kingdom and North America; problems of freedom of movement throughout the Caribbean have perennially produced serious tensions among Caribbean countries. The issues of inter-Caribbean migration featured prominently in the decision to dissolve the ill-fated West Indian Federation in 1962; and the treatment of Haitian migrants, especially in the Bahamas and the Dominican Republic, has continued to be a source of grave concern and regional embarrassment.

The Barbadian economist DeLisle Worrell, in his Scott Lecture (Barbados) in 1986, referred to emigration as the "ultimate sanction Caribbean people have on governments which try to confine them in an insular ghetto." But he also recognized that it has made a "major contribution to the development of the Caribbean economy ever since emancipation." He suggested that the loss of talent has often been compensated by the remittances to the region and the enhancement of skills by the returning migrants. He warned governments not to alienate their citizens with "burdensome proscriptions," which drove away the "knowledgeable, the inventive, the determined – the pathbreakers on the road to development."[4] It is instructive to note that in 1978 no fewer than 2,700 Jamaican emigrants took away with them managerial, administrative, and technical skills. The statistics from Guyana in the decade of the 1980s are even more alarming.

If migration has always been an integral part of Caribbean life, why is it regarded as an area of crisis, especially since the remittances from migrants are crucial to the Caribbean economy? Several reasons may be cited. First, those who are born and reared in an atmosphere of social contempt are (not surprisingly) motivated to seek a supposedly more wholesome existence elsewhere. Emigration provides such an escape valve. Second, the rapid brain drain from the region to the rich North is further exacerbated by the often overwhelming evidence of material success abroad. Third, when many of the region's talented people are removed from their immediate proximity, younger generations are robbed of proper role models and mentors to emulate. Also, the youth are likely to associate progress with emigration. Fourth, with the reduction of local talents and skilled personnel, there is a far more ready reliance on foreign substitutes to fill the gaps. The quality of their contributions is not always obvious.

The fifth result of the emigration problem has to do with the local engagement in Caribbean development, for emigration undoubtedly undermines the goals of authentic development by weakening the commitment of those who move out. Emotional commitment to a home region is hardly bankable in physical terms from afar, although the material support from overseas nationals does make a real difference to the Caribbean livelihood. Sixth, cultural pluralism is made more complex through emigration, since the interconnectedness of foreign value systems with those of the region often leads to increased dependence and new forms of alienation. We will discuss these matters further on. Seventh, the tensions between those who remain at home and those who return after their sojourn are not always easy to conceal or to control. Feelings of suspicion, insecurity, jealousy, and intolerance lead to a reduction in solidarity, which militates against the collective naming of the real common enemy in the Caribbean. Finally, as if tourism were not bad enough in characterizing the region as a place of resort, emigration slowly transforms the Caribbean into a place of retirement for its own sons and daughters. Most emigrants dream of returning home, although many never make it. Thus, the Caribbean becomes for some of its own offspring more a place of peripheral attachment and less the center of their sense of place. For the place that gave them birth is not always able to provide their bread. All this denotes a complex and continuing crisis for the Caribbean at the very heart of its struggle for full human dignity and development.

Cultural Alienation

Although we have insisted that there is indeed a distinctive Caribbean culture, we must also admit that cultural alienation exists, primarily as a direct result of the plantation mentality. Plantation society thrived principally on some very basic characteristics: rigid social stratification, a weak community structure, minimal social responsibility, poorly developed educational systems, high levels of social instability, and a perversion of human values emanating from the "great houses" on the plantations.

The official colonial policy of "divide and rule" was relentlessly pursued and rigidly woven into the fabric of Caribbean social life. Thus, under a dominant policy that stressed their natural inferiority and the inconsequential nature of their basic cultural heritage, Caribbean people became mutually contemptuous. They began to assume that anything foreign and white was good, whereas that which was local and nonwhite was not good enough. People became institutionally and systematically alienated from their own inherent characteristics and their own natural cultural endowment (race, color, language, belief systems, relationships, preferences, entertainment and leisure, work schedules, family mores, aspirations), and also from their rightful access to the corridors of power, social mobility, and participatory citizenship. Power, prestige, privilege, and participation had a distinctly white bias, and the legal and institutional framework of Caribbean colonial society ensured that this bias remained entrenched.

Nevertheless, the effects of cultural alienation are not as severe among the lower classes of society as they are among the aspiring middle classes. In our next chapter, we shall examine how the African heritage in Caribbean religion managed to survive some of the deliberate efforts of the official policies to eliminate it. But while religion served as a bastion of resistance against some forms of cultural alienation among the lower classes, the education system effectively produced a virtually deculturated, culturally alienated middle class. These men and women were educated to deny their inherent self-worth and the value of their own environment, and they were made to acquire a preference for skills and aptitudes that were largely unsuited to their own authentic development.

Caribbean history, for example, was given much less attention than British and European history. Local music was treated as demeaning, and much of it could not be sung on Sunday, the Lord's Day. In any case, calypso music was scorned by the upper classes. Similarly, the local Patois in St. Lucia and Dominica was frowned on by the elite. It was not to be spoken in their homes; they stuck only to the King's English. Education was therefore a process whereby the Caribbean middle classes, in an effort to gain upward social mobility, looked outward to Europe for their values and upward to the white ruling classes for their survival.

The crisis of alienation continues unabated in the Caribbean today—after decades of enlightened self-government and political changes, after attempts at more realistic and appropriate educational policies, after consolidated efforts at indigenizing institutions and expanding social opportunities, and even after the global collapse of the myth of white superiority. The Caribbean societies have passed through successive stages of slave-plantation society, colonial society, postcolonial society, and international community; but the residual attitudes of cultural alienation have remained constant.

The influence of the foreign electronic media, communications, and travel abroad has combined with tourism to perpetuate many subtle forms of cultural alienation that assault the inherent dignity of Caribbean people. Styles of dress are determined extensively by Sears catalogues. Air-conditioned Japanese cars refuse the fresh winds that cool the air naturally. Patterns of entertainment replicate the latest fads in North America. Intra-Caribbean travel hardly is contemplated at vacation time; foreign trips are generally preferred in a region that depends so much on tourism. While the collective struggle for cultural sovereignty generates new forms of emancipation, pervasive alienation provides fertile ground for new forms of dependence.

Dependence

Caribbean society has historically passed from one form of structured dependence to another, and it is the persistence of structures of dependence that has made life in the region so hard. Dependence has been not only an endemic economic reality but also a political and attitudinal reality. The Jamaican economist George Beckford maintains that the plantation created an "ethos of dependence and patronage," which deprived the people of the Caribbean of dignity, security, and self-respect.[5] Patterns of dependence have permeated every aspect of Caribbean life to such an extent that the accession to independence of almost all the former colonies in the region has not radically changed the nature of their relationship with their former colonial masters.

It is true that the locus of authority has been relocated into the region from European cities, but many of the traditional forms of dependence for survival still remain and have been overlaid with new forms of dependence. Colonialism has given way to neocolonialism, which in many ways sometimes appears to be worse than colonialism. That is because neocolonialism has been accompanied by patterns of internal colonialism in the region, and the rise of local political hierarchies has created added burdens on the masses of people, who have to depend on the favors of the political directorate for much of their livelihood and well-being.

In all these newly independent territories, economic sovereignty has not accompanied political sovereignty, for there is still foreign ownership and control of key economic and industrial sectors, plus a substantial infusion of foreign aid for public financing and a heavy reliance on preferential and concessional arrangements in international trade. For the most part, therefore, there is still a close relationship between a politically dependent directorate and a common fear of retarding the pace of economic development. The poverty that results from dependence is matched only by the dependence that results from poverty. Today, "the economic and political realities in Caribbean society sustain a web of dependent poverty," which confines the human spirit and "creates serious obstacles to social change for the better, and full human development."[6]

Dependence is indeed a critical form of bondage from which Caribbean people urgently need to be emancipated. Their formal independence paradoxically accentuates their persistent dependence, since they still lack the power to make their own decisions and the courage to make their own mistakes. That is, they are unable to determine their own priorities, to articulate them fearlessly, and to accept the full consequences of such determination. As a result, they do not demonstrate the stuff out of which genuine independence thrives. The following observations by Clive Thomas point uncomfortably to this dimension of Caribbean reality:

> At the moment, the penetration of North American ideology, particularly through the electronics media, press and school system, is taking the lead in the region's cultural "development" in much the same ways as the TNCs, with their dogmas about the efficiency of the market place and the private pursuit of private gain, are taking the lead in the region's economic "development." A balkanised region is unfortunately easy prey to these new forms of dependency.[7]

The recent history of the Caribbean has repeatedly demonstrated that revolutionary approaches to political or economic change, ideological preferences that run counter to the dominant Western policies, or new alignments in the geopolitical sphere are considered to be grave threats to the status quo. Cuba, Grenada, Guyana, and Jamaica have all had to pay the price for their excursions. The general reluctance in the Caribbean to accommodate ideological pluralism continues to challenge Caribbean freedom and sovereignty. But Caribbean sovereignty is also threatened by yet another area of crisis.

Fragmentation

Fragmentation among the Caribbean countries continues unabated. Geographical realities in the region already create wide disparities in size, resources, and capacities for self-sustaining growth among the people. At the same time, geographical endowments do not always ensure a country's stability and well-being. The island of Montserrat can boast of a much more stable and self-sustaining populace over the past two decades than Guyana. Historical realities also interfere. The four European colonizing powers have left their marks on the character of their former colonies, so that the relationships between the Francophone Caribbean and their Anglophone neighbors are not very strong; the Netherlands Antilles hardly feature in Caribbean affairs, except through nongovernmental bodies. We have already indicated how the Puerto Ricans think of themselves in relation to the Caribbean. The Haitians are treated differently in different areas of the region, and the Dominican Republic officially maintains a separate identity as a Hispanic country. Cuba continues to hold a unique place in the Caribbean constellation, not only because of its recent political history but also because of the patterns of migration early in this century. Cubans speak Spanish, while the vast majority of Caribbean countries are English-speaking; but some call Cuba an "Afro-Hispanic-Caribbean" country.

Geographical and historical factors may be difficult to counteract, but political factors are not. Yet it is the political factors, particularly in the Anglo-Caribbean, that often create crises of fragmentation. The effects of political imperialism serve to generate rivalries, mistrust, and bad communications between countries. The West Indian Federation (1958–1962) failed, not only because British imperial politicians attempted to pour new wine into old wineskins (by creating a federation without the necessary instruments of federal enterprise) but also because the economic and political strategies among Caribbean leaders were competitive rather than complementary. Gordon Lewis's study on this issue is most instructive. He contends, among other things, that "there was no exciting symbol around which federal sentiment might have rallied."[8]

Recent efforts at regional cooperation have been more lasting, and the regional bodies established by governments for purposes of trade, education, and regional security have survived. But rigid immigration policies and practices, excessive demonstrations of national sovereignty, and unenlightened chauvinistic sentiments exploited by politicians and other vested interests have reinforced the layers of fragmentation that have plagued the region for centuries. Not even the successful West Indies cricket team or the well-established University of the West Indies is immune from the pressures of such fragmentation. The crisis of dependence must therefore be placed alongside the crisis of fragmentation, for they reflect the ongoing realities of neocolonialism. Some would even say that they are the inducements for Caribbean recolonization. William Demas utters some very strong words when he contends: "We welcome foreigners, we ape foreigners, we give our national patrimony for a pittance to foreigners, and what is worse, we vie among ourselves in doing all these things. It is a state of psychological, cultural, and intellectual dependence on the outside world."[9] Demas therefore calls for greater levels of interdependence among West Indian territories, even for another Caribbean Federation. Yet the islands are much closer together in their encounter with a most pressing problem, which represents the final area of crisis with which we will deal.

Drug Trafficking and Narcotics Abuse

Caribbeans had just begun to grow accustomed to the fact that some segments of the community were growing and using marijuana as a drug, under the guise of religious sanction, when they suddenly discovered that hard drugs were being transferred through, or else imported into, the region. The natural openness of the region, and its close proximity to such South American countries as Colombia, makes the Caribbean a haven for the transmission of drugs to the lucrative markets in North America. In the process, various Caribbean countries have become involved not only in the transshipment but also in the actual distribution of the illegal substances. In addition, the heavy influx of tourists and the encouragement of various types of entrepreneurs from outside the region have compounded the problems.

Corruption of some leaders has now become a common scandal in the region, as prominent persons in the Bahamas, the Turks and Caicos Islands, the Cayman Islands, Trinidad and Tobago, and elsewhere have been allegedly implicated in the profiting from this illegal trade. It is now generally conceded that the drug crisis is a major political problem in the entire region, for drug barons have emerged to exercise considerable influence over important sectors in Caribbean societies. The prime minister of Barbados has commented on the problem in this way:

Not only are these barons, for example, able to provide money and arms to support their armies of cultivators, processors and traffickers but they have been able by devious means and through acts of intimidation to infiltrate law enforcement agencies and to corrupt public officials in order to protect their nefarious investment.[10]

The abuse of drugs and the illegal trafficking in them will continue to have devastating effects on the economic, social, cultural, political, and institutional fabric of the Caribbean. The generations of youth who will grow up to take such practices for granted as a way of life, and the underground economies that will continue to flourish as an alternative way to making progress, will together bring about a most debilitating assault on the values necessary for full human development. But as long as the demand for illegal substances continues unabated in the North American culture, chances are that people in the poorer neighborhoods of the hemisphere will do what they can to cash in on the supply.

As we bring this discussion on the crises in the Caribbean to a close, then, we need to reiterate that the six areas discussed do not by any means exhaust the list of crises that continue to affect the well-being of Caribbean existence. There is indeed a carnival of crises through which Caribbean people have to pass as they struggle to repress attitudes of aimlessness and experiences of frustration. Unfortunately, most Caribbean citizens today would be hard pressed to refute the late Eric Williams's assessment of their region in 1969:

> The contemporary Caribbean is an area characterised by instability; political and economic fragmentation; constitutional diversity; economic, psychological, cultural and in some cases political dependence; large-scale unemployment and underemployment; economic uncertainty; unresolved racial tensions; potential religious conflicts; the restlessness of youth; and an all pervading fear of the United States.[11]

That the people of the Caribbean continue to thrive in the face of these realities, and to maintain a distinctive set of human characteristics, is almost beyond explanation. But that their human spirit is such that they can still generate and promote a celebration of life through the Carnival sometimes borders on the incredible.

BEHIND THE CARNIVAL

It is inconceivable that anyone could reflect on the above mentioned crises in the Caribbean without being struck by the apparent hopelessness of it all. No serious analysis of the region can ignore the harsh realities with which the Caribbean is daily confronted. Soaring prices, rising unemployment, balance-of-payments deficits, shortages of goods and services, escalating costs of higher education, technological obsolescence, political corruption and uncertainties, inadequate medical services, and the unavailability of welfare subsidies—all converge on the human condition to make life very difficult. Because of the patterns of domination over the masses by local political directorates, human rights are sometimes elusive, and an individual's right to work is often contingent on that individual's political allegiances. All in all, to survive in the Caribbean inevitably requires the art of confronting various forms of economic, social, and political bondage. The struggle for emancipation is therefore no dispensable option, even if the intensity of the struggle varies with the perception of the bondage. How, then, do Caribbean people thrive under such conditions? The life behind the phenomenon of the Carnival spectacle helps us with a part of the answer, while the scenario of religious activism through the churches provides us with another. (For purposes of this discussion, we shall be using "Carnival" as a summary term for the festival arts and celebrative attitudes of Caribbean people, for the annual festivals actually bear different names in various islands.) We shall deal first with the Carnival aspects of Caribbean life.

Festivals are generally an important and indispensable part of social livelihood. The cycle of the year turns through its seasons. Because the Caribbean cannot boast of the four major climatological seasons of the year (there is only the hurricane season to deal with), the threat of monotony from a steady tropical climate can be very real. Seasons, therefore, have to be tagged to agricultural activities, to cultural festivals and religious observances, or to the commemoration of historical events. Rites of passage in the family circle awaken the celebrative urges, and major accomplishments in the context of drab social monotony often trigger great moments of merriment.

Every Caribbean country has its major national festivals. Many of them are related to the festival of Carnival, which usually occurs just before the season of Lent. Carnival in Trinidad is by far the most famous and elaborate of them all, but there are variations on the Carnival theme in other islands throughout the annual calendar. The Junkanoo and the Goombay in the Bahamas, Crop-Over in Barbados, Christmas Masquerade festivities in St. Kitts and Montserrat, Jonkonnu in Jamaica, Hosay and Divali in Trinidad and Guyana, Rara in Haiti — all point to the festive dimensions of Caribbean culture. But what is there to celebrate, given the pressing circumstances of daily living? Why are these festivals taken so seriously, and how can the apparently excessive amount of time, talents, and resources so expended be justified? Why would millions of poor people strive to live for the moment in such expensive pageantry and abandon? What does the Carnival factor really mean to Caribbean emancipation?

Carnival has to be seen as the major social process of "soul purging" for the people, the time when the lighter side of life takes over, when the harsh truths of daily social existence are altered for a while, when the rites of reversal become powerful statements of the other side of human life. Carnival parades provide a liberating experience for the people; life is energized to a high crescendo; spiritual rebirth is realized, if only for a moment; and different "personae" emerge behind the masquerades and festival costumes. Prim and proper (sophisticated) ladies, and the gentlemen of fame and fortune, are transformed as they dance without inhibitions in the bands. The lines of social classification are blurred (except perhaps for one's ability to afford the costumes), so that in a very real sense the Carnival becomes a powerful integrative force. Dolores Yonker says of the Rara in Haiti:

> For the hard-working Haitians, Rara is release, an abandon to their spirits, natural and supernatural. Flashing tinsel, mirrors, sequins, multi-colored scarves, and strips of cloth transform their clothing, just as Rara transforms ordinary life for a few precious days.[12]

Yet the contemporary expressions of the Carnival phenomenon should not be interpreted apart from its historical antecedents. When the Europeans started their Carnival festivals in Trinidad, they would not allow the slave populations to participate. But that did not stop the Africans from maintaining their own patterns of celebration. Eventually, the will of the people prevailed in the festivals, and the festivals became the means whereby the people's pent-up feelings and emotions were brought to the fore.

The Jamaican scholar Rex Nettleford says that the "sustaining lifeblood of these events was the creation by the participants of masks to disguise, of music to affirm, of dances to celebrate, as well as the germination of ideas beyond the reach of those who brutishly supervised them for the rest of the year."[13] He refers to the festivals as mechanisms of affirmation, "part of the quest for appropriate designs for social living." They seek to blend the old with the new and to establish a fusion between that which is native and that which is not. Nettleford refers to the point made by the Trinidadian scholar Errol Hill who sees in Carnival a synthesis between "folkforms and artforms, between native and alien traditions."[14] Thus, in Carnival the historical strands of Europe, Africa, and India meet in creative imagination and celebrative style. In Nettleford's words, Africans and East Indians in the Caribbean are "marginalized souls," and for them "metaphor, the mask, and masquerading are among the tools of liberation from the uncertainties consequent on uprooting."[15]

Although the festivals have to be based in the particular islands, the music associated with them does not. The musical tradition of the Caribbean gives lasting vitality to the Carnival activity and permeates the spirit of the region from island to island. The Caribbean is indeed a musical region, and the rich musical forms created in the region have been exported to all parts of the globe. The calypso and the reggae are but two examples of these forms, apart from the musical sounds of the steel orchestra. These musical creations of the Caribbean people, exported with the Caribbean migrants and entrepreneurs, have formed the basis for a thriving entertainment and festival business in many metropolitan capitals. Carnivals in Brooklyn, New York, as well as in Toronto, Canada, and Notting Hill, London, have become world famous, the last named being the largest annual festival in Europe at the present time. There are also popular festivals associated with Caribbean musical forms in Miami, Amsterdam, and Paris. The demonstration of these spectacles in metropolitan centers conveys most poignantly the combined meaning of three Caribbean realities — movement, music, and migration.

Kenneth Bilby, an anthropologist associated with Johns Hopkins University, has researched and written extensively on the ethnomusicological traditions in the Caribbean. In *The Caribbean as a Musical Region,* Bilby points to a number of important features about Caribbean music that make it a unique and distinctive tradition. Among other things, he mentions the way in which the European and African musical heritages are blended together, and the enormous range of musical expressions that carry within themselves much of the historical antecedents of Caribbean social life. Two aspects of these expressions are worth noting from Bilby: the collective participation in most music and dance, and the "polymusicality" of Caribbean people.

With respect to the former, Bilby notes that the success or failure of a performance is normally determined by the level and quality of communication and interaction between performers and audience. The performance that does not inspire the people to participate enthusiastically will be deemed a failure. In the language of Caribbean people, any performance that does not motivate clapping, movement, tapping, or actual sing-along by the audience is deemed "not sweet." Bilby has this to say:

> This general criterion of collective participation is something that Caribbean musical traditions share with African and Afro-American music in general, and it constitutes one of the most powerful reminders of the depth of the African contribution to Caribbean musical life. It is an aesthetic canon, a sensibility, that permeates nearly all Caribbean music.[16]

Nevertheless, as Bilby points out, this strong collectiveness does not in any way diminish the emphasis on individualized expressions, personalized styles, and flamboyant originality. Nowhere is this originality in greater evidence than in the realm of the calypso, to which we shall turn shortly.

The other aspect of Caribbean music mentioned by Bilby is its "polymusicality." Caribbean musical traditions often appear to be made up of a patchwork of varying styles and cultures, and the instrumentalist is often capable of performing well in different areas of music. The musician is able to move across the "stylistic continuum" without any disjointedness, says Bilby, because Caribbean musical cultures are represented more as "integrated wholes than as jumbled assortments of separate and competing cultural traditions." The adaptation of musical compositions is a specialty of Caribbean polymusicality, as anyone who has heard Bach's "Jesu Joy of Man's Desiring" played to a calypso beat in the dance hall can testify.

Anyone who has heard Rossini's *William Tell* "Overture" played to Caribbean rhythms by a native steelband also shares that testimony. Anyone who has participated in a spirit-filled worship service and heard English hymns sung lustily by a Caribbean congregation, or anyone who has heard the common singing of hymns by the working gangs, or even the whistling of religious songs in rum shops, bars, or buses, will instantly recognize what all this means. Thus, Bilby concludes:

> Caribbean musical cultures—with their emphases on individual expressiveness, collective interaction, improvisation, and experimentation—are distinguished by their receptivity to new combinations of ideas and influences. Borrowing and blending between traditions, after all, has been occurring for several centuries; it is a part of the Caribbean heritage. Whatever else may be said about Caribbean music, it remains always ripe for change.[17]

Caribbean music remains everywhere, says Bilby, "a people's music."

No one who seeks to understand the strength of Caribbean life can ignore this important dimension of music, for it is deeply rooted in the soul of the people. It sustains them in their darkest moments, it gives them a sense of solidarity and worth, it nourishes the expression of their hopes and beliefs, it enkindles their spirits in the face of daunting material realities, it nurtures their young and gives marrow to the bones of their skeletal existence, it expresses their finest creative abilities as it interprets their innermost feelings, and it infects their environment with a force of cultural contagion that is almost irresistible. It liberates them from despair and from the pretensions of superiority and intimidation. It sweetens the fabric of physical work, reinforces social upliftment, and energizes the practice of spiritual worship. Music, to be sure, is the Caribbean voice of God. Caribbean people have been generally successful in sustaining most of their cultural heritage in music, dance, and religion, despite rigidly countervailing social structures and institutions.

Before we leave the study of Carnival, we need to deal with the function of the calypso in Caribbean cultural life. The calypso constitutes one of the most Caribbean of all elements in the region's social life, because it represents the creative response of local artistry to the realities experienced in varying sectors of the society. It owes its origins to the slave society, in which the slaves were able to mimic their masters, and to comment on the conditions of a slave's life, by putting their sentiments into rhyme and rhythm. The original calypso was not only the product of creative imagination; it was also the testimony of the political hopes and aspirations of a marginalized and oppressed people. It is therefore an important vestige of the historical circumstances out of which Caribbean society has emerged. Today the calypso plays a very special role in demonstrating popular sentiment as well as local creative artistry.

Calypso songs generate movements of celebrative activity that provide release for many subterranean feelings. In the calypso, the power of the politician is reduced, and artistic musical expressions provide the populace with a sense of justice that transcends the normal ascendancy of the ruling political elite. The Trinidadian scholar Keith Warner, who has made an extensive study of the calypso, suggests that in this special art form calypsonians are able to display a deliberate language and artistry in which social values are patently ambivalent, and where apolitical expressions take precedence over the power of political rhetoric. The people speak for themselves in a powerful way.[18]

The calypsonian becomes a national hero without excelling on the sports field or campaigning through the hustings for political office. The calypsonian, whether male or female, puts into music and song many of the characteristics of local identity, popular irony, and biting wit, and is able to make the "unpleasant palatable with wit and humour."[19] Calypsos therefore assume the social function of divining the popular sentiment through social comment and challenge, or open contempt for local authority. The spirit of nationalism usually runs high in the lyrics, and new visions for social change are often expressed or explored. Above all, the calypso often displays the insatiable capacity of Caribbean people to laugh at themselves and to "level down" those who take themselves too seriously.

Caribbean musical talent, particularly in its calypso art form, remains one of the primary instruments of social emancipation. It helps Caribbean people celebrate the measure of freedom they enjoy, and it provides for them, especially at Carnival time, a means of social release and renewal that extends beyond the boundaries of economic dependence or political control. What they seek to accomplish through the Carnival, they also hope for through the churches.

CHRISTIAN ACTION FOR CHANGE

Religion in the Caribbean has historically been maintained at two levels. As a part of the dominant culture, the Christian bodies have been able to enjoy the support of the establishment with relatively few tensions. The other level—the African heritage, mainly Yoruba related—will be examined in some detail in the next chapter. Islam and Hinduism have also survived in the region through the culture of the Indian population. But by far the most widespread religion has been a denominationally diverse Christianity, reproducing the divisions that centuries of missionary activity and the influx of outside resources have kept in place.

Christianity has had a varied history in the Caribbean. With relatively few exceptions, the historical development of the Christian church in the Caribbean may be plotted as follows. It began as a chaplaincy to the plantation establishment, and thus functioned as an engine of social control and an agency for such social benefits as were grudgingly allowed the poorer classes. Then it became the pioneer for the education of the masses, although such education was designed more for domestication than for development or social amelioration. As the masses of the poor became more involved in churches traditionally peopled by the upper classes, the church became more a collective mode of social identification and a community of social interpretation and interaction. But there was never any question of who maintained the upper hand, especially where foreign white missionaries remained fully in control of the leadership and administration of the religious bodies, or where foreign funding still ensured the survival of such a status quo.

Another side to the story of Christianity in the region has to do with the way in which the African slaves and their descendants interpreted and transformed it into a force for spiritual sustenance and social survival. Although there was not a distinctly formed church movement among the lower classes, as there was among the African Methodists or the Baptists in the United States, there was a distinct way in which the lower classes took hold of the religion for themselves and gave to it a social relevance and efficacy for which the missionaries could take no credit. Their concepts of sin and divine grace often diverged from the concepts held out to them; God was not a distant deity but a very present help in all circumstances. Their songs and daily rituals reflected a close allegiance to a divine presence that could be relied on. Thus, while they often found little affirmation in the established churches, they sustained mutual support and assurances among themselves elsewhere. They could still attend the conventicles of the upper classes without feeling that they were less than special in God's sight.

In the next chapter, we will pay attention to the strength of the African soul in Caribbean religion. It is sufficient at this point to note that Christianity in the region has had more than one face and that the groupings have largely reflected the denominational divisions originating outside, as well as the patterns of social stratification within. There has been no black church, or white church as such, for most churches have been peopled largely by the masses of the people. As long as missionaries remained in control, however, few changes could be expected in the role and function of organized Christianity. Nevertheless, notable changes began to take place in the 1960s. Missionaries began to retreat or to be otherwise withdrawn. The people became better educated and adopted a more enlightened approach to the value and functioning of all their social institutions. Political independence brought with it new bursts of popular demands and expectations, and the rise of nationalistic sentiments and discourse was accompanied by stronger moves toward Caribbean indigenization of all bodies and structures. Local governors, prime ministers, and executive managers had to be matched by local bishops, priests, and superintendent ministers. The sociocultural revolution—which was symbolized, for example, by the Black Power uprising in Trinidad in 1970—sent rippling effects throughout the region. No aspect of Caribbean life remained untouched, and the churches responded in kind to the growing demands of the day. Besides all this, ecumenical movements were proliferating throughout the Third World, and the struggle for self-determination and indigenous expressions was reinforced by the general political debates on the international scene.

The Christian churches in the Caribbean had little choice but to become fully engaged in the action sweeping the world. They chose to adopt a more progressive stance in their public concerns and pronouncements, becoming the social conscience for the region and organizing themselves to provide catalysts for social change. In 1971, at a historic ecumenical meeting on Caribbean development at Chaguaramas, Trinidad, the Caribbean people were called upon to pursue their own appropriate life-style and to become more actively involved in the running of their affairs as they sought to effect radical structural changes for their authentic development. The churches were also challenged to become totally engaged in the process of Caribbean development and to make every effort to bring about greater unity in the Caribbean.

Confronted with this challenge, sixteen major denominations in the region, representing all four major language areas, formed themselves into the Caribbean Conference of Churches (CCC) in November 1973 and ratified their constitution with the following preamble:

> We, as Christian people of the Caribbean, separated from each other by barriers of history, language, culture, class and distance, desire, because of our common calling in Christ, to join together in a regional fellowship of Churches for inspiration, consultation and co-operative action. We are deeply concerned to promote the human liberation of our people, and are committed to the achievement of social justice and the dignity of man in society. We desire to build up together our life in Christ and to share our experience with the universal brotherhood of mankind.[20]

The CCC constituted the first major regional grouping across languages and cultures outside of governmental structures. It set itself the task of focusing on two major themes—renewal and development. These were to have the widest possible implications, not only for the churches themselves but also for the societies that they served.

During the 1970s and 1980s, the churches have been engaged in a ground swell of collaborative activities. Many other churches have joined the ranks of the CCC, regional governments have become responsive or reactionary to the initiatives of the organization, and a virtually new generation of Caribbean consciousness has emerged through the prompting and the programs of the CCC. As it has attempted to interpret the crises in the region and the need for change, the CCC has worked with and on behalf of the churches. It has even found itself working in spite of the churches, when reactionary and conservative forces within have sought to inhibit the progress of Christian engagement in action for social change. The familiar charges of "communism" have been heard, but the CCC has managed to attract and sustain enormous support in the form of material resources and good will from internal and external sources.

The four major goals the CCC has been pursuing are these: (1) to promote a spirit of self-reliance by helping people generate and sustain indigenous development efforts; (2) to provide catalysts for regional developmental efforts; (3) to contribute to the material well-being of the poorer classes in society; (4) to promote wider participation in the social and political process, while encouraging greater reconciliation between estranged groups in the region. In Chapter Five, we will examine the CCC's recent activities, but it is crucial here to recognize that no other movement of similar importance has brought together the realities of Caribbean crisis and Caribbean Carnival into a creative and fertile tension. The work of the CCC has touched every segment of Caribbean life, including the regional intelligentsia, the politicians, the youth, and other networks of social endeavor (labor, agriculture, creative arts, social activism).

Far from being the sigh of an oppressed people, then, religion in the Caribbean has become an agency for awareness building and for social betterment. It no longer confines itself to its traditional role of promoting social survival and cultural resistance. Through the CCC in particular, religion has begun to challenge the Caribbean to face up to the areas of crisis discussed above, and has urged the people toward a vision of a new society by the pursuit of greater self-reliance and the fruitful exploitation of their own human resources and abundant strengths. What are these resources and strengths?

Caribbean people are poor in many ways, but they are nevertheless very resourceful; they make it possible for a little to go a long way. They have a strong spirit of resilience as they confront the pressures of social and economic life, and much of their strength is usually tested in the fires of all kinds of adversity. They do not give up easily; suicide is a rare phenomenon. Those who fail try again, even if failure threatens more mightily than before. In spite of their many crises, they remain a generous, hospitable, warm-hearted, and friendly people, who make allowances for friend and foe alike and sustain an openness of mind and a flexibility of spirit. The level of humaneness demonstrated by these people is hardly paralleled anywhere else in God's creation. A deep religious conviction runs through their veins, sustained by a source of religious vitality deeply rooted in the history of the people. Such a conviction often engenders some degree of self-esteem and self-assuring hope; there is a confidence that comes with each new day; for Caribbean people really believe that "while there is life, there is hope." Time is therefore always on their side; and they seem to have a measure of control over it, so that whatever fails to happen today might in all probability happen tomorrow. "Tomorrow is another day," they say; and when tomorrow comes, they are in some sense vindicated, if only because they have developed a stronger capacity to bear with new hardships.

As we bring this discussion to a close, then, we can do no better than to recognize that the Caribbean experience, with its shifting sands and changing circumstances, is always faced with tremendous paradoxes. There are crises of almost insurmountable proportions, and yet the people are thriving. There appears to be little to celebrate, and yet they sustain a Carnival spirit with which they infect all who deal with them. Crisis gives them a strong sense of resilience and survival, and Carnival gives them a strong sense of beauty and creativity. Religion serves as the integrative factor in all this, and the churches provide the avenues for ritual, ceremonies, hymnody, proclamation of the Word, communal discourse, a sense of belonging and spiritual expression, as well as a reason to hope for brighter days. But the churches could not do all this by themselves; the persistence of the African-related religions also contributes greatly to the Caribbean emancipatory practices discussed in our next chapter.

Caribbean emancipation is still to be realized in all its dimensions and structures, not merely as a political or economic objective of history but also as a concrete manifestation of the work of a Divine Emancipator. Change and renewal, liberation and maturity are constructs of the meaning of Caribbean humanization and freedom. The rest of this book will therefore seek to explore the contextual realities and connections through which God's emancipatory presence in the Caribbean and elsewhere can best be understood and reaffirmed.

CHAPTER FOUR

THE AFRICAN SOUL
IN CARIBBEAN RELIGION

Religion in the Caribbean is a complex system of beliefs, values, rituals, and behavior. It encompasses a shared experience of common relationships, common responses, common resistance, and common resilience or survival, toward the goal of social, spiritual, and material fulfillment. These four factors—relationships, responses, resistance, and resilience—need to be brought together by a fifth *R*, reconstruction. Current attempts to reach the commanding heights of Caribbean autonomy will continue to be frustrated as long as there is an accompanying reluctance to plumb the depths of Caribbean religion. Far from being the opiate of the masses, Caribbean religion has constantly been the bastion of Caribbean liberation. Caribbean reconstruction will not be fully achievable through religion without a rediscovery of the African soul.

Hardly another area in the world can more aptly qualify to be called a social laboratory than the Caribbean. Since the arrival of Europeans in the Caribbean in the sixteenth century, the region has been subjected to a process of perpetual experimentation. Europeans attempted simultaneously to procure African bodies and suppress African souls. While patterns of ownership and control may have changed over the centuries, and spheres of interest may have fluctuated, two historical factors have remained fairly constant in the Caribbean: the direct encounter between European power and African presence, and the unending series of fresh starts toward the reconstruction of social institutions and economic systems.

Poverty, dependence, alienation, and imitation remain as demons to be exorcised; and survivalism, communalism, creole humanism, movement, and fertile creativity are the powers by which they may be exorcised. Those who construct their vision of Caribbean society with the aid of those demons are generally at home with the prophets of doom, or else they take flight from the region with the shout that the Caribbean will never create anything. Those who seek to validate the powers of exorcism, however, generally emerge as purveyors of hope, wherever they reside; and they engage themselves and others in a relentless struggle for the construction of the new Caribbean society. It is therefore a major theme of this chapter that religion has functioned as a basic means of Caribbean survival and is an indispensable social instrument for the reconstruction of Caribbean society. Caribbean religion cannot provide strength for the purveyors of hope and comfort for the prophets of doom at the same time. Yet Caribbean religion itself could not have survived without its African soul. But what do these terms mean?

By "African soul," we are not referring to a part of, or spark in, the physical anatomy. We are using the term to depict an intangible yet energizing force, an invisible yet effective reality, a formless yet formative source, out of which actual feelings, fears, faith structures, and cultural preferences are born and bred. By "Caribbean religion," we mean the aggregate pattern of individual beliefs and social behavior in the region, which seeks for the deepest meaning in life and which thrives on a relationship with some supernatural form of existence. Both terms demand a considerable amount of investigation.

CARIBBEAN RELIGION

Just as there are varieties of religious experiences in the Caribbean, there are varieties of religious expression. These varieties closely reflect the historical developments that have turned the region into a heterogeneous collection of communities. After the virtual elimination of the original inhabitants by the Europeans, the Caribbean was peopled by Europeans, Africans, and most recently by Indians and Middle Easterners. At the various points of their arrival, they brought their religions with them. Thus, it is technically correct to speak of religions (rather than religion) in the Caribbean; for, although the Caribbean has produced no great religion, it has absorbed several from the outside: African traditional religions, Christianity, Islam, Hinduism, Judaism, North American cultism. Apart from a mention of the Jim Jones tragedy in Guyana and the pervasive technological cult of televangelism now sweeping the region, nothing more needs to be said about the last-mentioned phenomenon. Muslims, Hindus, and Jews have historically practiced the religion of their ethnic heritage, and the presence of small pockets of these religions is directly attributable to the existence of such ethnic groupings in the region.

The Europeans brought their brand of Christianity to the Caribbean, while they brought their slaves from Africa. But their slaves also brought their own religion with them. Could both religions survive? What would be the conditions necessary for their coexistence? The Europeans eventually left it up to their missionaries to decide, and they quite naturally exercised every available power to suppress African religious expression. But they did not succeed. Africa has survived not only as a physical reality in the Caribbean, through the millions of Caribbean people of African descent, but also as a spiritual reality. Although our principal concern here is with the continuity of the African vitality, or life force, or heartbeat in Caribbean religion, its soul, we cannot ignore the extensive work that has been accomplished on the African form and substance in Caribbean religions during this century.

Many scholars have been engaged in ethnographic studies of the New World during this century. The work of such persons as Melville Herskovits, Harold Courlander, Jean Price-Mars, Fernando Ortiz, Roger Bastide, William Bascom, Alfred Metraux, George Eaton Simpson, and J. D. Elder has been seminal in this field. We should also pay high tribute to the work of such persons as M. G. Smith, Donald Hogg, Frances Henry, Daniel Crowley, Leonard Barrett, Stephen Glazier, Maureen Warner-Lewis, Barry Chevannes, Jeannette Henney, Andrew Carr, and Jean Callendar. Many of these scholars are engaged in a longstanding debate about which aspects of Caribbean religion can be considered retentions from Africa and which aspects are reinterpretations of religious expression. Some are concerned about sources of ritual and language, while others are trying to find parallels between Caribbean expressions and contemporary African forms. Central to the debate are four important considerations. First, the Caribbean religious scene is a very complex area. Second, the Caribbean personality is incurably religious, and thus relates simultaneously to a wide spectrum of religious opportunity. Third, the religious factor in Caribbean society is inextricably bound up with factors of class, race, caste, power, and social access. Fourth, religion in the Caribbean is essentially a carrier of culture, rather than the reverse. Let us see what these points convey.

First, the complex nature of Caribbean religions results not only from the multiplicity of cults but also from the cultural pluralism in some areas. Simpson lists the religious cults in the region under five headings: (1) *Neo-African Cults*: Vodun, Shango, Santeria; (2) *Ancestral Cults:* Cumina, Convince, Big Drum, Kele, Black Carib; (3) *Revivalist Cults*: Revival Zion, Shouters, Shakers, Streams of Power; (4) *Spiritualist Cults*: Spiritualists in Puerto Rico; (5) *Religio-Political Cults*: Ras Tafari, Dreads.[1] Simpson's list is incomplete; for several other expressions of a cultic nature need to be accounted for: the Kromanti Dance in Jamaica, the Jombee Dance in Montserrat, Obeah in Guyana (especially since its official sanction by the paramount powers in that country), and the local cults of the Netherlands Antilles. We also need to consider the denominational groupings of the dominant religion, Christianity: Protestantism, Anglicanism, Catholicism, Pentecostalism, Evangelicalism, and "Nowherianism."[2]

Many Caribbean persons often claim allegiance to more than one religious grouping. This is particularly true in such places as Haiti, where Catholicism coexists with Vodun, and in Trinidad, where Catholicism coexists with Shango. Such pluralism is related to the range of social benefits that adherents derive from various settings, the sense of belonging that it engenders, the mutuality of support among members, and the sphere of personal freedom and release that is often enjoyed. This pluralism also reflects the cultural pluralism in Caribbean society as a whole, Trinidad being a clear microcosm of this reality. Daniel Crowley has made the following comment: "A Trinidadian may be a Negro in appearance, a Spaniard in name, a Roman Catholic at church, an obeah practitioner in private, a Hindu at lunch, a Chinese at dinner, a Portuguese at work, and a Colored at the polls."[3] It is therefore not difficult to understand the extensive amount of syncretism in Caribbean religious activity and the broad spectrum of beliefs and practices within the same religious groupings. The high level of religious tolerance in the Caribbean is due not only to pluralism and syncretism but also to the distinctive nature of the Caribbean personality.

Our second consideration has to do with the fact that the Caribbean person is incurably religious. Notions of atheism or agnosticism are quite rare in the region, and are often the result of ideological protest rather than metaphysical determination. Even overtly professing Marxist-Leninists in the region still appeal for prayerful support and religious solidarity with the divine. The traditionally Western dichotomy between sacred and secular spheres of life is often alien to the Caribbean mind, chiefly because the realities of life are so closely integrated for them and also because it is impossible for them to conceive of the divine absence from any aspect of human affairs.

The Caribbean person is always searching for relief from the tedium of social life, so much so that this search is sometimes callously labeled the "calypso mentality." But the deeply religious personality is often manifested in the singing or whistling of hymns or other sacred songs, the movement of the body in quasi-ritualistic modes, or the ready interpretation of daily occurrences as signs from above. Further, the way in which death and the afterlife are dealt with, not as tragic discontinuities but as natural sequences of life, points to a deeply religious mind-set in the Caribbean personality that also has a rich African connection. We shall return to this later on.

In sum, then, I think it is safe to say that the high level of religious tolerance, the constant search for religious meaning and human vitality, the capacity to be conservative and heterodox at the same time, the integration of believers from differing ethnic backgrounds, and the confident assurance with which ultimate factors of life are encountered, all combine to mark out the Caribbean personality as being unconditionally religious.

Our third consideration focuses on the relationship between religion and such factors as class, race, caste, power, and social access. Here we need to bear in mind that the advent of Christianity to the Caribbean was not originally meant for the spiritual health of the African slave population. The debate over whether Africans actually had souls that could be saved took a very long time to blow itself out. Christianity first took root in the region as a line of social demarcation. Christian missionaries later prevailed, and Africans were gradually admitted into the established religion, but not without social and political strings attached. Nonetheless, the African religious activities persisted, and the lower classes mainly sought admission to the religion of the upper classes for reasons other than religious fulfillment. With such a checkered history fully in place, then, Caribbean religion has continued through the centuries with considerations of race, class, caste, social access, and power functions still in evidence.

In general, systems of prestige and enhancement of social status are still closely allied to religious mobility. In addition to acquiring a sense of belonging in a particular religious grouping, adherents also find it possible to act out superior roles within, which are not possible without. For some people, Sunday mornings provide feelings of power and prominence that are not otherwise available during the rest of the week. Further, the religious cult or grouping ensures a certain amount of strength and loyalty to a social subgroup, and such strength is shared by most if not all the adherents. Yet there are other factors connected with power. In Vodun, for example, a great deal of syncretism often takes place between African traditions and Catholic practices—allegedly because of the need to conceal from whites and outsiders some precious religious traits. Power also means protection, which is sometimes assured by means of religious magic, or divination, or ancestor worship, or even through the ritual in established churches. As the faithful Vodun worshiper seeks protection from both Catholic practices and Vodun observances, it is said in some Haitian circles that it is better to rely on two magics rather than one!

Our fourth point has to do with the nature of Caribbean religion as a carrier of culture. In sharp contrast, in most Western societies, culture is the carrier of religion. Western culture is baptized by Western religion, and the object of worship in these societies directly reflects the norms and values of the dominant shapers of that culture. It is not surprising, therefore, that their God is understood to be the equivalent of a Supreme Military Commander or the chairman of a transglobal corporation whose profit-making and profit-sharing prowess is beyond question. Religion in such circumstances is simply a matter of inexhaustible good luck, and the prayerful preparation for a life of prosperity. But the Caribbean subsists in a scarcity of wealth and a rich abundance of humanity. Its culture has had to thrive against severe odds, not least of which has been the structural pluralism over which Europeans have long presided. Roger Bastide insists that in the New World there were three superimposed layers of folklore: African, creole, and white folklore. The first, he said, was "a pure traditional core, faithfully preserved."[4] No other mechanism existed by which this core of African folklore could be preserved except the songs, myths, drumming, dance, and ritual to which the African population hung tenaciously. Religion played a major role in this sociohistorical function. Nowhere is this more clearly to be seen than in Haiti, where Vodun has played a central part in sustaining the folk culture.

But Caribbean religion has had to carry several cultures—African, creole, European, and Asian. How has this been possible? The answer lies first in the nature of the pluralism of which we have already spoken. It also lies in the fact that, at the very roots of Caribbean existence, oppression and discrimination have produced alliances of solidarity, even across ethnic lines. So religion has served as a social mechanism of oblique protest against dehumanizing conditions and oppressive power structures. In Trinidad, for example, some East Indians are members of the Shango religion, whereas others are Spiritual Baptists; and tensions between the two groups are sometimes reported. However, what is interesting here is that, although East Indians are members of both cults, observers have noticed that East Indians usually are unable to become possessed by Shango spirits at their feasts, known as "palais." What accounts for this? Perhaps the words of W. E. B. DuBois about the depth of African spirituality can speak to such a situation. He noted that in the midst of an oppressed and downtrodden people "broods silently the deep religious feeling of the real Negro heart, the stirring, unguided might of powerful human souls who have lost the guiding star of the past and seek in the great night a new religious ideal."[5]

In addition to this search for a new religious ideal in the Caribbean, we must notice two related factors. One is the increasing tendency in the Caribbean, particularly in Haiti and Trinidad, to develop the Vodun and Shango practices, respectively, for the entertainment of the tourist sector. The other is the political ineffectiveness of most of the religious cults in the region. As early as 1972, Simpson suggested that "the time, thought, energy, and resources which are invested in shango, vodun, Revivalism, santeria, cumina, the Shouters, or in more conventional faiths, are not available as means for bringing about social, economic, or political changes. Also, the emotional release from accumulated frustration obtained from religious rituals often has the effect of reducing the amount of fervor available for political activity."[6] In spite of the continuing validity of Simpson's observations, however, there is increasing evidence in Trinidad, Haiti, and Jamaica that acceptance of the religious cults by the middle classes is being accompanied by some measure of political significance for these groupings. The quicker we rescue the invaluable assets of all our religious activities from the realm of the exotic, and strive courageously to place them as fully as possible within the mainstream of our socioeconomic and cultural life, the closer we will move toward our goal of Caribbean reconstruction.

THE AFRICAN SOUL

While the nation of Antigua and Barbuda was able to celebrate the 150th anniversary of emancipation from slavery in 1984, other countries — such as Jamaica, Trinidad and Tobago, and Barbados — held similar celebrations four years later. The historical reason is, of course, that the apprenticeship experiment between slavery and freedom was not implemented in Antigua. So there have been celebrations of emancipation in various Caribbean territories. Accounts of two events, which took place in Trinidad in 1988, help us to embark on our discussion of what I am calling the African soul.

The first event was a symposium of scholars dealing with the African past and the African diaspora, July 29–31, 1988. It was organized by a body known as the Confederation of African Associations of Trinidad and Tobago (COATT). In its final declaration, the symposium urged COATT to pursue the cause of African peoples in Trinidad and Tobago by responding to the "need for self-discovery, the quest for identity and the recovery, revival and re-assertion of African culture and heritage."[7] It called for an increase in consciousness about African history, art, language, culture, and literature. Toward the close of its declaration, the symposium noted that "the renaissance of African consciousness constitutes the basis of further and higher levels of contribution to the promotion of national development and life."[8] But is it possible for those who were not born in Africa, or who have never been there, or who have no direct parental linkage with the continent, to develop an African consciousness? Consciousness is formed by the power of the collective memory, perception, and sensation; it does not emerge from the creation of disconnected forms of social existence. What, then, does African consciousness mean to the Caribbean person whose existence is shaped mainly by the awareness of only Caribbean realities? Is African consciousness the same thing as the African soul? There is a strong case to be made that it is not and that, although the African soul can survive without form, African consciousness needs both form and substance.

The other event in Trinidad was the Orisa ceremony held to celebrate the visit of the Ooni of Ife (Nigeria) at the end of July 1988. A report on that ceremony is provided by Leo Bertley, a Trinidadian now resident in Montreal, whose maternal great grandfather, a Yoruba, came to Trinidad in 1854. As an Orisa High Priest, the Ooni presided over the ceremony, which Bertley describes in part this way:

> As he sat in regal religious splendour on a high ceremonial throne, ornately carved and specially prepared for him, one got the impression that one was in the presence of Greatness.
>
> The entire service was one of colourful but dignified pageantry, heightened spirituality replete with complex symbolism and deep mysticism.
>
> Those of us who allowed our spirits to merge with that of the Ooni and Oduduwa felt particularly charged and moved by the spirit of our ancestors....
>
> With this type of upliftment and real emancipation coming out of this memorable experience, it is difficult to understand how individuals of African descent could have refused to participate, directly or indirectly, in this Orisa service.[9]

Bertley bemoans the fact that one Trinidadian lady described the ceremony as an "obeah thing." The ceremony had been attended by the president and prime minister of the country. The Ooni himself had been accompanied on his visit by sixteen traditional African chiefs.

The question may well be asked, what did the Ooni really bring with him? Or what did he leave behind, in terms of the African consciousness? The deeply spiritual response of persons like Bertley should be respected, but it should also be borne in mind that millions of Afro-Caribbeans cannot trace their African ancestry and cannot be seized by an anonymous spirit. It is a cardinal principle of African religion that every spirit has a name and is somehow recognizable. Caribbean religion is comprised of many forms, but it does not provide a formula for the appropriation of all of them. The Ghanaian theologian John Pobee insists that "homo Africanus is a multi-headed hydra, displaying varieties not only vis-à-vis the non-African but also vis-à-vis other species of homo Africanus."[10] How, then, does one harmonize African pluriformity with Caribbean pluralism? The answer is that it is futile to try, for both cultures have been heavily infiltrated, or else seriously affected, by the heavy hand of European Balkanization in Africa or colonial domination in the Caribbean. It is precisely this historical encounter between the heavy hand of Europe and the indomitable African soul that merits some of our attention. We look first at Africa.

Europe's intervention in modern Africa is characterized by the slave trade. We are accustomed to dealing with the lives of the slaves in the New World, but we often neglect to reflect on what must have been left behind. In this regard, the words of the Nigerian scholar Emmanuel Obiechina are quite representative: "It would be right to say that the emasculation of African culture began with the slave trade when many of those who could have built a virile, thriving civilization on the continent were carted away and fear and psychosis were lodged deep in the heart of those left behind, menacing their psyche with fetters as heavy as the physical fetters of slavery."[11] Others speak of cultural imperialism and of the colonial experience of alienation, which makes them homeless even in their own homes.

Yet there is another side to this debate in Africa, and it has to do with the value of the civilization that the Europeans brought with them to the continent, and the radical change for the better that somehow ensued. Even if there is reason to believe that the noted African scholar Ali Mazrui has modified his position, his John Danz lectures in Seattle, Washington, in 1974 attest to an earlier position. In his lecture entitled "Language and Black Destiny," Mazrui suggests that the African experience of colonialism was both a political bondage and partially a mental liberation. He is particularly concerned here with the power of language. Mazrui makes the following comment:

The colonial impact might well have been the greatest liberating factor that the African had ever experienced, if by this we mean liberation from excessive subservience to ancestral ways. At the heart of this mental liberation was the world of new ideas. And this world was unveiled particularly well through the medium of the languages that came with those ideas. Of course once the stream of African thought was let loose, it was beyond the powers of the colonizers to determine the direction of its flow. Nor could the process of intellectual liberation be reversed.[12]

He proceeds to examine the process of Africanizing English and French with indigenous imagery, movement, myth, and metaphor. He concludes that the great challenge to blacks will be to create a means of communication that is both universal and particular. In a memorable word on the emergence of Afro-Saxons, Mazrui contends that Afro-Saxons "are not only here to stay; they may be here to multiply."[13]

Other arguments in favor of the positive results of colonialism in Africa point to the introduction to Africa of world trade, common languages, representative governments, a technological culture, new explanations (other than the traditional etiological explanations) for the phenomena of nature, and the immeasurable benefits from formal education. One Nigerian scholar goes so far as to claim, "It was colonialism that made so many hostile and warring ethnic groups into one country and kept them together by the might of *pax britannica.*"[14]

So the debate is still raging among African scholars themselves about the effects of Europe's historical presence and power in the continent, and the question of Westernization versus African cultural restoration is far from being settled. There is no question, however, that the African soul has flourished in the traditional religions, has converted Christianity and Islam (for missionary values were simply added to African values; they did not replace them), and has served as an integrative force for dealing with conflicting experiences. It was for this soul that E. Bolaji Idowu once made his plea with these words: "Africa must recover her soul; she must give the first and supreme position to her own God-given heritage, and be obedient to the teachings of her own God-appointed prophets."[15] Idowu's alleged elaborate pursuit of this ideal, however, has not gained wide appeal in Africa—probably because its people are reluctant to return to ancient forms as a way of expressing the vitality of the contemporary African soul. African life forms are changing, but the African life force is not.

In Africa, concepts of the soul are quite elaborate, and these concepts have somehow survived in Neo-African religions in the New World. In Dahomey, for example, all persons are said to have three souls, and adult males have four. Yoruba culture in Nigeria makes distinctions between the souls. There is the *emi* (breath), the *ojiji* (shadow), and the *ori* (guardian soul). In the Akan culture of Ghana the soul, although basically invisible, remains both corporeal and social; the departed soul can help the living solve mysterious crimes or locate lost possessions. In Haitian Vodun, each person has two souls—one to animate the body and the other to protect the person from dangers by night or day. Similarly, in Jamaica, Antigua,

St. Lucia, and elsewhere in the region, the concept of the multiple soul survives. Religious leaders claim special powers of consultation with invisible souls, and local entrepreneurs have been known to offer their souls for sale to the Devil at a crossroad in the dead of night, in return for immediate deliverance from financial ruin. Accounts of such transactions persist in Caribbean folklore.

But the African soul, or life force, has little to do with the configuration of souls or their spheres of influence. It has to do with the spiritual matrix—the source of meaning and worth for all that energizes African existence. It is that which accepts the continuing presence of God as the Great Ancestor and therefore seeks to share in God's creative activity. It is that which takes hold of time as a basic resource and as fundamental to the African self-understanding. Time is not a commodity for the African, something that can be measured, bought, or sold, as is the practice in Western societies; time is produced by the African in as much quantity and quality as the event warrants, for time is nothing more than a series of events. The acronym CPT (Colored People's Time) has much more to it than the lure of derision.

The African life force underlies the African people's deep sense of communalism—the sense that "I am only because we are." That "we" includes the ancestors, for in a very real sense many ancestors are the living dead. They may no longer be breathing, and their bodies may be buried, but they are very much alive in the affairs of the breathing ones. The African life force creates a strong need to memorialize these ancestors through family story and tradition, so that the past provides continuity with the present and assurance for the future. African people believe strongly in the immediacy of supernatural beings who share with ordinary persons a common existence and who must be appropriately addressed for the welfare of the whole community. This belief gives a concreteness to religion, a historical foundation to spirituality, and an integrated approach to the dominant view of the world, so that there is hardly any distinction between sacred and secular, or between matter and spirit, or even between consecrated and unconsecrated medicine.

Certain traditional African practices, such as divination, polygamy, animal sacrifices, and tribalism, often create difficulties for many non-Africans as they try to understand the dynamics of the African sociohistorical context. What comes naturally to African people, with all the practical wisdom informing their cultural traditions, provides grave sources of alienation for those who are on the outside looking in. But in every case where the African cultural scenario is brought up for close scrutiny, the African life force seems to empower Africans to hold tenaciously to their patterns of existence with great pride and determination. The debate about African polygamy at the 1988 Lambeth Conference, for example, took on a very challenging air when the African bishops came out in favor of a more sympathetic approach to what is for them a pastoral rather than a cultural problem. Serial monogamy in the West, the Africans contended, is a greater indictment of the sanctity of Christian marriage than serious polygamy in Africa. The bishops reminded their colleagues from the West that people who live in glass houses should not throw stones. Nevertheless, even if there have been some cultural discontinuities between the African and other traditions, there have been strong continuities between Africa and the Caribbean in the areas of symbolism, proverbial wisdom, music, movement, theodicy (that is, the power of evil in relation to the divine favor), the serial spirit, and myth. The African soul has subsisted in these principal substreams in the history of the Caribbean; but determined efforts have been made to counter its survival.

AFRICAN FOUNDATIONS IN THE CARIBBEAN SOUL

The white slaveholders experienced great difficulties in coping with the many cultural and religious practices that the Africans brought with them from their homeland: the ritual, drumming, songs, spirit possession, animal sacrifices, use of herbs, dances. Most of the time, they did not understand what was going on, and they derided these practices and took strong measures to suppress the slaves for fear of insurrection. Accounts of social situations in the early days betray a blissful ignorance about these practices. Here is the view of one Hans Sloane, who visited Barbados, Nevis, St. Christopher, and Jamaica early in the eighteenth century:

> The *Indians* and *Negros* have no manner of Religion by what I could observe of them. 'Tis true they have several Ceremonies, as Dances, Playing, &c, but these for the most part are so far from being Acts of Adoration of a God, that they are for the most part mixt with a great deal of Bawdry and Lewdness.[16]

And here is a report by a Roman Catholic priest about slaves on Saint-Dominque:

> Among these people song is a rather ambiguous sign either of gaiety or of sadness. They sing in adversity to while away their troubles, and they sing when they are happy to give vent to their joy. It is true that they have mournful songs and joyous songs, but it takes some experience to be able to distinguish the ones from the others.[17]

Christian missionaries and church leaders regarded Africanisms among the lower classes as manifestations of a heathenism that had to be suppressed, if not totally obliterated. Toward the close of the last century, we find prominent churchmen still adamant that the heathenism among the Negroes cried out for missionary activity. Bishop Bree of Barbados, writing to the Society for the Propagation of the Gospel in London in search of further financial support for West Indian missionary efforts, made the following claim: "It seems to me that it is quite as much work for God to preserve the black and coloured races of our old colonies from lapsing into heathenism as it is to break fresh ground in heathen lands."[18]

Bree's sentiments about heathenism point to a long train of official disdain for blacks in the nineteenth century. An 1825 entry in the vestry records of St. George's Church, Tortola, contains this directive:

> You have full permission to open the Church at any hour on Sunday or on any other day in the week that you may deem expedient, for the reception of such slaves as may be induced to attend Divine Service. At the same time it is proper to observe that the majority of the congregation is averse to having their pews occupied by the negroes, many of whom are afflicted with contagious diseases. It will therefore be necessary to confine them to the aisles and porch, in which benches shall be placed for their accommodation, and to the free seats in the gallery.[19]

This pattern of discrimination in church seating generally obtained in the established churches throughout the century, and served to reinforce the attitudes against Negroes and all that they represented to the ruling classes in Caribbean society. Elsewhere, I have already provided a substantial amount of discussion on this aspect of Barbadian history.[20] The evidence is overwhelming that white churchmen as a rule held West Indian blacks in generally low esteem.

Bishop Branch of Antigua held to the view that "our own West Indian negroes are still in the mass dark enough, ignorant and superstitious enough. The fact that they are such an emotional race accounts for much both of the good and evil in their religious character. Religion with them is peculiarly apt to be very evanescent."[21] This combination of attitudes to race, cultural habits, social deprivation, and religious tastes on the part of the whites made it difficult for blacks to find a ready welcome in the Christian churches, except perhaps the Moravian. The pervasive feeling of white superiority nurtured a strong notion of blacks as the inferior race, so that even Bishop John Mitchinson, the bishop of Barbados (1873–1881), who claimed that he had championed the cause of the Negro in Barbados, could not resist such feelings in his Ramsden Sermon at Cambridge in 1883.

In that sermon, Mitchinson allowed for three classes of humankind. The highest, of course, was the white European. The lowest was, according to him, "the savage pure and simple." Between both classes were those races who were inferior to the higher types of humanity but had come into contact with these "higher races." Of these, said Mitchinson, "the West Indian furnishes a good example; an example, too, the more instructive, because it is possible to compare the negro who has lived thus under Christianity with his heathen congener in Africa."[22] Mitchinson then proceeded to expand on his assessment of the West Indian Negro, based mainly on his experience in Barbados. His words speak eloquently for themselves, and about himself:

> But in the case of negro Christianity, at least of West Indian negro Christianity, the uneradicated faults and vices are much more palpable and apparent, and perhaps more generally diffused than those of European Christianity.
>
> They are the vices that either have come down to them from the days of their African heathenism, or were incident to their condition in the West Indies previous to emancipation and Christianity. Superstition of an abject and soul-enthralling kind, doubtless an indelible reminiscence of Africa, is widely prevalent among them, side by side with their Christianity, and, as is always the case where superstition and religion have to measure their strength against each other, proves the stronger motive power of the two. In every island the Obeah man, despite the efforts of the law to put the thing down, exercises a baleful ascendancy, and is by turns dreaded and sought after by his dupes. . . . Besides being enslaved by these iniquitous superstitions, the negro Christian has too often a very limited practical belief in the sanctity of truth and honesty; many an habitual Church-goer is prone to lying, cheating, and petty pilfering. He fails too often to bridle his tongue, and to the sins of evil speaking and lying many and many a one adds slandering.[23]

John Gilmore's recent book on Mitchinson, *The Toiler of the Sees*, fails to explain, or else explains away, the bishop's position on the Negro question in this historic sermon.[24]

As we approach the close of the twentieth century, we find that West Indian Christianity is firmly in the hands of the descendants of those whose very existence was grossly despised less than a century ago because of their African ancestry. The resolute attempts to suppress African religious and cultural evanescence in the established churches gave rise to Pentecostal-like groupings early in this century and somehow ensured the greater survival of Neo-African cults. Thus, both by European default and African determination in Caribbean religious history, we have witnessed the reality of African immortality in the Caribbean soul.

THE AFRICAN SOUL IN CARIBBEAN RELIGION

Edward Wilmot Blyden was born of free and pious parents on the island of St. Thomas in 1832. Refused entry to three theological schools in 1850 because he was black, he rose to become Liberia's ambassador to the Court of St. James (England). Blyden devoted his life and his substance to the promulgation of the Negro race and has come to be regarded as the spiritual father of black pride in the twentieth century. He insisted that the Negro race was not inferior, that it had produced many achievements worthy of great pride, that its rich culture was worth preserving, and that there was an intrinsic African personality characterized by spirituality, communality, and continuity. Blyden confidently believed that Africa might well prove to be the spiritual conservatory of the world.

The beginning of this century witnessed a tremendous upsurge of the pan-African spirit, in Liberia, the United States, Britain, and the Caribbean. The West Indian lawyer Henry Sylvester-Williams organized the African Association Conference in London in July 1900. The extensive efforts and influence of Marcus Garvey are too well known to be repeated; so, too, perhaps is the work of George Padmore.

The African soul has been nurtured and sustained not only on the mother continent but also in the New World, where it has taken root. Brazil has the second largest population of people of African descent after Nigeria; the United States is third in line. Africa is both a physical reality and a spiritual reality in the New World. African forms, styles, tastes, and substance may vary, because of cultural and historical factors, but there is an African soul, a life force, a vitality, a heartbeat, a spiritual substream that runs through this portion of the human family. Many have been the attempts to give expression to this African soul in the Caribbean. The Rastafarian movement, the Black Power advocates, authors like O. R. Dathorne and C. L. R. James, poets like Derek Walcott and Edward Brathwaite, and some folklorists have made sterling contributions to the promulgation of the African presence in our life and work.

But the theologians have not been generally active in this fundamental endeavor, for reasons directly attributable to the historical function of the Christian church in the region. It is nevertheless the task of the Caribbean theologian to demonstrate systematically that to be of African descent is not the result of a divine mistake, and that the lingering sin of self-contempt no longer finds justification in the devices of former rulers. Emancipation and self-affirmation are inseparable. Theological emancipation is on the way, however, and discussions such as this are to be taken as small efforts in the greater task of full human emancipation and development in the Caribbean.

It is not the back-to-Africa movement that we uphold; it is the forward-with-Africa spirit that we proclaim. It is not the myth of the Negro past that we must dwell on; it is the myth of the Negro present and future that we must construct. It is not the Western dichotomy between head and heart, sacred and secular, means and ends that we must sanctify; there is an irrefutable place for the African fusion of ideals with materialism, body with soul, feeling with thinking, art with sensuality. It is eminently respectable to emotionalize our spiritual experiences, as it is to physicalize those emotions in the movement of our bodies—whether in dance, ritual, or quiet homage. The black Anglican archbishop in solemn procession in his cathedral has much more in common with the Spiritual Baptist archbishop in his mourning ceremony, or the Orisha priest at his palais ritual, than he may realize. Their forms may vary quite considerably, but they are spiritual cousins. There is an African soul in Caribbean existence, permeating its institutional, cultural, and political life. If only we had the collective courage and political will to give a more honest expression to this reality, our total engagement in Caribbean emancipation would be far more effective.

Life in the Caribbean is a hard form of existence, and those who can survive in the region are generally preconditioned to finding life somewhat easier elsewhere. Further, that determination of Caribbean people elsewhere to contribute to an easier life in the region often obscures some of the harsher realities of Caribbean existence. The ethic of communalism exists where old-age pensions, social welfare systems, and unemployment benefits do not. Could not this ethic be matched by the politics of communalism, where adversarial partisanship would give way to the paramountcy of the common good, and where political acumen would come to mean sacrificial service and not individual prowess? Can there really be true emancipation in the Caribbean as long as the predilections of the few, however constitutional and valid, continue to define the predicament of the many?

The social principle of popular participation is especially significant here, for all Caribbean people must struggle together to achieve many common goals. There is the goal of self-reliance, which must diminish all forms of insufficiency or dependence on others at home or abroad. There is the goal of cultural sovereignty, which must diligently seek to Caribbeanize foreign ideas, gifts, or package deals. The inherent dignity of the African soul resists any notion that the region should become a dumping ground. There is the goal of emancipatory education, by which we develop our wits and our sensibilities to be creative, resourceful, and mutually affirming; to enrich and enhance our art of communication and social intercourse with the imagery, beauty, and wisdom that we have inherited. There is the goal of social justice, whereby we seek to be fair and equitable in matters of need, access, rights, and privilege. But the pursuit of none of these goals will be authentic without the radical acknowledgment that Caribbean life and institutions also have religious foundations. Caribbean religion is not a lost cousin of Caribbean home life; it takes its full place in the duties of social reconstruction.

Caribbean religion is not only a basic carrier of our culture but also a transforming agent. Instead of serving as a means of escape from social realities, Caribbean religion can encourage our escape from indifference and complacency toward the task of emancipation. Instead of serving as a means of manipulation, Caribbean religion can manipulate the creative human spirit toward a better quality of life for our people. If Caribbean religion is still seen as a form of social protest, the focus must be on the enemy within, since the enemy without can no longer carry the blame.

Above all, Caribbean religion must become a collective form of social engagement, making its own unique contributions to Caribbean reconstruction in the following ways.

First, the restoration of strong family values is fundamental for the strengthening of our social fabric. The extended family must again be cultivated to provide supportive mechanisms for the nuclear family structure. The sense of the continuing family, comprised both of the living and the departed, must not be trivialized by psychological theory or psychic fantasy. Our ancestors are still very much alive in us. The dignity of womanhood must radiate from the matriarchal nature of our family culture, and the virtues of respect for the elders who earn respect should once again be unchallenged.

Second, Caribbean religion must continue to meet the common needs of the human condition, resisting the subtle forms of evil, responding to the hardships and limitations of human life, coping with the meaning of death and the quest for salvation. Yet Caribbean religion must also give strength to the black serial spirit within its people—the spirit of pilgrimage, which impels the people to move from state to state, always seeking a brighter future, always hoping that their present state of belonging will bring fulfillment, but always searching nevertheless. This serial spirit in Caribbean life finds its rootage in the African soul, but it strives persistently for meaning and wholeness within the limited constraints of Caribbean existence.

Third, Caribbean religion must become more intentional about establishing fertile linkages with Afro-Americans and Afro-Brazilians. For too long there have been breaches in communication and understanding among the peoples of Africa in the New World. Those who have divided us have enjoyed ruling over our divisions. Caribbean reconstruction cannot afford to ignore the rich heritage we share with our cousins in the United States and Brazil. The primacy of tourism as an industrial base in the region offers an invaluable framework for establishing stronger linkages. The Black church in America is the only major organization that Afro-Americans can truly call their own; it is the source of vitality for most of America's thirty million blacks. And yet the Caribbean knows little about it. We shall be discussing the contextual connections for emancipation between the Caribbean and African-American communities under the rubric of the "Black Story" in Chapter Six. Programs of exchange visits and mutual encounter with Afro-Brazilians would release incalculable insights about the vast wealth of spirituality and culture that Brazil's ninety million blacks possess. It is always instructive to compare the experience of the Caribbean with that of Brazil, where African culture was officially encouraged in order to perpetuate class distinctions. The African soul is a long-suffering life force.

Our fourth issue has to do with ecumenism in the region. There is a natural ecumenism of concern in the Caribbean; it touches the political ethos, the social morals, the economic development of the region, and the crises that generally affect the well-being of our people. People come together quite naturally across religious boundaries, but they need to stick together even when there is no crisis. Efforts at religious integration need not be interpreted to mean uniformity, but those who share an African soul should not allow accidents of religious persuasion to obscure their common hope and the solidarity of their ideals. Radical integration at the religious level in the Caribbean can usher in a deeper level of integration at the political and social levels.

Our final issue deals with the Caribbean sense of beauty. Caribbean people love to "dress up"; their inherent sense of beauty, nurtured by the African soul, expresses itself in various forms of aesthetics, in ritual and ceremonies of all kinds, and in the flowery forms of verbal expression. Whether in religious ritual or social activity of any kind, this innate sense of beauty and style is never obscured. Caribbean religion must play a major role in continuing to foster this special area of Caribbean freedom and creativity, in music, speech, song, or the proclamation of the Word through proverbial wisdom and soul-building myth.

In conclusion, it is important for me to stress that the claims made for Caribbean religion cannot be understood in isolation from other forms of Caribbean endeavor. The Caribbean continues to be an open society, susceptible to the winds of change and vulnerable to the powers of external self-interest. But the Caribbean has survived where pundits predicted otherwise. Its survival is in large measure due to its religious foundations, and its religious foundations have been sustained by a persistent African spiritual reality. African dashikis, hairstyles, and first names may still upset existing Caribbean prejudices, but the deeply rooted African soul cannot. Forms of religion may conflict, but the sources of that religion cannot; for we all share a common need for a relationship with some great Other, whether Ancestor, Orisha, Saint, or Savior. Caribbean emancipation and reconstruction must go hand in hand as we seek to carry the strengths of our past into a brighter future. May the words of a famous Barbadian hymn writer at the turn of this century, Arnold J. Ford, still bring spiritual empowerment today:

> O Africa awaken!
> The morning is at hand,
> No more art thou forsaken
> O bounteous motherland,
> From far thy sons and daughters
> Are hastening back to thee,
> Their cryings o'er the waters
> That Africa shall be free.[25]

Can the theological task for the Caribbean be readily identified out of the context that has so far been charted in this book? What is the project of emancipation to which all this discussion about changing circumstances and grave crises seems to point? What does it mean to be a Christian at this critical juncture in Caribbean historical development? Is the Caribbean church up to the task of social change and full human emancipation, or will it cede its pioneering role to other groupings of people? As an open society, can the Caribbean draw any emancipatory insights from other areas of the Third World which are struggling for liberation and social wholeness? What about Africa, India, and Afro-America, with which it has had historical connections? Can any lines of solidarity be established between their respective stories? In short, where is the emancipating hand of God in the Caribbean context?

The rest of this book will seek to deal with these and other related issues as we explore the meaning of an emancipatory theology in the historical and cultural context of Caribbean existence, and as we seek to make a contribution to the wider global discourse on intercultural theology and the theology of liberation.

CHAPTER FIVE

CARIBBEAN THEOLOGICAL FOUNDATIONS

In recent times, Christians the world over have been seeking new ways of articulating their faith contextually. The wave of renewal that began with the pontificate of John XXIII and the Second Vatican Council was reinforced by the global influence of the World Council of Churches and other bodies over the past three decades. The rise of popular movements in Third World countries has been the driving force in building new forms of social consciousness on the part of the poor, the powerless, and the oppressed peoples of the world. The liberation movements in Southern Africa, the genesis of newly established nationalist movements in other areas, and the thrust of the United Nations in promoting human rights and dimensions of social and economic justice — all have contributed to an increased awareness of what it means to take one's faith seriously.

Further, the traditional hegemony of Western theology over the minds and conduct of an inordinate number of Christians has been seriously challenged. This challenge has come about not because of any perceived bankruptcy in the theological marketplace but because of the increased irrelevance of such theological norms and concepts to the actual conditions and expectations of people in the Third World. It has been increasingly acknowledged that the Christian theological enterprise is not the preserve of the West. The development of Western civilization was indeed closely allied with the evolution of the Christian theological and missionary enterprise; for this was the basis on which colonialism and slavery were given sacred approval for centuries. Yet at no point could the interpretation and proclamation of the Gospel of Jesus Christ ever become the exclusive right of the North, or even of the West. Christianity did not begin in the West. Indeed, the very universality of the Gospel has consistently challenged Western claims to superiority and power, and has eventually produced a new wave of theological initiative among Third World Christians.

A consultation held in Seoul, Korea, in September 1984, under the sponsorship of the World Alliance of Reformed Churches, paid special attention to the issue of Gospel and culture. The assembled church leaders and theologians agreed that a new freedom was required in order to relate the Gospel to the culture of Asia. They also said this:

A careful analysis of Western culture is required. It must not be mistaken for Christian culture. The Gospel must be liberated from Western civilization; it must be made clear that the Gospel implies a radical critique of many of the values on which Western civilization is based.[1]

Gustavo Gutiérrez has rightly suggested that "the greatest refutation of a theology lies in its practical consequences and not in intellectual arguments."[2] The practical consequences of the traditional Western theological formularies had failed to promote a sense of freedom to affirm local realities, especially the cultural and social realities among Third World and oppressed peoples. As a result, one of the practical consequences of the new search for liberation was the search for the liberation of theology itself. Theological liberation had to be seen not merely as the reconstruction of religious freedom, or the freedom to define the nature of faith, but also as the freedom to put that faith to work in the struggle for historical and concrete manifestations of freedom.

Gutiérrez insists that "theology becomes a liberating and prophetic force which tends to contribute to the total understanding of the word which takes place in the actions of real life."[3] The real-life context is important, since it rejects the constellation of abstractions and intellectualisms and provides for the people of faith—especially the poor and alienated—the main indications of what authentic liberation entails. Hence, "a theological reflection in the context of liberation takes its point of departure from the perception that the context obliges us to rethink radically our Christian being and our being as Church."[4] It is therefore not possible to expect an authentically liberating theology until the poor and alienated are entirely free to reflect creatively and to express appropriately what is the meaning of their faith as the people of God.

In the fascinating journal of his exploratory visits to South American countries, Henri Nouwen pays particular attention to the prominence, meaning, and vitality of liberation theology. He was impressed by the fact that it stayed close to the daily lives of the people:

> What makes liberation theology so original, challenging, and radical is not so much its conceptual content as its method of working. A true liberation theologian is not first someone who thinks about liberation, but someone whose thought grows out of a life of solidarity with those who are poor and oppressed. Liberation theologians do not think themselves into a new way of living, but live themselves into a new way of thinking.[5]

Many European and North American centers of learning have now committed themselves to appropriating Third World theological initiatives to Western religious experiences and behavior. It is not without significance that many Western theologians are attempting to educate themselves about the new theological surges emanating from the Third World. They have finally realized that there is no universal theology; that theological norms arise out of the context in which one is called to live out one's faith; that theology is therefore not culture free; and that the foundations on which theological structures are built are actually not transferable from one context to another. Thus, although the Gospel remains the same from place to place, the means by which that Gospel is understood and articulated will differ considerably through circumstances no less valid and no less authentic.

The new global Christian consciousness, which has been emerging in the wake of the new wave of theological initiatives, spells freedom from Western dominance in thought, beliefs, styles, and expectations. It also spells freedom for a new understanding of human freedom itself, and of the concrete imperatives that such freedom engenders in different contexts. Local theologies of freedom, or liberation, or emancipation are therefore being constructed across the Third World. Robert J. Schreiter has identified three models by which such local theologies are being constructed. He speaks of translation models, adaptation models, and contextual models. Translation and adaptation models are clearly part of the legacy of Western missionary enterprise and experimentation, and have largely failed to forge for oppressed and alienated people any genuine struggle for social transformation or cultural liberation. The models that have taken context seriously have found their points of departure in the Gospel, the local church, and the local culture. They have attempted to take into account the necessary dynamic interaction of these three foundational factors, and they have provided for their promoters a new understanding of human freedom in the light of historical faith.[6]

Genuine Caribbean sociocultural and historical foundations provide adequate impetus for the construction of a contextual theology. The theological traditions in the region have historically been patterned along lines of adaptation, or extension, or imitation; for Caribbean people in their home region have been the victims of colonialistic and neocolonialistic insensitivity throughout their existence. Economically, they have experienced poverty— structured, endemic, and persistent. Politically, they have had to grapple with problems of dependence in its pluriform manifestations. Dependence has been overlaid in the Caribbean with layers of unvarnished racism and external exploitation. Culturally, survivalism has fed itself on patterns of alienation and self-contempt, and Caribbean people have had to struggle for their existence by turning away from their roots through emigration and miseducation. Theologically, there has been a wholesale importation of ideas, literature, ethical and religious norms, and forms of articulation. Imitation has been the predominant policy. Caribbean theological and religious vessels have historically been carriers of many non-Caribbean goods and services to their own people.

During the past two decades, however, Caribbean indigenous religious leaders have begun to develop new patterns of prophetic and theological consciousness. This new consciousness has led to a new articulation of, and reflection on, the persistent poverty, dependence, alienation, and imitation. In turn, this new articulation has emerged under the rubric of emancipation, the major event in Caribbean history, which in August 1834 should have heralded the genesis of the new Caribbean society. Over a century and a half later, emancipation has yet to be translated into the actual structures of political, economic, cultural, and theological independence. The call of Caribbean religious leaders and theologians to their own people, to work out in practical and concrete terms what true emancipation means, is the ground of contextual theological construction in the region.

"Emancipation" is the Caribbean word for liberation, not only because it denotes the major Caribbean event but also because it evokes a sense of accountability to the Caribbean forebears in slavery and to the Caribbean descendants in freedom. Emancipation is still an event to be fleshed out, structured, refined, and reinforced in the Caribbean life system. It beckons Caribbean people away from their poverty, dependence, alienation, and imitation, and thus challenges them to reconstruct a social and historical reality that will banish the "old days" forever. Emancipation is the story that Caribbean people seek to tell with their lives — their politics, economics, culture, and relationships. It energizes their migratory tendencies to search for a better life in foreign lands. They carry their story with them, however, and they return occasionally to their native region, if only for spiritual reinvigoration. Most Caribbean people, wherever they live, work to fulfill their dream of returning to the Caribbean. Many never make it.

Theological initiatives in the region have therefore tended to take the meaning and exploration of human freedom very seriously, without much of an attempt to translate versions of liberation theology from other parts of the Third World into the language of the region. Racism, classism, self-contempt, nonresponsibility, and exploitation have been the major manifestations of sin in the region. When these have been theologically assessed in the context of poverty, dependence, alienation, and imitation (to which we will repeatedly refer in this chapter), some fundamentally new categories for theological construction have suggested themselves in the light of emancipatory faith, and in the context of Christian praxis for social and spiritual transformation. The Gospel of Jesus Christ has indeed been accepted as the word of salvation; but when the meaning of salvific truth and human freedom has been placed alongside Caribbean historical consciousness, a new formulation of theological priorities has emerged. At the heart of it all has been the persistent affirmation that God has accepted Caribbean people just as they are, with all their cultural baggage and traditions, and that God wills that they should not persist in self-negation or self-contempt.

The foundations of a Caribbean theology have historically been smothered and made ineffective by repeated attempts to erect patently inappropriate patterns of thought and articulation. Patterns of colonization, of domination and imposition, have shaped the theological enterprise in the region, just as they have shaped the rest of Caribbean existence. The reflections on the interaction between God and Caribbean humanity have never been allowed to flourish. Caribbean sociology, anthropology, and history have hardly ever been taken into account in the theologies dispensed in the region. Several Caribbean theologians have therefore called for the decolonization of Caribbean theology, and have suggested in various ways how such a process might best be embarked upon. Our present concern is to examine how an indigenous and relevant theology for the region might be constructed.

TESTING THE STRUCTURES

Caribbean society owes the genesis of most of its structures to the spirit of European expansionism (as indeed does North American society). The social institutions that have persisted within such a framework—church, school, court, plantations—are chiefly to be explained or assessed in that context. The origins of Christian "churches" in the region must also be understood apart from the origins of Christian "missions." The churches were brought with the settlers and their kith and kin as an extension of what they had been accustomed to in the "mother country." It was as if they had brought their god with them, not only for heavenly sanction but also for earthly protection. The English brought their "Church of England" with them, while the other Europeans brought the "Church of Rome." Both of these "churches" were integral parts of the establishment that defined, controlled, and contained the new plantation societies. On the other hand, the Christian "missions" came later, long after the churches had been established in full sway, and long after it had become obvious that the churches were mainly ineffective or unenthusiastic in addressing the basic personal needs of the masses on the plantations; for the churches were never intended for them in the first place.

As was evident in our previous chapter, the history of religion in the Caribbean and the history of the church in the region are not identical in the least. The structures of the church have not always been compatible with the structures of religion, deeply embedded as it has always been in the very soul of Caribbean people. Religion has extended far beyond the reaches of the church, and without it the observable structures of the church could not have survived. The church itself could not have survived in the region without the foundations of a religion for which it was not accountable, and for which it rarely provided adequate nurture.

The church has therefore passed through four phases in its relationship with the people. Phase One may be termed "The Church and the People." Here it functioned as an institution of the power structure to maintain the status quo as best it could. Phase Two we might label "The Church for the People." In this phase, the church was used as an instrument of socialization, in such processes as education and social welfare. There was no change of the power base for the broad masses of the people within the structures of the church. Phase Three can be termed "The Church of the People." This phase represents the first major shift in the life and ethos of the church in general, where more of the ordinary members began to assume some importance, many of the men earlier denied leadership positions (including ordination) were now being promoted, and earlier signs of indigenization began to take full shape.

The church in the Caribbean is now in the throes of a complex transitional phase. It is rapidly moving out of the Phase Three stage, but paradoxically it is slowly moving into Phase Four, which I choose to call "The People's Church." Most of the missionaries have left, and most of the foreign financial support has been curtailed. The meager resources of the members are grossly inadequate to maintain the physical structures inherited from a former time, and most of these structures are in need of extensive repair or replacement. New models of management, ministry, and mission are still being discussed, but none has been seriously implemented. Thus, the poverty, dependence, alienation, and imitation also find concrete expression in the realities of Caribbean church existence today. And yet no other institution in the region is better placed to make the best use of the roots of emancipation than the Caribbean church, for these roots are basically religious. We need to ask what roots we are talking about, and to look at some of them.

We are talking about a people who are largely ancestorless in ethnic character. The rootedness of a people is based on their ability to recount where they came from and who their forebears were. Most rooted people have a family story that is passed on from generation to generation. The rootedness of Caribbean people has been broken by the Middle Passage, the crossing from Africa and India to the Caribbean. Names were changed, linkages were broken, records were never kept, spirits were crushed, and the soul was submerged. Caribbean people are essentially a New World people. For example, I know that my maternal grandmother was called "Missie Burton," but I do not know what her mother's name was. My grandmother was certainly the grandchild of a slave, whose name I have never heard. Thus, my own sense of matriarchy begins with "Missie Burton," and she died in the 1950s. Caribbean people are today more the ancestors of the generations to come than they are the descendants of a line of ancestry. Slavery and indentureship created such a radical discontinuity in the Caribbean human tradition that it is not unreasonable to maintain that Caribbean people are themselves the foundation of a new ancestral tradition, especially since the threat of extinction has now been eliminated.

Caribbean society is essentially matrifocal—the mother has historically been the center or head of the family. Most of the children in the Caribbean are still born out of wedlock, and the function of marriage as the formation of the nuclear family has never been fully acknowledged. Many historical factors account for this, including the inability of slaves to legally marry, the loose morals of plantation owners, and the inability of Caribbean males to provide bread to those for whose birth they are partially responsible. Therefore the mother, or the grandmother, has been the focal point of family stability. However, modern psychological theories about the effects of absent fathers on the lives of children have not found much support, since most Caribbean children grow into adulthood in family settings, where close, warm, and affectionate relationships are generally experienced and where expressions of mutual care and responsibility between elders and children (even in extended families) are the norm. The matriarch creates this atmosphere and core of mutual relationship and caring, and therefore provides for the Caribbean society a foundation of humanity and a consciousness of worth and value that is irreplaceable.

There is a very real sense in which Caribbean people are incurably communitarian in nature. They live in the community, and the community lives in them. Their sense of community regulates a good deal of their social behavior and is far more powerful than the force of legislative action. The power of gossip can always be felt, and choices of actions, relationships, and life-styles are heavily determined by the consideration of what others in the community are likely to think or say. Since most communities serve as protective environments for their members, these feelings of allegiance to the community hinge more on respect than on fear. The power of community feeling is therefore very important in Caribbean society, so that even if individual members of the community are not articulate enough to express their beliefs or feelings, the community does it on their behalf.

Certain considerations follow from this basic underlying communitarian nature of Caribbean society. The various aspects of Caribbean life, of which we have already spoken in Chapters Two and Three, find their context here: the sandlike nature of Caribbean fortunes, the many ups and downs that the people constantly have to face, the crises we have outlined (including the fragmentation and the drug trafficking). Because of their sense of community, Caribbean people are strong enough to cope with these pressures and still remain warm and celebrative. They find it easy to forgive and forget, to pick up the pieces and move forward. They have an attitude of tolerance that often causes non-Caribbean people to marvel, and they cope with a wide array of contradictions and pain that often defy the more "enlightened" minds of sophisticated societies. Many of the "sins" that cause heads to roll in other cultures are taken in stride in Caribbean culture. Caribbean people are often stunned by the fuss that is made of "small" crimes while the big ones are allowed to get away.

Furthermore, Caribbean people are extremely resourceful and adaptable. They have been habituated over the years to make the most of the little at their disposal, and to adapt whatever was available to suit their own perceived needs and circumstances. They have never been in the habit of allowing others to interpret their needs for them; nor have they allowed others, especially self-serving overlords, to interpret their real strengths and priorities.

Still other characteristics have made it possible for Caribbean people to survive within the structures of the church, as well as in spite of them. We can refer to these human attitudes as the structures of reception, respect, reinterpretation, and response. Let us look briefly at each one of these in turn.

First, there is the structure of *reception*. Most of the preaching and teaching in the churches were adapted from models and images of other cultures. The literature and the music, the liturgies and the theologies, the vestments and the sacred vessels, the patterns of holiness and the canons of saints—all were given sanction and approval from abroad. Nothing that the people saw and heard bore any relationship to how they lived, or to what meant most for them in daily living. Thus, there was a radical discontinuity between what was sacred and blessed by the church and what was indigenous to the people. Their manner of birth and pattern of life, their relationships, and their modes of getting and spending were regarded by the church as sinful. The structure of reception made it possible for the people to hold tenaciously to the belief that behind all that church performance there was still a God who could be better understood, and who really understood them, in spite of what they looked like or what they did, mostly through no fault of their own. Circumstances made them who they appeared to be.

Second, the structure of *respect* has always been an important cultural instrument in the hands of Caribbean people. It is sometimes a weapon, sometimes a shield, sometimes a decoy, sometimes a badge, sometimes an envoy, sometimes a conduit. Whatever its function, respect has always paid great dividends for Caribbean people. No wonder, then, that most children are brought up to "have manners and respect." Where did all this begin? Did it begin on the plantations, where the planters inflicted the need for respect on their subordinates? Or did it begin earlier, in a more wholesome society, where respect for the elders was found in the very marrow of society's bones? I think it is the latter, and although in slave society "Massa" insisted on being respected, such respect came naturally, for there was something more than respect which "Massa" could not command. External respect did not always enjoin internal allegiance, and for most Caribbean people the latter is far more important than the former.

Much the same thing has traditionally happened in organized religion in the region. In the established churches, the religious leaders—priests, pastors, ministers, bishops—have maintained the respect of most of the membership. Much of what they have said and promulgated has been benignly received and calmly respected, but there has been no guarantee that genuine allegiance has been in place. Thus, although the church has enjoyed a high position of respect in the Caribbean community, and its formal influence has been considerable, such respect has not frequently translated itself into the true and genuine allegiance of its members, especially where ethical, moral, or political options have been at stake. The church has received respect but has yet to gain the moral authority it should have in the lives of the people, primarily because it has never been "The People's Church"; that phase of its history is yet to begin.

The third structure, *reinterpretation*, was critical in the lives of Caribbean people, as far as their religion was concerned. The work of the Christian missionaries was made easy because they did not encounter an irreligious people. At the same time, it was made more difficult because they could never get the people to do exactly what they said—chiefly because the people did not agree with them. Caribbean people took hold of the Gospel in their own way, reinterpreting its main tenets and then passing it on to their offspring—often in contradiction to all that the churches were proclaiming. It is precisely because the people were able to reinterpret the Gospel message, and to find for themselves a pattern of good news that would otherwise have been missed, that the foundations of a Caribbean theology are so much in place, in spite of the inappropriate structures that have been inherited. The spirit of reinterpretation, then, has always been in evidence—whether in the singing of hymns or songs, the reading of scripture, the preaching of sermons, the recitation of prayers, or even in their address to God. Caribbean Christianity has always undergone a process of serious reinterpretation, and this has in no little way frustrated the efforts of those who would have preferred to preside indefinitely over what Caribbean people could not believe or profess.

The fourth structure is *response*. A people's response to the structures of reality is generally indicative of their response to reality itself. In the Caribbean, the rigors of poverty and dependence have often produced a hardiness and a strategy of survival, as well as a philosophy for living, that can make a difference for all of life. In such an existence, there are hardly any divisions between forms of reality; there are hardly any dichotomies to be made, for all of life is one.

It is this tendency toward a holistic pattern of life and experience that has characterized the Caribbean structure of response, to such an extent that the lines between sacred and secular are as blurred as those between good and not so good. This tendency also has far-reaching implications for Caribbean people's notions about the past, the present, and the future. Sometimes, to their own apparent detriment, they will assess the present in terms of the past, rather than assessing the present in terms of the future. Who you were often tells most about who you are. Nevertheless, this pattern of holistic response has within it the groundwork for a theologically emancipative framework.

SOUNDINGS OF FAITH

Caribbean people make a clear distinction between "Churchianity" and "Christianity." A well-known saying in the region goes like this: "Nearer to church, farther from God." God is real in the Caribbean, even more real than the sun and the sky. God is more than just the God in the Bible. In general, because of the way it has been presented to them, Caribbean people cannot identify with the people depicted in the Bible—apart from the slaves in Egypt or the people of the land struggling under the extravagances of kings. Yet they accept many attributes of the biblical God and even add many other attributes, derived from their experiences with fortune and misfortune. For example, "Tief from tief mek God laugh,"[7] conveys a traditional sense of divine justice mixed with mirth when the thief (slave owner) loses at the hands of the one from whom so much has already been stolen (slave). God is the ultimate source of justice, truth, love, wisdom, life, healing, and hope. The real God does not like "ugly," a local way of speaking about evil. Yet evil is real. The reality of evil manifests itself in a number of different ways, but Caribbean people are able to distinguish the effects of sin and wrongdoing from other evils, which cannot be explained: Some things just happen, that's the way life is, and there is nothing we can do about it. Drought, disease, hurricanes, natural calamities or deformities, mysterious accidents, and other unfavorable phenomena—all find their place in the list of the mysterious and unexplainable, for God moves in a mysterious way. Yet God never gets the blame. We are just too limited in power or wisdom to understand all the mysteries of life. And these mysteries provide new ground for strengthening faith rather than weakening it. Thus, Caribbean people maintain a strong faith in a God of love even though there appear to be many "grounds" to believe otherwise.

The other side of the question of evil has to do with sin. This is historically a debatable issue in the Caribbean, chiefly because the primary notions of morality often vary in relation to the class or status of the "sinner." The sins of the upper classes are accorded a different status and classification from those of the lower classes. Euphemistic terms become more frequent as the same lapses in moral behavior appear further up the social ladder. Caribbean people have never been fools in this respect at all, and they have not been hesitant to call sin by its right name, regardless of the sinner. The question, therefore, is not whether all persons—regardless of their rank—are sinners but, rather, "What is the nature of the Caribbean sin?"

The missionaries regarded it as the sexual immorality that produced thousands of children out of wedlock. Most Caribbean people believe that being born out of wedlock is better than not being born at all; and, in any case, many of those born out of wedlock were fathered by married men. So sex is not where we need to look for the Caribbean sin. We need to look for it in the area of nonresponsibility, for this is the area that touches every class of Caribbean citizenry. Two things are clear in the Caribbean groundings of faith: (1) Caribbean people, like the rest of humankind, live in a sinful world. (2) The structures of sin are deeply rooted in the ways of social intercourse, and only someone like Jesus Christ is able to rise above it all or to deliver those who are encumbered by it. No human agency is untouched by sin, nor does any find exemption from the need to be set free. Caribbean harmatology therefore forms the basis for Caribbean cosmology and Christology.

Caribbean people are deeply devoted to the reality of a God who not only creates the world but who also loves the world. Many of them live very close to nature, not only by their constant relationship with the sun, sea, sand, and land but also because of their close communitarian links through family and human relationships. The world is the constant sphere of God's loving and providential activity on behalf of Caribbean people. Therefore, they can affirm with the psalmist that the earth is the Lord's and the fullness within it. Cosmology consists in the basic belief that while there is life in the Caribbean, there is always hope. The Bible thus becomes an important tool for the interpretation of, and response to, the world as God's creation, and it also provides the continuing story of how God faithfully persists in dealing with the problems of the world through the meaning of the life, death, and resurrection of Jesus Christ.

The character of Jesus in the Gospel takes on historical significance for Caribbean people, not merely because he was human but more especially because he assumed the figure of a grass-roots leader who successfully confronted the authorities. Jesus is important because he led a movement of resistance against the Devil, as well as against the most debilitating forms of human existence – disease, hunger, poverty, social rejection, hopelessness, and death. The miracle stories provide hope and strength; the parables become meaningful for those who live close to nature and the pastoral life. The encounters with the poor and dispossessed make it possible for the underclasses of this world to be in touch with the God of Jesus. Jesus ushered in then, and continues to usher in now, a new era of liberation, emancipation, survival, and change. No wonder they sing: "What a friend we have in Jesus / All our sins and griefs to bear." Questions of whether Jesus is divine are not important. What is important for Caribbean people is that Jesus tells them supremely what God is all about. To continue to be unjust and cruel to Caribbean people is to reenact the Crucifixion of Jesus. Every Good Friday has its own Easter, say the Caribbean Christians.

All this sense of allegiance to Jesus Christ of the Gospel finds fertile expression in the strong attachment to the life of worship in all kinds of churches and congregations. The established churches began to lose their hold on the masses at the turn of the twentieth century, after the Pentecostal movement from North America began to spread its wings. Many people who were denied permission to express themselves in their own way in the established churches started their own congregations. In the Caribbean, the present century has witnessed a tremendous emancipatory surge of religious fervor, whereby hundreds of independent churches with faint connections to North American bodies have sprung up all over the region. The one great thing about this phenomenon is that it has provided for thousands of Caribbean Christians the outlet by which their allegiance to Jesus Christ has been nurtured and expressed, without the official sanction of the historical churches. When we connect these expressions with the other religious expressions of the African soul, of which we spoke in the previous chapter, we have before us a most overwhelming story of the emancipatory theological foundations of Caribbean human existence.

The church in the Caribbean is therefore alive and well, but not necessarily in the way it was originally intended. Nevertheless, this active church membership sometimes takes fundamentalism so seriously that it has slighted the more urgent problems of Christian engagement in the social emancipatory process. North American fundamentalism still sanctions a passive acceptance of things as they are, instead of pointing Caribbean people toward a more realistic embrace of their historical groundings of faith. These groundings are centered on the Caribbean understanding of the immeasurable and matchless grace of God. Caribbean people are not able to define grace in intricate theological terms. They simply experience and testify to its efficacy. God's grace has sustained them in spite of the other ungracious acts by which their existence has often been surrounded. The Caribbean understanding of divine grace, therefore, does not necessarily translate itself into the ease of life or into an escape from the harshness of Caribbean physical existence. Yet it enables Caribbean people to be warm, gracious, generous, forgiving, tolerant, kind, friendly, and hospitable. The fact of human grace reflects the human understanding of divine grace. To that extent, Caribbean people have managed to maintain what can only be called a very gracious, if not always a graceful, society. The grace of God in the Caribbean is without question in the minds and hearts of those who seek out their meaning of life in that part of God's vineyard.

These groundings of faith provide for Caribbean people a new framework out of which the old realities can find fresh theological expressions. These expressions will be more oral than written. They will be narrative in framework rather than systematic; they will be existential rather than metaphysical; they will reflect the lives and hopes of a people yearning to be free rather than a people who continue to be domesticated by the ancient formularies of a bygone era. We therefore need to reassess the theological imperatives arising out of the need to confront poverty, dependence, alienation, and imitation. These still constitute forms of human bondage, and from all of these the people of the Caribbean urgently need to be emancipated.

NEW CARIBBEAN THEOLOGICAL STRUCTURES

The integrated matrix out of which new theological structures for the Caribbean experience can emerge must surely include all the historical, cultural, sociological, anthropological, political, ecumenical, and physical realities that we have been piecing together in this book. Above all, the basic underlying experiences of Caribbean existence must be treated holistically, and integrated by the religious factor. No other factor is consistent or compelling enough to demonstrate how the Caribbean has survived as it has, in spite of the poverty, dependence, alienation, and imitation that have persistently entrapped most of its inhabitants.

The new theological structures must be fully reflective of those groundings in faith that we have been outlining. They must be evocative, culturally affirmative, ecumenical, and provisional; they must directly address the four basic problems as the manifestations of the bondage and rigors of oppression; they must empower Caribbean people to put their faith to work in solidarity with one another and in strategic connections with other oppressed peoples. Further, they must point out clearly that Caribbean people are responsible for their own liberation and development, for the endemic Caribbean sin still consists in the area of nonresponsibility. We shall discuss the new structures in the light of the four basic problems of poverty, dependence, alienation, and imitation.

Poverty

Caribbean people are poor, mainly because they live in a poor region, and will hardly ever be able to reach a level of self-sufficiency, as far as the basic available resources and demographic demands are concerned. Full employment was possible only once in Caribbean history, and that was during slavery. The Caribbean was never meant, or expected, to be a self-sustaining region. The emancipatory goal, therefore, is not to create a wealthy region but, rather, to enable the people to move from absolute poverty to relative poverty, from economic decay and despair through resource depletion to economic growth in resource exploitation. Such a process clearly requires imaginative and purposeful creativity, which Caribbean people have often demonstrated abroad but not at home. The same determination that has enabled them to be productive abroad needs to be more readily obvious in the home region.

This focus on economic growth through imaginative creativity and resourcefulness finds its religious motivation in the fact of God, and in the meaning of God's assured and favored presence in the Caribbean condition. God is not only the One who is on their side but also the One who has made it possible for them to survive when all conditions seemed to point to their sure and steady demise. God has been their continuous creator, and their own ability to be creative under conditions of deprivation and oppression has found its source and origin in God. In the areas of child bearing, child rearing, and child care, they have already proven themselves to be procreators with God. Caribbean people accept their children as gifts from God. Their children are their life support, the symbols of God's good favor, persons of loving demand, and charges of supreme obligation. Caribbean people need only to match the making of their own "bread" with their understanding of the making of children as an instance of divine-human collaboration; and the theological implications and imperatives for economic growth and creativity, productivity and self-determination will cry out no longer for articulation.

The ethical imperative here is clearly the need for moral persistence. Because this is a region of starts and stoppages, shifts and turns, hopes and promises dashed to pieces, strange beginnings and mysterious endings, moral persistence is especially difficult. "In the Caribbean," the people say, "nothing lasts for long." This notion must be contradicted and renounced. The emancipatory ethic of persistence is therefore clearly enjoined at this point. If it draws its nurture from an understanding of the favored presence of God, who wills that they should be creative and resourceful, then the resilience that is demanded by the need for sound and stable economic growth will surely empower their wills toward the steady rejection of structured and persistent poverty. The poverty of will, the low level of expectation, and the depressed standards of self-worth come into play here; for structured poverty is often reinforced by one's inability to appreciate the true extent of one's actual needs, as well as the worth and value of one's own available resources.

Dependence

The political problem of dependence is inextricably linked with the economic problem of poverty. Caribbean people often lament, "When a man is poor, even his very words are poor." Dependence, then, is not simply a temporary, or transitory, state of the Caribbean human condition. It is a built-in characteristic, which cannot be removed by the formal creation of sovereign states (sometimes referred to as "village-states") or by the perfunctory admission of small territories to the conclaves of international discourse and decision making. In these international settings, the smallness and dependence often become more gravely accentuated. Political sovereignty is often compromised by the need to translate it into economic advantage, and in most cases the power of transnational corporations grossly overwhelms the genuine national priorities of local political directorates. In other words, they who pay the piper still call the tune.

If dependence is the form of bondage from which Caribbean people need to be emancipated, then—given the economic realities of the perceived need for bread at a price—what is the goal on which they might focus? Independence as a form of political arrangement has meant the cessation of external decision making, but it has not provided much substance for the validity of internal authority or decision making. Distant voices still make sounds, and their echoes are heard loudly and clearly in the region. The goal is thus to achieve self-reliance, in the sense of self-determination: the ability to determine one's priorities; to articulate them fearlessly, honestly, and clearly; and to be fully disposed to accepting the consequences of such determination and articulation. That is the stuff out of which national sovereignty is made, and on which genuine independence really begins to thrive. To achieve such a goal, one needs moral consistency—consistency with local values, realities, and priorities; with long-term goals and objectives; and with the highest ideals of national prestige and human self-esteem. The popular will must insist on such moral consistency instead of the political norms of expediency and the principle of the zigzag. Caribbean vacillation on important matters of national integrity has made political independence virtually meaningless, to the point where citizens of the region have openly wished (in their weaker moments) for the return of colonial rule. There was more consistency then, they say, even if the colonial masters painfully and systematically assaulted their sense of pride.

At this point—that is, as a way of speaking to the Caribbean concern for emancipation from dependence—Caribbean Christology comes into its own. Caribbean Christology likens human conditions in the Caribbean to incidents in the life and times of Jesus of Nazareth: his humble birth, his love of simplicity, his persuasive speech, his colorful miracles, his resistance to oppressive establishments, his confrontation with the authorities, his loyalty to his friends, his filial obedience to God, whom he called Father (who is also the Caribbean Creator God) even up to death, his innocent suffering, his conquest of death and the grave. All these characteristics and events are parts of a constant narrative that informs the Caribbean people's understanding of who Christ is. Caribbean people do not just speak *of* Jesus; they actually speak *to* Jesus. Theirs is an active, concrete, and existential Christology. Christ is the mediatorial presence of God the Emancipator. The consistency of Christ in his faithfulness to God, as well as his faithfulness to Caribbean people, is in no doubt at all; and the Christological motivation to be self-determinative, in the light of the will and favor of God, is far more powerful than the fear of repercussions and consequences that might induce the people to compromise their high principles of independence. There must be some built-in religious and political guarantee which lets the world know that the Caribbean people are no longer for sale and that their dues have already been paid, not only by their ancestors in slavery but also by their brother Jesus Christ.

The virtue of courage is undoubtedly the moral imperative here. Not only does it follow on the ethic of persistence and moral consistency, but it also is inherent in the very character of Christ himself. Here the meaning of faith is expressed—not merely faith in one's cause but also faith in God, which evokes trust, confidence, hope, purposeful assurance, and loyal obedience. It takes courage to assert one's self-determination in the face of those to whom one must still look for help and assistance. We are not required to sell our souls to those from whom we ask for aid. It takes divine courage to determine aloud, and in concrete historical terms, where the asking ends and where the selling begins. Judas Iscariot is the vendor character in the Gospel narrative, and Caribbean people are generally apprehensive of any Judas-like tendencies in the region.

Alienation

Cultural alienation has perhaps been more devastating than either poverty or dependence. The official policy of divide and rule was relentlessly pursued by the colonial overlords and rigidly woven into the fabric of colonial social life. It encouraged Caribbean people to become mutually contemptuous and to accept patterns of self-contempt, sometimes as a means of social progress or acceptance by others. That which was foreign was good; that which was local was not good. So people were alienated from each other by inducement. They were also alienated from their natural cultural endowment (race, color, language, belief systems, relationships, preferences, entertainment and leisure, work schedules, family mores, personal aspirations) and from their rightful corridors of power, influence, opportunity, and social access. Children born out of wedlock were baptized in churches on weekdays, while children born within wedlock were baptized on Sundays (the Lord's Day). Unmarried fathers were regarded as social outcasts by self-righteous priests and pastors; so that mothers would sometimes present their own brothers as the fathers of their babies to the unsuspecting priests. Cultural alienation has run deep and wide throughout the social institutions and communities as a whole.

In the light of such social conditions, therefore, the major goal must be to ensure social justice—that is, all the rights, privileges, opportunities, incentives, and guarantees that promote full personhood in the Caribbean and enable Caribbean people to participate together in the sociopolitical and cultural processes of the region. The imposed forms of alienation have tended to decimate the people's communitarian spirit, by pitting neighbor against neighbor and class against class. The virtue of community involves not merely collectivity but, more particularly, the rights and obligations of communicating and sharing; the responsibility to resist fragmentation in all its forms, as a continuing regional crisis; and the need to contribute to the creation of a more wholesome generation of self-affirming, self-accepting, de-alienated young people, whose pride in their heritage would render the return to alienation an impossible dream.

This sense of community surely takes its nurture from the Caribbean understanding of God the Holy Spirit—the unseen (but not unexperienced) power of God in God's world, particularly among God's people, but not only among them. The Holy Spirit is not the part-time, absolute God, but God in the nearness and powerful presence of love, protection, guidance, and forgiveness. The Holy Spirit empowers, enlightens, endears, enriches, and encourages. The Holy Spirit creates community, for it is particularly in community with others that the overwhelming power and presence of that Spirit is experienced. So—just as traditional theology understands the Trinitarian God as the embodiment of solidary love, the Holy Spirit being the bond of love between Creator and Savior—Caribbean people understand the solidarity of communal love which the Spirit gives, and they seek to identify the meaning of a Caribbean spirit of solidarity with the concrete manifestation of the work of God the Holy Spirit. The Holy Spirit is undoubtedly the Caribbean spirit.

The ethical imperative here is for respect (which has already been identified as a distinctive structure of the Caribbean spirit). The need for Caribbean self-respect, mutual respect, and respect for the primacy of Caribbean cultural endowments has never been more acute and urgent. Respect itself builds persistence and courage. Many fresh starts have been followed by quick falls because their initiators failed to gain the necessary support and respect of their fellows or of those who were to be the primary beneficiaries of such initiatives. Enforced respect for authority must now be replaced by voluntary and enlightened respect for one's fellow sharers in the struggle for true and lasting community and for a better quality of life for all. Nothing violates the spirit of Caribbean selfhood more than the blatant denigration of the spirit of Caribbean community in all its dimensions. The legacy of alienation will not be laid to rest until Caribbean people, inspired by the Spirit of God, struggle together for social justice through their mutual support and respect for each other in community. Caribbean political and religious leaders are called upon to set the highest possible standards in this regard, and to ensure that the rights and freedoms of the least among us are protected as much as the rights and freedoms of the greatest among us.

Imitation

Imitation is simultaneously a religious, a theological, and a social problem. Patterns of dress, music, status symbols, and domestic comforts are rapidly being defined by the Caribbean middle class in accordance with observed standards in North American culture. Social interaction with tourists and other visitors, extensive travel to European and other centers, and the tremendous pull of sophisticated technologies have made a serious impact on the Caribbean middle-class mentality. Even styles of management and commercial arrangements have been gravely influenced by imitative tastes. Madison Avenue of New York has extended itself, at the very time that Caribbean history has embarked on a search for independence and self-determination. The borrowing of tastes and values has been far from judicious among the Caribbean middle classes, and yet they continue to be models of advancement for their less fortunate fellow citizens.

Much the same has been true in the area of religious developments in the historic churches. The traditional pattern of adopting initiatives from the older churches overseas continues. The vestments, styles, themes, controversies, and patterns of intercourse are imported without much variation into the life of the local churches. Even the Pentecostal and newer churches have not been exempt. They have been less than discriminating in their adulation of foreign evangelists and preachers, and of alien styles of church promotion and renewal. There is still far too much prepackaged, ready-made, ready-for-use consumption of religion in the Caribbean, originating from outside the region. Too much of the formal Christian practice is still being proclaimed and promoted by rote importation and imitation, and there is too little intelligent conversion or adaptation.

What is the antidote for such social, religious, and theological imitation, which eats away at the very soul of Caribbean spirituality? The answer lies in the direction of imagination and boldness; of accepting Caribbean realities as endowments of divine creativity, not the results of divine mistakes (for Caribbean people do not believe that divine mistakes are possible); and of affirming the forces of indigeneity in the inner and outer workings of the Caribbean spirit. This move toward indigeneity would not be new to Caribbean spirituality, for it has survived in the cultural substream of Caribbean living. It would only be coming to the surface with an openness, a level of respectability and acceptance, and a measure of divine approval that was presumed missing in former years. The process, then, is one of building an awareness of the Caribbean selfhood, the Caribbean value system, and the Caribbean structure of faith and religious expression, which answers to no external authority for legitimacy or salvific assurance.

Where else can the Caribbean understanding of God's grace be more fully experienced or expressed, if indeed grace means favor, acceptance, loving-kindness, and steadfast mercy? How else can Caribbean people understand that God has accepted them just as they were made and that they do not have to use the services of intermediaries to find favor with God in matters of their theology or religion? How else can their use of the Bible, their love of the church as the fellowship of the Spirit, their loyalty to the efficacy of the Christian sacramental disciplines, and their fervor in prayer find full meaning and significance? It is through the grace of God that Caribbean people are able to come to a fresh awareness of who they are called to be, and to renounce all forms of religious imitation as degrading forms of flattery and aspects of spiritual abomination. With Saul of Tarsus, Caribbean people can fully affirm that by the grace of God they are who they are, and that that grace, which was fully bestowed, "was not bestowed in vain."

The ethical imperative of all this seems to lie in the area of the search for integrity. This is a search of tremendous importance, for we are dealing here with integrity at several levels: the integrity of the Gospel, the integrity of faith as the response to that Gospel, the integrity of the Christian tradition without compromise or dilution of ethic or ethos, the integrity of indigenous cultural antecedents, the integrity of common relationships with Christians in other cultural and sociohistorical settings, and the integrity of common purpose with persons of other faiths. There is no fixed concrete formula for Christian integrity as such. The object of the struggle is to insist that the highest level of Caribbean integrity is reflective of the faithful response of Caribbean people to the demands of the loving and gracious God. Not only must Caribbean theology and religion come to have an integrity of their own, but Caribbean people must also demonstrate a level of spiritual maturity and integrity that speaks for itself without compromise, apology, or equivocation.

We may therefore summarize the foregoing discussion in the following way:

1. The economic problem of poverty must have as its solution genuine and realistic economic growth. This goal can best be pursued through imaginative creativity, inspired by the power of the Creator God and maintained by the ethical imperative of enlightened persistence.

2. The political problem of dependence must be eliminated by increasing levels of collective self-reliance. The example of Jesus Christ, the Caribbean Christ, is the major empowerment here; and it is mainly through moral consistency and Christian courage that endemic dependence can be counteracted.

3. The cultural problem of alienation should best be confronted by the deepening of community and the struggle for social justice. Theologically, the Caribbean experience of the Holy Spirit, as the lifegiving presence of God, generates such a movement. By the moral force of mutual respect and the personal increase in self-affirmation, this colonial legacy can be radically attacked.

4. The religious problem of imitation persists as long as there is a denial of indigeneity. The need for human conscientization is matched only by the recognition that the grace of God is already at work in the Caribbean. A full response to God's grace in the Caribbean can dispel the last vestiges of social contempt and spiritual anemia.

Such a scheme merely represents one attempt to look at the many problems of Caribbean existence in an integrated way, since no Caribbean problem exists in isolation from the others. It suggests a theologically illuminating way of interpreting the where, how, why, and what of Caribbean existence, and offers a framework for understanding the structures and priorities needed for the reconstruction of local realities. Caribbean emancipation is both a divine promise and a human project, and the theological initiatives mandated by the call to human freedom render it necessary for theology itself to be emancipated. The four steps toward such emancipation are (1) identifying the problem, as we have done; (2) positing the salvific goal, as we have done; (3) suggesting the process that is required for the pursuit of such a goal; (4) reflecting on the preceding steps and then taking appropriate action. Theology in such a case is not simply the handmaid of a faith tradition but, more particularly, the illumination of a historically concrete emancipatory praxis, which puts faith to work in a distinctly challenging historical context. How some Caribbean initiatives have attempted to do just that will require our review in the next chapter.

CHAPTER SIX

PRAXIS FOR THEOLOGICAL EMANCIPATION

What are the overriding concerns that relate to theological formation in the area? How have they been addressed? How can a relevant and viable process of theological education be instituted for the region? Should it be an ecumenical venture? If so, what about the denominational interests and loyalties that remain important to Christians in the region? How can the new Caribbean pastors serve the spiritual, material, and social needs of the people committed to their charge? What are the continuing linkages with metropolitan theological methodology that need to be maintained? What linkages need to be cut if Caribbean people are to work out for themselves the meaning of emancipation, independence, self-reliance, development, cultural renewal, and justice in their daily lives? Is there a need for an indigenous Caribbean theological methodology; or does such a methodology already exist, needing only to be recognized, affirmed, and proclaimed without apology? What are to be the new forms of ministry? All these questions have occupied the minds and discussions of church leaders and theological educators in the region for the past two decades.

Most of the churches in the Caribbean are aware that theological education means much more than ministerial formation, but they have been unable to restructure their institutional programs and priorities, or to redeploy their scarce resources, to reflect these realities. They will obviously need to promote new methods, within the context of local communities, to respond to current pressures: the need for more formal training of women, the growing inability to sustain appropriate standards of living (economically) among their clergy, the revolution of ethical perspectives and rising expectations in the Caribbean, and the inevitable imperatives of ecumenism. Whether they have the will to respond purposefully to these pressures is sometimes in doubt. What is not in doubt, however, is that the mission of the church in the Caribbean is to proclaim in word, sacrament, and action that the Gospel of Jesus Christ is Good News for today and tomorrow. We are not permitted by God to function in the yesterday of history.

The North American influence on Caribbean theological formation has been increasing. Most of the postgraduate theological courses of study that

Caribbean persons now pursue are provided in North America, and they are paid for by the North Americans. The University of the West Indies offers a master's degree in theology, but this program has not yet had wide appeal. Most of the current theological literature and language in use still reflects a close North American connection. It is difficult to resist the tremendous pull of North American religion. But does the shape of theological formation in the Caribbean have to be determined by North Atlantic realities in perpetuity? Can a more rigorous attempt be made to develop a comprehensive theological education program, both in the seminaries and in the churches, that would more readily reflect the realities of Caribbean religious priorities and indigenous theological perspectives? The answer to this question, I believe, is a resounding "Yes." Let us explore some of the factors that would need to be taken into account.

METHODOLOGICAL PRIORITIES

The need for theological self-reliance is just as urgent in the Caribbean as in other spheres of regional endeavor. The traditional dependence on forms and methods from the metropolitan North has been long ingrained, and these old habits die hard. Further, these methodologies appear to offer a ready-made set of solutions to complex theological problems, so that the temptation to import them is stronger than the will to seek new and indigenous ones. However, if Caribbean theological educators were to embark on the creation of a radically new theological methodology, the following insights would need to be borne in mind.

An appropriate theological methodology does not necessarily require the total abandonment of that which is currently employed, but it does require a radical assessment of the needs of the Caribbean constituency which is attempting to interpret the meaning of the Gospel of emancipation in the Caribbean context. In the study of the Scriptures, for example, educators — instead of paying so much attention to the lively debates among European and American scholars over esoteric issues or philological technicalities — could make an extensive study of the ways in which the Bible has been interpreted by generations of local Caribbean religious leaders, and to good spiritual and social advantage. The material for such study can be gathered from many sermons and other teaching material in local congregations. These need to be collected systematically.

Again, the traditional ways of pursuing a study of systematic theology or moral theology — that is, through a heavy emphasis on what the so-called "divines" have proclaimed over the years — need not continue to be the basis for contemporary theological and moral insights. After all, Caribbean people have been able to express their faith over the years in the face of the greatest odds. They have been able to cope with family duties and responsibilities when most of their rights were being denied. These achievements suggest that somehow they have been living out a theology and an ethic deeply rooted in an abiding faith in God. Such a theological and ethical heritage must challenge Caribbean theological educators to conduct intensive research and codification, in order that the spectrum of theological exploration might be enlarged. The contemporary debate about polygamy in Africa, and the appropriate Christian pastoral and ethical response to the challenges it poses for the Christian, should be instructive in this regard. Thus, with such basic disciplines as theology, Scripture, and ethics, and with all the other curricular pursuits, Caribbean theological methodology should be as intentional about globalizing the scope of the system and material as it should be about indigenizing the moral and spiritual formation of those who would assume leadership in the Caribbean churches.

In addition, theological educators cannot afford to ignore Caribbean folk wisdom and cultural history. In our previous chapter, we paid special attention to the significance of the African soul in Caribbean religion. We pointed out that indigenous religious activity had long been a source of spiritual and cultural power for the underclasses of Caribbean societies. Those religious and cultural antecedents have not disappeared, even if the outward forms of religious observances have been overtaken by Western traditions. The proverbs remain in place, deeply rooted and loudly echoed in the consciousness of Caribbean people, from generation to generation. The songs, myths, dance, movements, dietary habits, domestic customs, music, and even creole technology remain firmly rooted in the Caribbean structures of response. They all have to be taken into account as an essential part of the matrix from which appropriate theological reflection and praxis take their departure.

The mention of praxis brings us to the question of how theology is practiced in the life and sociohistorical circumstances of the Caribbean. The focus of the emerging discipline called practical theology has not always been clear, and the priorities for Christian engagement in the rough and tumble of social and political life are not altogether apparent. Caribbean theological methodology cannot afford such vagueness or ambiguity. Theological formation must take place in the midst of congregational life, social and political witness, and the actual hands-on situations of ordinary people who struggle on the margins of poverty and frustration. This means that prophetic dimensions of theological formation must not be left to chance or caprice, nor must the formidable mission of the church be confined to statements of synods and church councils. Preparation for the practice of theology in the world must not be isolated from the practice of prophetic and missional service in the context of that formation. In short, the lines between theory and practice must be so blurred that the learning-by-doing option takes precedence over the learning-before-doing option.

Women are by far the more dominant sector, numerically, in the life of the church in the Caribbean, just as they are in other areas of the Christian world. The lifeblood of the church would be seriously malnourished if women were to withdraw their full participation and support. Yet church leaders in the Caribbean continue to be ambivalent and hesitant about the significance of such participation and about the value of women in the leadership structures of the Christian movement. Can women be ordained? Some people in the Caribbean doubt it. Should women be ordained? Many more are decidedly against such a proposition. Caribbean society has been overwhelmingly a matriarchal society. Women have played the dominant and leading roles in the survival and shaping of the mind of the Caribbean. They have been the shapers of the Caribbean conscience, for they have nurtured most of those consciences singlehandedly, or carried many of them on their backs and cradled them in their arms.

Caribbean women have indeed been the major preservers of the Caribbean cultural foundations. They have even provided most of the plantation labor, especially for the export crops that have provided bread for the region and profits for the wealthy outside the region. Their ministry and service in the church and the society are without question. The church has an inescapable obligation to improve the lot of women in every possible way—not only through ordination but also through a recognition of the significance of motherhood and feminine strength and a determination to secure the rights and privileges of women.

The matter of lay training and participation in the life of the church, and even in the process of theological formation, is of tremendous urgency in the Caribbean. Any appropriate methodology for theological formation in the Caribbean must resolutely avoid a cleavage between clergy and laity. They must be exposed to much of the same training together, and the metropolitan propensity for establishing an elitist approach to clerical training should be intentionally avoided in the Caribbean approach. Caribbean churches rely so heavily on their lay personnel that it is becoming increasingly difficult to justify the low level of training for their lay leadership. In keeping with this line of thought, theological formation of congregations as a whole is just as important as the theological formation of the laity. I therefore contend that effective programs of research and development for congregational nurture and reinforcement are necessary corollaries to the training of lay leadership in the church. The importation of social psychological theories from other contexts needs to be judiciously guarded, for models that work in the North are not automatically transferable to the Caribbean. There is much to be learned from Caribbean congregations. There is also much to be gained from serving the needs of such bodies over and above the traditional pastoral ministrations.

The matter of pastoral ministrations also raises interesting questions about the methodology for theological formation appropriate to the Caribbean. We referred earlier to the continuous stream of Caribbean ministers who made the trek to North America to pursue graduate training. One of the most popular courses of study is "Pastoral Counseling and Care." However, because much of the pedagogy in this field is based on a clinical approach to human suffering and social deviance, and because the social context in the Caribbean differs materially from the North American setting, grave difficulties emerge when North American–trained counselors (mainly pastors) attempt to implement their skills in an area for which their training has not prepared them. The whole question of continuing education for the clergy is of major importance for the Caribbean church. Two basic problems persist. One is that, because of the scarcity of such provision in the Caribbean, the clergy justify the need to emigrate in search of it. The other is that these clergy often fall prey to the temptation of staying away indefinitely in places where the pastures are much greener. So the Caribbean loses immensely by its failure to provide full and appropriate programs of continuing education for its leadership.

Finally, appropriate methods of theological formation will continue to be wanting as long as opportunities for ecumenical sharing and ecumenical engagement are overlooked or strategically neglected. The need for Caribbean integration was discussed in an earlier chapter, and we mentioned the work of the Caribbean Conference of Churches. But much more needs to be accomplished by the churches themselves apart from their formal ecumenical structures. More use should be made of the structures and program facilities provided by the CCC; in addition, more effort is needed toward establishing joint programs of training at all levels of church life. Realistic and serious dialogue between groupings of different persuasions is required, as well as formal opportunities for fellowship and mutual learning between Christian and non-Christian bodies. Caribbean theological formations must seek Christian unity at all levels of the church, as well as Caribbean unity at other levels. The unity of the Christian church and the unity of the human family in the Caribbean cannot be maintained in separate compartments. The emancipation we seek cannot afford to be at the expense of human division and religious bigotry.

If there is to be an appropriate methodology for theological formation that principally relates to the work of the institutions of learning, there must also be a broader agenda for theological emancipation in which the Caribbean church as a whole is engaged. And there are indications that such an agenda for Christian theological renewal is being developed.

SIGNALS FOR CHANGE

A martyr church does not exist in the Caribbean, although there are sometimes threatening signs of such a development. Some religious leaders have been attacked for their open and prophetic witness on some issues, and there have been serious tensions involving church leaders in places such as Guyana and Haiti. There are no basic ecclesial communities such as those found in Brazil, for example. Liberation theology, as it has been developed and proclaimed in Latin America, is not generally understood or admired in the region—possibly because relatively few people can speak or read Spanish and Portuguese. Most pastors and church leaders have not read extensively on the subject. The global fervor to fight for bread and justice, as a matter of Christian duty, is more or less translated in these islands into a natural fervor to fight for bread as a matter of human justice. Religious sensibility is not required here, and Christian duty is peripheral, they would say, for everyone has a basic right to eat.

Organized engagement in theological praxis for change is therefore regarded as generally exotic, occasionally exciting, but not ordinarily compelling. Caribbean spirituality does not necessarily rely on inherently religious or theological imperatives to such an extent that Christians would get together, because of their common confession, and share their sufferings or their joys in the light of their faith. Theological solidarity is not a generally attractive principle when there are no visible or concrete rewards to be grasped. Theological initiative is therefore scant and scrappy, as far as systematic and organized reflective thought and praxis are concerned. Such an initiative rises and falls in relation to the demand for it in seminars, conferences, and spasmodic publications, or else in response to some extraregional impetus.

In the light of this state of theological praxis in the Caribbean, a number of considerations must be borne in mind. First, the harsh realities of human dependence have not been substantially lessened because of formal political independence or the emergence of indigenous leadership in church, state, and society at large. Consequently, human initiative at all levels is still encumbered by the pragmatic efficacy (albeit a superficial and farcical one) of being imitative, or at least responsive to some external initiative. To understand the need for the emancipation of human initiative in the Caribbean is to touch the very heart of its sons and daughters yearning to be free.

Second, Caribbean people are so preoccupied with survival that theological reflection—when it is not directly related to food, shelter, and work—would command little attention from ordinary laypersons, or even from pastors, who virtually survive to preach by struggling for their livelihood.

Third, although the rate of literacy is comparatively high in the region, most of the people prefer to read people—by listening, conversing, hearing about others, or by personal encounters—rather than literature. Erudite books do not sell well in any intellectual discipline; newspapers that sensationalize the latest events or highlight the latest controversies are considerably more popular. Christianity, as a religion of the book, is not popular in the region, so that systematic theological expositions in print emerge with the built-in disadvantage that hardly anyone will eventually read what is written. Furthermore, the few ambitious theological authors know very little about each other's work. Such is the islandic and unintegrated nature of much of the theological enterprise in the region.

Fourth, the real theologizing among Caribbean people is done orally, narratively, and informally. I have argued earlier that the real theological workshops in the Caribbean are the homes, the fields, and the street corners, rather than the seminaries or the churches. In other words, while written theology struggles, oral theology flourishes.

What, then, can we say about recent theological initiatives in the Caribbean? Four major areas of discussion will occupy our attention:

1. The debate concerning a "Caribbean theology."
2. The general areas of theological reflection.
3. The specific areas of theological praxis.
4. The fundamental imperatives for Caribbean theological initiative.

CARIBBEAN THEOLOGY

Is there a Caribbean theology at present, or is there one in the process of being born? We will have to assume some acquaintance with the pioneering work done by the late Idris Hamid in such publications as *Fambli, In Search of New Perspectives, Troubling of the Waters,* and *Out of the Depths*; with the work of the late David Mitchell in his editing of *With Eyes Wide Open* and *New Mission for a New People*; with the various CCC reports of theological seminars and conferences; and with *Moving into Freedom*, which I edited and published in 1977.

Edmund Davis, the Jamaican theologian, in his book *Roots and Blossoms,* refers to "Caribbean theology" as an emotive phrase, a slogan of vindication, a concept that is driving us toward establishing "the value of Caribbean religion and culture."[1] He expresses the fear that Caribbean theology might become too narrow in its focus and concern, and therefore urges cautious use of the term "Caribbean theology" if it is to be "meaningful and powerful for men who live in the open predicament."[2] But Davis's fear is unfounded, since he ignores the basic fact that the Caribbean itself is an open society and that religious trends and theological ideas—like other trends and ideas—enjoy voluminous traffic in both directions. If there is any fear for Caribbean intellectual enterprise, it is in the other direction—of being too broad rather than too narrow.

More recently, Davis has modified his position. In his latest book, *Courage and Commitment*, he calls on Third World theology to return to the historical roots of Christianity by pursuing the concerns of the poor, the weak, and the powerless. "Freedom from the enslavement of personal sin and death must be coupled with transformation from structures of injustice, conflict and oppression. Third World theology identifies the process by which oppressed peoples begin to question and to challenge economic exploitation, social deprivation and the violation of basic human rights."[3]

Burchell Taylor, another Jamaican theologian, suggests that the phrase "Caribbean theology" itself must denote "that we are assuming our theological responsibility, a responsibility that no one can rightly assume for us."[4] Taylor calls for Caribbean theology to be "both reflective on and responsive to the particularities of the Caribbean context in the light of the Word of God."[5] He suggests that we should make use of the social sciences, which provide useful interpretive tools, but we should also retain the use of metaphysical analysis. The corporate and structural nature of religion should receive greater focus than the individual and personal, the theme of liberation should be high on the agenda, and the concept of memory should also play a significant part. Taylor calls for a theology that is neither neutral nor apolitical—one that will motivate the church to take the side of justice, peace, love, freedom, and salvation. If Caribbean theology becomes wedded to any one system or method of achieving its end, he warns, "it will end up being no better than the theology it replaced, and it could in turn become supportive of oppressive and tyrannical structures."[6]

The late Idris Hamid in 1979 expressed a preference for the phrase "Caribbean perspectives in theology" rather than "Caribbean theology." In his view, the main theological task in the Caribbean consists of four elements: (1) The ways in which Caribbean people have experienced God over the years should be analyzed, structured, and clarified, so that "the power of intellect [will] make that experience persuasive to the rest of the community, and keep it alive."[7] (2) The deeply rooted understanding of freedom and dignity in Caribbean people must be fully expressed. (3) The experience of the consolation of God among Caribbean people, because of their suffering and pain, also must be expressed. (4) The cumulative effect of these experiences on our people should be carefully and clearly analyzed and expressed. Hamid therefore believed that "the important and continuing task of doing Caribbean Theology is that the mine is yet to be dug and one is amazed again at its depth, and its profundity, and its beauty."[8]

In 1981, a book entitled *Towards a Caribbean Theology*, and dedicated to the memory of Hamid, was published in Trinidad. It chronicles most of the major thoughts, themes, and discussions from seminars held between 1976 and 1981 at St. Andrews Theological College, with which Hamid was associated. The book ends with a quotation from a group seminar, in which it is suggested that Caribbean theology should focus on a sharing of the good things that each territory possesses, and that the phrase "liberation theology" should be withheld from the struggle for liberation, since "there is a danger that the revolutionary connotation of the name 'Liberation' might bring about a rejection of the Christian ideals contained in it."[9] Nevertheless, the Caribbean theologian should be a revolutionary, "calling for change of attitude, 'metanoia,' so that courageous and wise action can be undertaken."[10]

CARIBBEAN THEOLOGICAL REFLECTION

Our second major focus is on identifying the general areas of Caribbean theological reflection. These areas can be listed under two main categories—the ecclesial and the societal.

1. ECCLESIAL

The Liturgy. Clergy representing most of the historic churches in the region have attempted to reformulate their theological understanding of their liturgical traditions, and to revise what they do in their churches in the light of their experience of God outside.

Cultural Identity. The general awakening to the fact that Caribbean cultural identity is not European or American mimicry has created new imperatives for the churches. Thus, in their polity and organization, they have been attempting to relativize themselves, so that there can emerge a "People's Church" rather than a "Church for the People."

Ecumenism. Through the efforts of the CCC, great strides have been made in developing ecumenical approaches to theological reflection and theological education, and the mutual sharing of ideas and material between Caribbean churches has been increasing. We shall return to this area later.

The Bible. Renewed emphasis on the place of Bible study and the importance of scriptural exegesis has been observed. Michel DeVerteuil has suggested some new ways of studying the Bible in the Caribbean, particularly within the ambit of narrative exegesis. George Mulrain, a Trinidadian theologian now teaching in Britain, has suggested that there is such a thing as a calypso exegesis, since the culture of the exegete influences the exegesis. His thoughts on the viability of a calypso exegesis make very provocative reading.[11] The CCC has also promoted Bible studies on such subjects as the poor, power, the kingdom, glory, peace, and development.

Christian Education. This has been an area of significant progress and moderate success, for a new curriculum for church and day schools called *Fashion Me a People* has been produced by the CCC and widely distributed in the region.

Historical Reflection. Here again, a substantial amount of work has been done and is currently in progress. It is indeed true to say that much of the genuine and authentically indigenous theological initiative has been related to a radically new and refreshing historical reflection that has been taking place in the Caribbean. The history of the churches is being rewritten.

2. SOCIETAL

Peace. As a result of superpower rivalries and increased militarism in the area, there is a growing awareness of its geopolitical and strategic importance. The Grenada crisis of the 1980s has greatly challenged the Caribbean church. Because Caribbean people do not wish to be caught in the superpower crossfire, or to be a party to the struggle between the joint superpowers and God over who controls all of human destiny, the church has been actively calling on all concerned to designate the region as a Zone of Peace.

Human Rights and Justice. There has long been a passionate concern for human rights in the area, and for the proper pursuit of justice among all classes of Caribbean society. Theologians are becoming increasingly articulate on this issue, which now constitutes a significant element in the Caribbean integration process at the nonformal, extragovernmental level.

Development. Although the massive impetus of the early 1970s on the part of the churches has been overtaken by the efforts of other groups in the region, the most significant advance has been made within the framework of the churches themselves, and new theological approaches to development are now taking root within the church community. The churches are beginning to appropriate to themselves what was said on their behalf a decade before.

Political Involvement. The debate about the church's role in politics continues, and the theological perspectives are sadly blurred by widespread ambivalence and strategic pragmatism on the part of many church people. Often, the politics of personalism supersedes the politics of principle. *Homines non principia* is an appropriate motto for Caribbean politics today, and the task of theology in the face of this situation is not always and everywhere being fully acknowledged.

Ideological Pluralism. After most territories became sovereign states with formal political independence, it was expected that the logical successor to colonialism would be full freedom and that the trappings of sovereignty would bestow a sense of importance and worth on Caribbean political leadership. In any event, Cuba's revolutionary story, it was thought, would never be repeated in the Caribbean. These assumptions have been challenged (for instance, in Grenada, Guyana, Jamaica, and Suriname); and the theological perspectives for an ideological pluralism in the region—rejecting both capitalism and communism as the only ideological options for social reconstruction—are pointing toward the possibility of a third way.

Social Ethics. Specific ethical issues have surfaced quite conspicuously in the Caribbean, because of recent legislative, behavioral, and economic trends. These ethical issues include gambling, sex and sexuality, drug use, political power, AIDS, abortion, capital punishment, and family law (divorce, "legitimate" versus "illegitimate" children, rights of common law partners). Theologians have been active and vocal in setting the tone for a general debate, or else in setting the cat among the pigeons.

Corruption. Since the advent of the European, Caribbean history has been attended by flagrant manifestations of the corruptibility of the human spirit. The vestiges of racism and slavery, of capitalistic spirituality and plantation ethic, of colonialistic experiment and militaristic endeavor, of structured poverty and endemic alienation—all have combined to implant within the Caribbean breast the practical value of human corruption. Theological enterprise in the region is heavily weighted against this notion, but the attractions of metropolitan success and the lure of instant personal fortune are winds too heavy to be withstood most of the time.

CARIBBEAN THEOLOGICAL PRAXIS

In four specific areas, among those listed above, theological praxis has been especially significant, challenging, and creative. These areas are peace, development, ecumenism, and Christian education. We have to bear in mind, however, that laypersons are not engaged in theological reflection and praxis in any organized and systematic fashion. The layperson is usually referred to as the "person-in-the-pew" and often prefers to remain there.

Who, then, it may well be asked, are the persons actually engaged in theological reflection and praxis? Who are the persons taking the Caribbean initiatives in theology at a level that is dialogical and communicable? The CCC plays an important role here. Some progressive church leaders succeed in registering concerns and initiating action in their church synods that are hardly possible at the parish level. Besides these, there are the occasional pronouncements of church leaders. They are not normally lacking in courage or sensitivity in identifying the areas for urgent theological attention. Several Caribbean theological educators, pastors, and ecumenical executives make contributions to the theological debate. It must sadly be acknowledged, however, that comparatively little in the way of creative theological discussion actually emerges in print from the theological seminaries. The possible reasons for this require a separate study in its own right.

Peace

Seminars on peace have been held in Trinidad, Grenada, and other islands. Several articles have appeared in *Caribbean Contact* pointing out that—in order to achieve justice, independence, and a participatory and sustainable society—the region must eschew violence. The Third Assembly of the CCC, which was held in Curaçao in November 1981, passed resolutions calling on the Caribbean governments to establish a Zone of Peace in the region. It deplored the existence and escalation of political violence in the region and declared its support "for such movements as are attempting to redress the results of any form of political violence in the area."[12] It urged the CCC to "stimulate greater political awareness in the region in order to live our faith through greater participation on the part of all our peoples in the creation and development of a new Caribbean community, one where all may live in the dignity of being truly human and free—free to be and to become."[13] The Fourth Assembly (Barbados, 1986) reaffirmed similar concerns.

Most of the regional governments have expressed their support for the establishment of the region as a Zone of Peace. A Caribbean delegation visited several North American cities in 1982 to consult with the churches on behalf of Caribbean churches. As a result of this visit, an experimental program was established to develop liaisons between counterpart church bodies. In answer to the question "What can Christians and churches do?" the CCC has been promoting the following suggestions:

1. Organize programmes of education for peace.

2. Promote discussions on questions such as violence, order, and subversion.

3. Attempt to inculcate concerns for a better quality of life and the environment into formal educational systems and the media.

4. Challenge the pervasive manifestations of the culture of violence in media, dress, advertising, political activities, and other areas.

5. Become sources of alternative information on questions of peace and development.

6. Become more informed about topical issues related to peace.

7. Take positions on human rights issues.

Information is not readily available on how actively the local churches have responded to these important suggestions. In January 1983, the Centenary Provincial Synod of the Anglican Church issued a communiqué to all its congregations, strongly urging that serious study be given to the CCC publication *Peace: A Challenge to the Caribbean*.

Development

The CCC and some of its constituents have been helping to keep the development debate alive and up to date. The rapid increase of wealth in Trinidad and Tobago, along with the steep decline in wealth and living standards in most of her CARICOM neighbors (principally Guyana), motivated the Caribbean countries to search for new and appropriate paths for development. However, the more recent cataclysmic decline in the economic and industrial fortunes of Trinidad and Tobago has ushered into the Caribbean debate new dimensions of concern about a massive influx of wealth into previous contexts of poverty. Judicious distribution and administration of wealth are not always guaranteed by its fortuitous acquisition. Beyond economic growth as an indicator in Trinidad, self-reliance as an ideal in Guyana, and social justice as a developmental theme in Jamaica, development must lead to cultural liberation and self-determination, human rights, and new forms of relationship with the regional and global community, together with better ecological attitudes. Theological initiatives in such areas have been of great significance.

Development action groups have been established in most of the territories, and financial resources have been transferred to enable them to implement some of their decisions. Most of these groups are part of the CCC network or else work in close collaboration with it. There have also been frequent seminars and meetings to discuss specific issues related to development, and several church leaders have been involved. The move away from mere economic development has been especially significant. At the formal opening of a Christian Action for Development in the Caribbean (CADEC) meeting in Grenada in May 1981, the Roman Catholic bishop of Grenada, Sydney Charles, emphasized that authentic development concerns the whole man and every man. It seeks to instill self-reliance, self-determination, and self-government. It is based on love and is directed at both rich and poor.[14]

The CCC also sponsored an important Consultation (or "Think-Tank") in Barbados in December 1980 to deal with the broad area of "Caribbean Theology and Development Issues in the 1980s." The three-volume report of that Consultation was published by CADEC in 1981. Unfortunately, financial constraints severely limited its wider circulation.

The Third CCC Assembly paid much attention to development issues. It passed resolutions dealing with tourism, racism, foreign aid, economic relations with the developed world, the Haitian refugee problem, Belizian full sovereignty and independence, and the need for cooperation between the CCC and other development agencies in the region.

The Antilles Episcopal Conference of the Roman Catholic Church in the Caribbean issued a Bishops' Pastoral Letter in February 1982 entitled *True Freedom and Development in the Caribbean*. Although this document is not as earthshaking as its predecessor, *Justice and Peace in the Caribbean* (1975), it nevertheless demonstrates that the leaders of this important Christian community in the region are eager to express their pastoral concerns for "the full human development and authentic liberation of our Caribbean peoples." My own major work *Mission for Caribbean Change*, published in the summer of 1982, represents, as far as I am aware, the first systematic attempt by any Caribbean theologian to examine a historical study of Caribbean developmental praxis as a theological enterprise. That work already needs to be updated in the light of more recent developments in the region.

Ecumenism

The measured success of ecumenism in the Caribbean represents a significant dimension of theological praxis. The organizing of councils of churches around specific agendas of common concern and interest has paid great dividends. The churches have been attempting to speak with one voice and to express solidarity on a number of crucial social and political issues. Furthermore, the old practice of playing off churches against one another is being forced out of existence, and many governments in the region now face the added challenge of having to deal with solidarity among churches, as if solidarity among trade unions were not bad enough. Ecumenical action on the part of churches in Guyana, Grenada, Antigua, Jamaica, and Suriname has been remarkable. It has given further support to the principle that metropolitan-inspired denominationalism may be tolerated but not worshiped as an arrangement made in heaven. The churches still have far to go, however, and I have suggested elsewhere that a new ecumenical agenda should focus more persistently on in-church concerns, such as the Bible, hymnody, baptismal policy, the agape, marriage services, the ordinal, and a Christian family liturgical service.[15] It is confidently expected that the CCC will spur the churches on to greater levels of ecumenical cooperation.

Christian Education

The Sunday School curriculum material known as the *Caribbean Christian Living Series* was widely used in many Protestant churches. In recent years, however, a number of factors brought about a decline in its use. The CCC therefore mounted another Christian education program, which included three major planks: (1) the training of church leaders and teachers of teachers; (2) the collective identification of relevant and appropriate religious educational methods and materials; (3) the production of a new curriculum for Sunday schools and day schools by a Caribbean-wide team of writers, including Roman Catholics, Anglicans, and Protestants. The result has been highly successful, and the CCC can be justly proud of *Fashion Me a People*, which has been adopted by many churches and some governmental Departments of Education for their official use. The series was published in 1981 and was designed to respond to the following objectives:

To enable persons to:
Experience value and meaning as members of the household of God
Grow in their relationship to God and with other persons, as revealed in Jesus Christ
Respond to the challenges of the gospel in their individual and corporate life
Appreciate and live in harmony with the world God has created.[16]

In the preface, the then general secretary, Roy Neehall, explained: "The Sessions deal with concerns of our identity and development as a Caribbean people and as Christians. Basic concerns are of work, family life, ecology, inter-group relationships, crime, social and economic development and spiritual development. All this is dealt with in the light of scriptural teaching."[17]

We come finally to an overall look at the state of theological enterprise in the English-speaking sector of the Caribbean, and we ask the question "What is fundamental to the theology?" We understand theology to be the critical reflection on life in the light of faith in God toward the generation and sustaining of orthopraxis. Theology is the active search for that right relationship between God and the world, and between persons in the world. Its genesis cannot be external to its praxis, so that there can be no externally devised and administered canons of theology. There is a pervasive temptation for such to emerge, and new theological insights often surface in the region in the wake of external promptings that are not relevant, imaginative, or even viable. Caribbean theology is to be a home-grown system rather than an externally motivated enterprise.

The former president of the United Theological College of the West Indies (UTCWI) in Jamaica, William Watty, once made the following statement: "Liberation in the Caribbean is primarily and essentially a liberation of the mind, both from self-depreciation and imitation on the one hand and from dreaming the impossible dream on the other hand."[18] He further contended that a theology should first of all confront and destroy the false values that have always corrupted human relationships. This need for higher and nobler levels of value and human excellence is particularly acute in the Caribbean. The Pastoral Letter to the Methodist Church in the Caribbean and the Americas, which was issued by the church's leaders in May 1978, ends with these challenging words:

> Within a changing situation in our Caribbean lands and territories we are urged to allow our treasured foundations to be shaken so that what is real and relevant and meaningful may remain. To be unwilling to accept change is as serious as sin itself. But to face change with courage and complete trust in the Lord Jesus Christ is to transform it into a creative opportunity for righteousness.[19]

The CCC is currently pursuing a program called "Theological Reflection and Conscientization." Among its many objectives, this program has been attempting to create a greater consciousness among Caribbean people about (1) the importance of the biblical and theological imperatives for solidarity with the poor; (2) the meaning of oppression and liberation in the light of the Kingdom of God; and (3) the need to renew a commitment to social change in the developing world. It has encouraged the work of theologians and theological institutions, and it has developed theological networks to support and enhance Caribbean ecumenism and renewal and to promote social change for the better. It also claims to place a high premium on the development of indigenous traditions and forms.

TOWARD AN EMANCIPATORY THEOLOGY

The historical and theological significance of that great event of August 1, 1834, cannot be emphasized enough. Slavery was abolished. Emancipation from bondage became law, and, except for a few minor adjustments and hesitations, freedom was to be the new bond between ex-slave and ex-slaveholder. Emancipation was to be *the* change, making possible all other changes in the Caribbean human condition. During the 1980s, the region has been celebrating the 150th anniversary of emancipation from slavery. Opinions differ greatly about how much there is to show for that period, or how much there is to celebrate. "Emancipation" is for Caribbean people a strong emotive word, connoting that spirituality of freedom which they are pursuing. The word "liberation" does not offer as much. "Emancipation" links us existentially with the struggle of our slave ancestors, since we are the inheritors of that struggle; it also keeps before us the strongest warning away from the bondage to which God wills that we should never return. In Caribbean terms, "emancipation" is the word that tells us and the world that "Massa day done." Slavemasters are no more, nor are there to be slaves anymore.

What is it in the Caribbean experience that still hinders the process of full emancipation? Is there not a need to dig deep into our own historical consciousness and to reapply ourselves to the task that was arrested or deferred somewhere along the line? Is it not true that the most crucial human need in the Caribbean at this time is neither trade, nor aid, nor arms, nor even the liberation of the mind, but rather the *emancipation of the disvalued self*? Is it not true that this disvalued self is the product of our own misconception of truth, beauty, goodness, and human dignity, and that others have willingly joined us in our self-deprecating miscegenation of values? The culture of our mind has been assaulted by the culture of our environment, and our historical values have been radically disfigured by misguided modes of belief. We are trapped most of the time within the confines of our disvalued selves, and we seldom realize that we are.

Emancipation is still possible; it is still a fundamental historical promise of the emancipating God. Perhaps the major initiative in the Caribbean must therefore be the theological one—that radically new and critical reflection on life which will engage not only the mind but every aspect of our collective selves in the thrust toward emancipatory experiences, expressions, and relationships. The theological initiative must be emancipatory in thought, language, and praxis. I am therefore suggesting that we must be engaged in the process of emancipatory theology rather than the theology of emancipation. The former creates instant light and heat for power; the latter induces light but can never radiate heat for praxis. The one is experiential and energizing; the other is cerebral and entertaining. The Caribbean show is over; the work is long overdue.

What, then, of this emancipatory theology as the major initiative for the Caribbean church? A number of factors appear to be indispensable for the comprehensive construction of such a process. Emancipatory theology should be understood to take place at a deep, comprehensive level. It should seek to give concrete and systematic expression to the following:

1. The steady and disciplined release of the creative imagination in the use of folk wisdom in proverbs, myths, folktales, symbols, and cultural imagery.

2. The selective and judicious borrowing of values and modes of reflection from other cultural contexts.

3. The constant and concrete affirmation of human life in the light of faith in Jesus Christ.

4. The priority of the communal will over individualistic predispositions.

5. The God-oriented virtues of faith in the church as the family of God and an authentic sign of the Kingdom.

6. A prophetic interpretation and proclamation of the realities of social and historical existence in the light of the Kingdom.

7. The unending search for the transformation of present resourcefulness into emancipatory praxis toward full humanity.

8. The collective and disciplined pursuit of an emancipatory social ethic.

9. The conscious reconstruction and proclamation of the Black Story in the light of the emancipatory experience.

10. The deliberate and systematic attempt at a Caribbean hagiography.

11. The openness for constant dialogue and communication with people of other faiths and other modes of interpretation and praxis.

All these factors represent, or seek to respond to, the varieties of need for authentic Christian witness in the Caribbean today. They point beyond themselves to a region of human expectation and suffering, of human alienation and spiritual poverty, of human failure and general anomie. But they also stem from a people who have not lost hope, and whose faith in the power of God is only occasionally distorted by those who would almost pass themselves off as divine agents bringing in another kind of kingdom. Emancipatory theology is for Christians who call the Caribbean their home.

It is the place where it has pleased God to place them; it is the center of their world. They understand God in terms of such realities as their island homes have to offer, and they are ready to respond to that understanding of God in the light of their earnest desire to be free. The Caribbean church must announce to all its people that God has willed everyone to be free and to inherit life in all its fullness. For some non-Caribbean persons, "the Caribbean is a very important passage-way for our international commerce and military lines of communication."[20] We thank God for that. But for Caribbean people themselves, it is the only place they can call home; it is the Gate of Heaven. Caribbean emancipatory theology is to be the major protagonist of this fact for today. The most urgent theological task for the Caribbean now is not to think and talk ourselves into new ways of acting but, rather, to act ourselves into new ways of thinking. Therefore, in the next three chapters, we shall consider the doxological significance of an emancipatory theological praxis and the contextual linkages between the Caribbean people and other oppressed peoples. For God's emancipation does not take place in isolation; it takes place only in solidarity with all other people who—in the context of their oppression, suffering, and poverty—press forward on the way toward that unconditionally free God, who is already on the way toward them.

CHAPTER SEVEN

EMANCIPATORY EXISTENCE: CHRISTIAN LIFE AS PRAISE

New ways of theological thought and praxis have been taking shape in Latin America, in Africa, Asia, the Caribbean, and Afro-America. Theological initiatives have been flowering throughout the oppressed world, and the struggle for the pursuit of human freedom as the gift of the God, who wills all persons to be free, has been gaining momentum. The new wave of articulation of the faith and the search for common dialogue and solidarity among Third World theologians have made an impressive mark on the consciousness of Third World Christians. Black theology, Minjung theology, liberation theology, and emancipatory theology have all been promoted as authentic expressions of understanding the faith in Third World contexts. Local theologies proclaim the Gospel of freedom as the essential meaning of the person and work of Jesus Christ. A central theme is Paul's dictum in Galatians 5:1, "For freedom Christ has set us free; stand fast therefore, and do not submit again to a yoke of slavery."

It is really difficult to overstate how significant a role the church plays in the lives of those whose claims to full humanity and dignity have been historically and systematically denied. It provides the last and sometimes the only bastion of affirmation available to them in their community. When the church has failed to fulfill their need for spiritual strength and social acceptance, they have taken their sense of God's presence with them and freely gathered together elsewhere for worship and witness. Nevertheless, the church continues to be the major wellspring for the generation of that doxology through which God's abiding care and presence are acknowledged, and by which the realities of social existence are reshaped. "Thank you, Jesus" and "Praise the Lord" are not vain repetitions; they emanate from a life rooted and grounded in the church.

Authentic doxology is not by word alone, though words of praise often rise from a deep and rich substream of experience. The sense of gratitude and thanksgiving, the struggle for holiness of living, the readiness to share God's blessings in a context of material scarcity, and the courage to bear even unbearable sufferings—all constitute the essential meaning of the church as source of doxology in the practice of emancipatory theology. We dare not reduce the language and life of such a spiritual encounter between the believers and their God to the psychology of the theater or the sociology of the hospital. God meets with God's people in the context of freedom, and emancipatory spirituality can utter nothing but praise.

In spite of the many advances made in liberation theology—advances that have caused reactionary governments to take countervailing action and to encourage theological espionage—there remains a need for a substantial range of active reflection. Because the notion of "liberation" has been heavily overlaid with exclusive, and even divisive, ideological and political concerns, the term "liberation" seems to be in urgent need of emancipation. When North Atlantic liberals speak of "liberation," they often seem to mean something different from what the word stands for in the lives of those on the underside of history. And yet both types of people are genuinely in search of freedom. Therefore, the importance of context must be borne in mind, since what is wine for one might be poison for another. For those on the underside of history, the historically poor and oppressed, the notion of emancipation is more meaningful than the notion of liberation. It ushers in a deeper range of theological reflection and response than is usually offered in the varieties of contemporary theologies.

The vision of emancipation is understood in all languages, cultures, and contexts of human society. Indeed, it was Karl Marx who said that "all emancipation is the reference of the human world and of conditions to man himself."[1] Marx, however, believed that emancipation from religion must supersede all other forms of emancipation. His own sociohistorical context had caused him to regard religion as a part of the superstructure that had to be dismantled if the dominated classes were to realize their full human worth, economic power, and historical control of their freedom and destiny. Religion was, for him, the "sigh of the oppressed." Other contexts have often led other people to regard religion as the hope of the oppressed. Such is the power of context.

In emphasizing the importance of context in relation to emancipation, we are not concerned merely with a notion of emancipation—as, for example, a "theology of emancipation" or an "ideology of emancipation." We are in fact searching for the deeper emancipatory experiences of human life that are made available to us in the heart of a spiritual encounter with our context. Emancipation is not a gift of the British Parliament, or Abraham Lincoln, or P. W. Botha of South Africa. Indeed, legal instruments of emancipation have historically created new forms of enslavement for those who sign them. Gail Bowman (a former student of Howard University's School of Divinity) once wrote in an essay: "America turned upside down in the 1960's but somehow managed to right itself with much of its oppression intact and with a frightening willingness and ability to recreate its flaws. One might ask why Christians still believe in Christ's emancipation."[2] Martin Luther King, Jr., in even stronger words, once said: "No Lincolnian emancipation proclamation or Johnsonian civil rights bill can totally bring this kind of freedom. The Negro will only be free when he reaches down to the inner depths of his own being and signs with the pen and ink of assertive manhood his own emancipation proclamation."[3] King was, of course, referring to what he called psychological freedom, which could engender self-esteem even in the enslaved.

Emancipation as a divine activity is even more profound than psychological freedom, for it originates in the sovereign action of the God who not only creates but also re-creates and sustains. It is a lifelong encounter that has to be fleshed out, structured, refined, reinforced, and fleshed out again for more restructuring. It is an ongoing response to an authentic divine-human encounter, for no one can truly meet with God and still feel enslaved. Emancipation is therefore both a divine promise and a human project, and the theological initiatives mandated by the call to human freedom render it necessary for theology itself to be emancipated.

There is, as mentioned, a vast difference between "emancipatory theology" (the existential search of faith for freedom of expression and praxis) and the "theology of emancipation" (the cerebral systematization of intellectual notions that may not bear direct relationship to actual human engagement). Emancipatory theology demands a constant openness of the self toward the realization of the context in which it lives. Such openness will always require the steady and disciplined use of the creative imagination and a realistic appraisal of the wide range of human values in the light of faith, human dignity, and freedom. It requires a courageous integrity of thought, self-perception, and human relationship, and it demands the acknowledgment that persons are always more valuable than things.

Emancipatory theology is the constant purification of hope, through faith in God. It responds to present conditions in the full assurance that greater emancipation is already on the way. It seeks always to listen to other contexts and to share what it has discerned with a wider context, without attempting either to dominate others or to be dominated by others. Emancipatory theology does not seek merely to use the word "emancipation" as a "kind of epochal catchword for our contemporary experience of reality."[4] It is the struggle for real life and liturgy, real purpose and praxis, real context and conduct, real hope and happiness. It is the source of understanding, as well as the sign by which those who live it are to be understood. It resolutely confronts domination, tutelage, paternalism, disadvantage, and injustice; and it gives radically new meaning to life even in the physical context of continuing poverty, oppression, and pain.

We have already spoken of theology as a science; we have called it a science for freedom. We now need to go further and to recognize that theology is much more than a science; it is also an art. As a living and captivating art, emancipatory theology seeks to integrate at least eight sources of the life experience and promise into a rich tapestry of historical responses to contextual realities. These sources need to be identified and briefly discussed.

First, emancipatory theology bases its fundamental rootage not in the choice between God on the one hand and freedom on the other, as Western liberalism suggests in our post-Christian era, but rather in the affirmation of God as freedom. Such an affirmation is not an intellectual presupposition for a range of ideological nuances and social strategies, but rather the basis on which God as ultimate reality is experienced as intimate reality. God is not simply a god without a name; God is that God-experience which brings freedom. Thus, in emancipatory theology, the assertion that God has created humanity in God's image means that human beings are capable of the God-experience. As Martin Luther King, Jr., said of the free God, "God is not interested merely in the freedom of black men, and brown men, and yellow men; God is interested in the freedom of the whole human race."[5] And as Desmond Tutu has told the South African youth: "We were created freely for freedom and when we are free we are able to set others free to be themselves, not letting them live up to our expectations of them, but remembering that God believes in them as He believes in us."[6]

Second, the chief and pivotal locus of that God-experience is the human body. God cannot be experienced by us apart from our bodies, since we are in fact what we were made by God. Emancipatory theology therefore stresses the significance and dignity of our bodies. Our bodies are not our possessions; our bodies are us. They constitute the point of our encounter with God. God becomes enfleshed in our existence; it is through our flesh that we are joined with the divine. The African theologian Tertullian reminds us that "the flesh is the central point of our salvation." How poignantly does that giant fifth-century preacher John Chrysostom speak of this enfleshment: "He has decreed that ignominy shall become honor, infamy be clothed with glory, and total humiliation the measure of His Goodness. For this He assumed my body, that I may become capable of His Word; taking my flesh."[7] A giant preacher of this century, Howard Thurman, speaks in this way: "The time and place of a man's life on earth are the time and place of his body, but the meaning and significance of his life are as vast and far-reaching as his gifts and the passionate commitment of all his powers can make it."[8] Emancipatory theology acknowledges the human body as the divine promise of freedom and salvation, while liberal theology regards it as a project, and conservative religion treats it as a problem. The apostle Paul regards the body as the center of doxology: "You were bought with a price," he says. "So glorify God in your body" (1 Corinthians 6:20).

Third, the meaning of Jesus as the Christ of God and Savior of the world emerges from the reality of the freedom in the God-experience. Such freedom does not seek to evade the pain and suffering in the body, or in the structures of society, but rather to confront them concretely. Jesus is not only the one who gave himself wholly and unconditionally to accepting the freedom of God in radical obedience, but he also refused to allow himself to be deterred by any other guise of freedom or power. So emancipatory theology acknowledges Jesus as the Son of God, the free God, and accepts the words of that Jesus: "If the Son makes you free, you will be free indeed" (John 8:36). That freedom is assured through the resurrection of Jesus from the dead, and that is why emancipatory theology is essentially a resurrection theology. It agrees with the following assertions of Jürgen Moltmann: "The ground of freedom is the cross of Christ. The power of freedom is the resurrection of Christ. The truth of freedom is love."[9] But the Christology that informs the construction of emancipatory theology focuses attention on the meaning of Christ for those on the underside of history. Mays says that Jesus had a bias for the man who was the farthest down: "It is the man farthest down who needs to remember that he, too, is the salt of the earth, and that he, too, is a child of God. It is this man who needs the assurance that he has the right to walk the earth with dignity and pride. It may be ... for this reason that we usually find Jesus on the side of the 'least of these.' "[10]

Fourth, emancipatory theology draws its nurture from the wisdom of the folk culture—proverbs, stories, songs, spirituals, calypsos, and hymns. Through the medium of such folk wisdom, the spirituality of freedom has been generated and sustained even in the face of great forms of historical bondage. The use of proverbs, the collective function of Negro spirituals, and the lessons from stories, whether legendary or historical, have all given a distinctive context to emancipatory theology. It is distinctive because it speaks to the whole person in community, and it develops an oral, aural, visual, and visional framework in which to function.

In his seminal work on the Negro spirituals, Howard Thurman shares with us some important insights about the people whose lives gave rise to such songs. These songs, he points out, denote that for the Negroes life carries its own restraint, that people do reap what they sow, regardless of who they are. "This notion is a dynamic weapon in the hands of the disadvantaged. It makes it possible for them to ride high to life, and particularly to keep their spirits from being eaten away by gloom and hopelessness."[11] Another insight from these songs, says Thurman, "is that the contradictions of life are not in themselves either final or ultimate." The vicissitudes of life could not use up all of God's resources. Thurman contends that "the awareness of the presence of a God who was personal, intimate and active was the central fact of life and around it all the details of life and destiny were integrated."[12] He also demonstrates that the songs portray an authentic belief in personal immortality. The works of such persons as James Weldon Johnson, Eugene Genovese, Alain Locke, John Lovell, Jr., Wendell Phillips Whalum, and Wyatt Tee Walker, among others, help us enter deeply into the emancipatory world of folk wisdom, especially in song. It is here that emancipatory theology as doxology finds much of its strength and substance; but there are several other sources as well. The words of W. E. B. DuBois continue to ring in our hearing today, when he says that the Negro folk song "still remains as the singular spiritual heritage of the nation and the greatest gift of the Negro people."[13] We turn our backs on freedom when we mute the sounds of the Negro spirituals.

Our fifth dimension in the construction of an emancipatory theology has to do with the nature of the church and its effect. The church commands a cardinal place in the lives of those who seek to give meaning to their faith through the freedom of the God-experience, and in the context of an oppressive and alienating world. Varying images of the church converge in emancipatory theology, chiefly because the church has to provide for the nurture, the sense of worth and calling, the reassurance of the value of life in God, and a taste of freedom of belief and expression – all of which would otherwise be denied. So the church is indeed God's household of God's people; and the confluence of prayer and praise, of word and movement (whether in rhythm or ritual), of service and mutual support makes it an indispensable part of one's reason for living.

This brings us to our sixth dimension of emancipatory theology, for the doxology that is generated through the Spirit of God in the church, and that is radiated in the most contagious way in the daily expressions of such theology, finds its source material mainly in the biblical tradition. It is important to stress that we are talking about the biblical tradition, rather than the Bible as literature, or as the "Book." In emancipatory theology, the biblical tradition is a living experience. Characters, passages, and episodes come alive in a most liberating and invigorating way. Thus, it is at the point of doxology that the living encounter with the God of the Exodus and Easter, the provider of manna and sender of the rain, makes possible the full meaning of a grateful response and confident assurance.

Patient study of the doxological portions of the biblical tradition produces an enormous treasury of material from which to understand the ground and scope of doxology as the first duty of the people of God. The songs, psalms, and acclamations all affirm that God is freely to be praised for what God has done and will do; that God's sovereignty is without conditionality or compromise; that those who experience the absence of the free God for a time are soon reassured that such absence is merely short-lived if not illusory; that emancipation by God is not in doubt, regardless of the overwhelming terror of human and historical bondage. How else can we enter into the spirituality of Moses or Miriam on the safer side of the Red Sea (Exodus 15), or the exultation of the Levites in Nehemiah 9:5: "Stand up and bless the Lord your God from everlasting to everlasting. Blessed be thy glorious name which is exalted above all blessing and praise"? This is the spirit that pervades the words of Deutero-Isaiah after the mysterious experience of the fourth Servant Song (Isaiah 52:13–53:12). God speaks in the rest of that Isaianic encounter, and the One to whom praise is due evokes praise from those whose emancipation is assured.

The world of the Psalter stands unparalleled in the tremendous surge of the human spirit to offer back to God so much of what has been experienced in the heat of sin and suffering, or in the maze of struggle and success. It is chiefly in that world of ancient spirituality that the Christian church has come to a deeper understanding of the close encounter between the God of history, as the sovereign Lord of creation, and the people of God, whose history has been shaped by the certainty of that encounter. So the psalmists tell the story and reflect on their experiences through it, and in that reflection they encompass the whole range of the human condition as it comes under the scrutiny of God's judgment and as it is illumined by the radiance of divine glory.

Those of us from the Caribbean who have been brought up in the rich liturgical tradition of chanting all the psalms with regularity and devotion, and who have meditated incessantly on the treasury of this sacred tradition, have largely been blessed by the freedom and strength we have found in such a discipline; and we have been able to apply the doxological imperatives toward an emancipatory interpretation of our historical existence and our societal relationships. Through the constant repetition of Psalm 8, we work out in doxology what is the core of Christian anthropology; through the affirmations of Psalm 29, we defy any claims to ultimacy other than God's; in the exaltation of Psalm 150—"Let everything that has breath praise the Lord"—we hear the unmistakable sound of emancipatory theology as doxology. One cannot live in the world of the Psalms and feel enslaved to anyone.

In spite of all that we have said so far about the Psalter and our modern attachment to it, nothing should detract from the prominent use that is made of it by the New Testament writers. The strongly doxological flavor of much of the New Testament material reflects quite faithfully the liturgical background in which the writers were steeped. Emancipatory theology draws on the heritage from the New Testament, whether it is the doxological interlude in the Lazarus story of the Fourth Gospel, or the canticles in the Birth narratives in the Third Gospel, or the numerous acclamations of praise in the Book of Revelation. Listen to the dialogue between Jesus of Nazareth and the heavenly voice at the conclusion of his public ministry: "Father, glorify thy name." "I have glorified it, and I will glorify it again" (John 12:28). Then, of course, there is the world of Pauline literature, which is replete with such doxological passages as, "O the depth of the riches and wisdom and knowledge of God! How unsearchable are his judgments and how inscrutable his ways! . . . For from him and through him and to him are all things. To him be glory for ever. Amen" (Romans 11:33, 36).

Emancipatory theology finds fertile ground for doxological responses to reality not only *in* the biblical tradition but also *through* that tradition as the basic norm for understanding Christian faith and freedom. The need to understand Christian faith and freedom is especially crucial for those who face situations that threaten to reduce the efficacy of faith itself. It is precisely at the point where faith itself is threatened that emancipatory theology strives to be intensely doxological. Such an intensity generates a kind of doxology that permeates the very being of the believer who struggles to discern the mission of God and the moment—the "kairos"—of the free

God. Thus, we can say that emancipatory theology as doxology is both missional and "kairotic"; it claims the power from the God who sends, and it names the moment for the God who empowers. We need to identify the characteristics of such doxology as it is experienced in the freedom of creative hope. The doxology to which we refer is not merely verbalized; it envelops the totality of one's being and determines human attitudes, aptitudes, life-styles, and relationships. True doxology is that which is lived out in the freedom of faithful dependence on the God who is absolute freedom.

Yet in the Caribbean religious experience, nothing exceeds the power of singing and music as a vehicle of praise and worship. The experience of God in worship is most powerfully to be felt and observed in the singing of the Caribbean worshipers. The spirited manner in which hymns and songs are learned and sung from memory; the way in which church musicians are frequently frustrated by their congregations' self-directed styles; the luster and feeling that often accompany even otherwise drab liturgies; the use of tambourines, guitars, drums, and other loud instruments besides organs—all these are integral parts of the Caribbean religious experience, and they testify to a wealth of spirituality and fervor that mark out the emancipatory dimension of Caribbean praise.

Caribbean hymnody is deeply rooted and grounded in the cultural life, so that even the workplace and the playing field become spheres of doxology. Whistling and humming hymns and religious songs can often break the monotony of the hour. The hymns and songs learned from early childhood (through regular attendance at worship) provide simple means of release and relaxation for the burdened heart. Most worship services are assessed for their value less on the standard of the preaching than on the enjoyment of the music. Of course, both enrich the quality of the event, but bad preaching is often saved by good singing in the Caribbean ecclesial life. The traditional hymns of Charles Wesley and Isaac Watts are well known by most Caribbean people of any denominational persuasion, and they provide a strong incentive for social interaction wherever they are sung. Caribbean people have made these hymns their own by their lusty and inimitable way of singing them, and by the creole interpretation of rhythm or meaning they appropriate to them.

As a life of praise, then, emancipatory theology is often linked with a passion for justice, for we cannot glorify the freedom in God while at the same time renouncing the justice that God demands for God's people. Everybody talks about heaven, we sing, but not everybody will get there. Doxology affirms the ethical demands of love and strives to link them with the basically new commandment of Jesus that we love one another as he has loved us. This love of Jesus is the ground of sacrificial obedience to which we are constantly called by God. King said, "Power at its best is love implementing the demands of justice, and justice at its best is power correcting everything that stands against love."[14] There may be risk involved in meeting the demands of justice, love, sacrifice, and obedience; but, as doxology, emancipatory theology proclaims a Gospel of the victory that has already been won for us in Christ, so that the risk of faith is countered by the assurance of emancipation. And yet, even with this assurance, there lingers in the human heart a sense that it is unworthy of God's gracious freedom. Doxology invites us to acknowledge such unworthiness and to recognize that unspeakable grace of God, who dares to love the unlovable.

As doxology, emancipatory theology inspires us to be led by the Spirit of God because we are the children of the free God. Such leading by the Spirit challenges us to accept the full force of the truth—not simply the truth that convicts or condemns but, more significantly, the truth that transforms. For, in the final analysis, unless we can allow ourselves to be transformed by God's truth, we cannot expect to enjoy the glorious freedom that belongs only to the children of God. Mays has said, "No man is really free who is afraid to speak the truth as he knows it, or who is too fearful to take a stand for that which he knows is right."[15] Truth and freedom are absolutely inseparable. Therefore, doxology spells engagement in God's world, not withdrawal from it. It spells confrontation with all that creates unnecessary divisions and unjust systems—racism, ageism, sexism, classism, intellectualism.

Mays has left us these profound words:

> When we build fences to keep others out, erect barriers to keep others down, deny to them the freedom which we ourselves enjoy and cherish most, we keep ourselves in, hold ourselves down, and the barriers we erect against others become prison bars to our own souls. We cannot grow to the mental and moral stature of free men if we view life with prejudiced eyes, for thereby we shut our minds to truth and reality, which are essential to spiritual, mental, and moral growth. The time we should spend in creative activity, we waste on small things which dwarf the mind and stultify the soul."[16]

Doxology breeds inclusivism and scorns discrimination; for when we dare to accept the full truth about ourselves, we dare not take ourselves too seriously. Emancipatory theology can serve as an effective antidote for overweening conceit and sophisticated pomposity. Those who spend their time praising their God have no time left to seek praise for themselves. We live in a world where human praise is often used to numb the pain of divine truth, for the truth that emancipates is often the truth that hurts. It is in the strength of emancipatory theology that we are often saved from our friends, for we already know our enemies.

We have said earlier that emancipatory theology as doxology is not only missional, but also kairotic. It is seized by God's kairos, God's moment. What does such doxology look like? Doxology is the band of South African young people on the trot with clenched fists upraised and moving against the police and their bullets. "Freedom is coming," says Desmond Tutu, as they trot on. "We will be free whatever anybody does or does not do about it."[17] Doxology is the spirit of defiance fleshed out in taking hard choices when softer options were being offered—so that we can say with Mays, "I am glad that I did what I did .... I have done what I understood to be God's will for me and will continue to do this until I die."[18] Doxology is the fortitude of faith that trusts unconditionally in the trustworthiness of God in the midst of oppressive or depressing circumstances. Doxology dares to profess that the God who has brought us this far will not leave us here alone. God, who has been the help in ages past, will continue to be the shelter from all the stormy blasts—even if we know not how. "Only God is able," thundered Martin King. "It is faith in him that we must rediscover. With this faith we can transform bleak and desolate values into sunlit paths of joy and bring new light into the dark caverns of pessimism."[19] So life's moments are provisional rather than permanent, says emancipatory theology, and we cannot afford to treat relative experiences as if they were of ultimate value.

There can be no place for fear in the world of emancipatory theology, for the whole point about the emancipatory work of Christ is that we are set free from fear—especially the fear of death. Such an absence of fear is cause for doxology, and it also becomes the ground for facing the threatening structures of unrelenting oppression and injustice. It was in the strength of this faith that King was able to proclaim: "I am happy tonight. I'm not worried about anything. I'm not fearing any man. Mine eyes have seen the glory of the coming of the Lord."[20] Such a doxology could not even be silenced by the bullets that silenced King a few hours later. Or let us listen to Oscar Romero of El Salvador two weeks before his brutal death in March 1980: "May my death, if it is accepted by God, be for the liberation of my people, and as a witness of hope in what is to come. You can tell them, if they succeed in killing me, that I pardon them, and I bless those who may carry out the killing."[21]

Such an attitude toward the realities of life empowers us to speak out boldly and to call things by their right names. Whether in the difficult society of Latin America or in the oppressive environment of South Africa, true emancipation must lead one to an enlightened analysis of one's social context and to articulate such an analysis with courage. Winnie Mandela speaks with beauty and boldness while her husband emancipates the meaning of a prison from the inside. Another Christian once imprisoned in South Africa, Cedric Mayson, recognizes that "the problem of liberation is not to control bad people at the bottom, but those in positions of leadership who think they are good."[22]

As doxology, emancipatory theology gives concrete meaning to the evangelical vision of a new heaven and earth by seeking to bring into historical reality the freedom of heaven on earth. This emancipatory vision of present conditions in the light of future possibilities enkindles the heart with joyful courage and the lips with joyful praise. "I will sing a new song," says Howard

Thurman. "As difficult as it is, I must learn the new song that is capable of meeting the new need. I must fashion new words born of all the new growth of my life, my mind and my spirit."[23] Such a vision eventually won for Martin King the Nobel Peace Prize in 1964. On the occasion of accepting that award in Oslo, King spoke these words: "I have the audacity to believe that peoples everywhere can have three meals a day for their bodies, education and culture for their minds, and dignity, equality and freedom for their spirits. I believe that what self-centered men have torn down men other-centered can build up. I still believe that one day mankind will bow before the altars of God and be crowned triumphant over war and bloodshed, and nonviolent redemptive good will proclaim the rule of the land."[24] Doxology at work thus seeks to change the limits of our belief about the participation of our God in our historical circumstances, and enables us to recognize that hand of God as it enlarges and enhances the master plan of freedom in our lives.

We have been attempting to demonstrate in this chapter that the Christian life of praise, which is deeply rooted in the Caribbean religious experience, is an authentic expression of the emancipatory experience emanating from the relationship between God and the people whom God wills to set free. Such life of praise, such doxology, is not peculiar to the people of the Caribbean; other oppressed peoples have also demonstrated the centrality of praise in their struggle for freedom and their fight against historical oppression. Such doxology provides the strongest cultural and theological linkages across several contexts, and Caribbean people find themselves at one with their sisters and brothers in other contexts of the struggle. The practice of emancipatory theology is impossible without the free expressions of personal and collective praise to the unconditionally free God.

So freedom sings what Freedom brings. Human freedom sings what Divine Freedom brings. It sings because it acknowledges the glory with which God continues to create human life with dignity, beauty, and freedom. It sings because it is not simply absorbed by what we are emancipated *from* but, rather, by what we are emancipated *for*. It sings because freedom brings not only creative empowerment but also creative hope. It sings because its highest role is to make our lives "not only a benediction breathing peace but also a vital force of redemption to all" we touch.[25] It sings because humanity created in the image of God is made chiefly for communion with God, chiefly for participation in the divine life that is patently experienced in history. The goal of history is to become unhaltingly doxological—to declare the glory of God in every dimension of our endeavor. The song of freedom is no song of abandon or illusion; it is a song of engagement and action. We act out our doxology in the context of our freedom, for we hold to the confidence that only in the service of God is perfect freedom assured. As freedom sings, no one is excluded or alienated, but no one is elevated either—for God shows no partiality. Emancipatory theology thus offers us a most illuminating way of dealing with our common purpose for living. It provides us with a means of release from those historical accidents of birth or fortune that often obscure the basic truths of our existence. That is why it is doxology, and that is what the Afro-American bard Paul Laurence Dunbar would have us all feel in that stupendous poem "When Malindy Sings":

> Who dat says dat humble praises
> > Wif de Master nevah counts?
> Heish yo' mouf, I hyeah dat music,
> > Ez hit rises up an' mounts -
> Floating by de hills an' valleys,
> > Way above dis buryin' sod,
> Ez hit makes its way in glory
> > To de very gates of God!
>
> Oh, hit's sweetah dan de music
> > Of an edicated band;
> An' hit's dearah dan de battle's
> > Song o' triumph in de lan'.
> It seems holier dan evenin'
> > When de solemn chu'ch bell rings.
> Ez I sit an' ca'mly listen
> > While Malindy sings.
>
> Towsah, stop dat ba'kin', hyeah me!
> > Mandy, mek dat chile keep still;
> Don't you hyeah de echoes callin'
> > F'om de valley to de hill?
> Let me listen, I can hyeah it,
> > Th'oo de bresh of angels' wings
> Sof' and sweet, "Swing Low, Sweet Chariot,"
> > Ez Malindy sings.[26]

CHAPTER EIGHT

THE BLACK STORY:
EMANCIPATORY CONNECTIONS

The powerful theme of the Black Story has great emancipatory significance to many who are engaged in the relentless struggle for meaning and
personhood, both in the Caribbean and in America. Theology is an important dimension in the study of human existence, and those who engage in
theological reflection should always take full account of the intercultural
nature of our common experiences and aspirations. The intercultural theological process must play a crucial role if we are to engage in an authentic
search for sustained personhood, spiritual maturity, authentic emancipation, and common growth toward the measure of the stature of the fullness
of Christ. This is the goal of all of our participation in theological reflection
and Christian witness; this is the *missio Christi* to which we profess allegiance. In this chapter, we will therefore seek to explore the meaning and
scope of the Black Story as an intercultural matrix in the search for a new
theological process with distinctive emancipatory connections.

PARTICIPANTS IN THE BLACK STORY

Religion means different things to different people, and the concrete
manifestations of their religious behavior often indicate what is their defi-
nitional approach. If religion is used merely as a systematic attempt to
supplement felt insufficiencies in the human order, then the rise in human
sufficiency will create a corresponding fall in the need for religion. A fleet-
ing glance at post-Christian Europe will illustrate this quite clearly. If, on
the other hand, religion consists in the movement of one's purposeful
response to ultimate reality and the pursuit of total fulfillment, then it grows
with the person and undergirds all human experiences. The Black Story is
the integrative experience of a people whose religion is characterized by
this latter approach. Because their God has been a help in ages past, Caribbean and African-American people hold unflinchingly to the assurance
that, in prosperity or poverty, God is the hope of years to come. For such
people, atheism is hardly a serious option.

In this discussion, "black" does not merely stand for "nonwhite" or "nonrich" or "powerless" or African. It denotes that dynamic spirituality of a particular type of people who have had the distinction of being the only ones in history whose claims to being human have been systematically called into question, in Europe, the Americas, the Caribbean, and Southern Africa. It signifies the vitality of a people who have had to subsist culturally at the underground level but who passed on from generation to generation a quality of spirit that loved human life and dignity in the face of threatened extinction and overwhelming dehumanization. It is the sign of a people with a relentless trust in the future, in spite of the fact that they have been alienated from their ancestors, their inheritance, their land, their power. Their past is still ahead of them.

We use the term "story" because, in every cultural tradition, the story is a most important tool for chronicling the wealth, prestige, and achievements of ancestry. It is the means whereby a people ensure that succeeding generations not only tread in the footsteps of their foreparents but also develop the determination and the need to achieve. The story encompasses the rich promises that have to be fulfilled in contemporary and future eras. The story is a dynamic chain of human events and experiences. It links people together in the face of enforced fragmentation at other levels. Normally, the story is attached to a place. The Black Story is attached to nowhere in particular, although its roots are in Africa, and it transcends realities of race, power, and status in its degrees of relevance and vitality.

The Black Story is much more than the underside of Western history. It is not so much the retelling of the story from the black perspective; neither is it merely the attempt to bring into open and full recognition the story of a people whose existence was historically undermined. It is the totality of the cultural traditions, organizations, institutions, and systems of oppressed people in their struggle for meaning, dignity, and a better life. The Black Story is that indefatigable attempt by Caribbean and African-American people to transform the meaning of slavery and oppression, poverty and dependence, failure and weakness, into powerful signs of promise, achievement, fulfillment, and historical emancipation. The Black Story historically begins in Europe and passes through Africa to the Caribbean and the Americas, where it establishes its ontological rootage. Who would dare deny the historical facts of the systematic development of racism today? Racism was conceived in Europe, incubated in the Caribbean, baptized in America, ordained in North Atlantic trade, and canonized in Southern Africa. So the Caribbean and the Americas are a major spiritual center of the Black Story.

The following testimony from an outstanding African-American scholar, Roger Wilkins, also reflects the sentiments of generations of Caribbean people:

There we were, little kids, enveloped and almost crushed by an insidious fantasy that was reinforced daily by the most powerful society on the face of the earth. In order to gain human strength and integrity, we had to purge all that garbage from our spirits. We had to come to know in some fundamental way that no matter what the power of wealth relationships in this society might be, we were not invented by American white people and we did not stand on this earth at their sufferance. One good way to start was to understand that before the European invasion of Africa five centuries ago, the people from whom we got the contours of our lips and the curl in our hair walked their land in their way and arranged their lives according to their own lights.[1]

A significant part of the spirituality of the Black Story has been developed through Caribbean linkages with North America. Many in the Caribbean today continue to sing with the psalmist that "salvation comes neither from the east, nor from the west, nor yet from the south." Again, an age-old refrain in the Caribbean acknowledges the good fortune of Caribbean proximity to the American mainland. The spirit of gratitude for all that America has made possible and meant for them is quite pronounced in the expressed consciousness of many Caribbean people. No theological exploration on the Black Story can afford to ignore this fact, in spite of the current geopolitical tensions between the United States and the region.

THEOLOGY AND THE BLACK STORY

Four types of theology appear to be at work during any ordinary week of the year. First, there is the "Monday-morning" theology, with which academics and students have exercised their minds and burned the midnight oil. Very little of this ever leaves the place where it is dispensed. Second, there is the "Tuesday-afternoon" theology, by which the church boards conduct their affairs and complement the predilections of the church hierarchy. "Monday" and "Tuesday" are often suspicious of each other. Third, there is the "Saturday-night" theology, by which the preacher prepares a monologue for Sunday morning after a week of unrelated chores, appointments and off-days.

The fourth type is the "Sunday-morning" theology, which, for the sake of its own survival and efficacy, seeks to insulate itself from the other three types, except when its built-in selective mechanism discovers something worthwhile in them. "Sunday-morning" theology is sustaining and wholesome; it is impervious to irrelevance and arrogance, to threats and false promises. It motivates the faithful to and from the pews week after week, and it keeps them going all through the week. Its workshop is not in the church but in the home, the fields, and the shops, on the buses, by the rivers, at the street corners. It produces its own liturgy and rediscovers its own links with antiquity. In the churches, it only reaffirms its vitality and acknowledges its source — the God in the Black Story.

"Sunday-morning" theology is not merely *fides quaerens intellectum* or critical reflection on life; it is principally a passionate response resulting from that critical awareness of an inner reality which God makes known in the roughness of life. It is full of feeling, and folk wisdom, and pain, and humanity. "Sunday-morning" theology thrives on the contradictions of life—in the world, in the church, in the heart—and enables its practitioners to cope with the pressures of living by faith even if they are short of sight. In view of all this, therefore, the most authentic theologians of the Black Story are often the unlettered, the unenlightened, and the sometimes unloved.

What are the relevant characteristics that should inform an appropriate theological framework of the Black Story? Nine such considerations suggest themselves.

1. There must be a constant determination to plumb the depths of our common historical experience, to search for the underlying factors that constitute our intercultural identity and provide distinctive religious foundations.

2. Without attempting in any way to sanctify the socioeconomic institution of slavery, we must identify the divine disclosures within that historical era of the Black Story and try to establish their significant contribution to the religious foundations of our people. If we are to look back at ourselves through the slave days with any sense of pride and achievement, rather than with guilt or shame, we must be determined to identify that "finger of God" which kept our humanity intact while the outward selves of slaves and the inner selves of their owners were being brutalized and wasted away.

3. We should give ample recognition to the fertile and creative tensions within our human experience which have given birth to a basic resilience in the face of adversity and deprivation, together with the imaginative skills of survival and movement, of preservation and progress. These skills, evident as they are, cannot be accounted for apart from the framework of religious motivation.

4. A basic commitment to God—an acknowledgment of God's power, and love, and righteous demands—is constantly indicated throughout the Black Story. Even if there is sometimes an element of bargaining and compromise in this commitment, the realization of a covenantal relationship with this God is never diminished.

5. In our theological construction, we would also need to take full account of the predominant structures of response to reality. The way in which our people deal with the varieties of experience, natural and supernatural, accidental or determined, favorable or unfavorable, has much to say to us. In particular, the structure of the community response over against that of the individual response is significant, for the sociality of our personhood carries far greater weight and more valuable currency than its individuality. Indeed, the individual response is constantly nurtured and refined by the community response. Thus, when we are dealing with the

structures of religious response, the need for deprivatization is crucial for the Black Story. Individualism is the gate of sin.

6. Our theological search must identify the appropriate modes of human engagement, or involvement, in Christian witness and service. In a very real sense, we should struggle to determine orthopraxis rather than mere orthodoxy, and to be agent-oriented rather than merely action-oriented. The Black Story is the dynamic process of being and becoming, and the most appropriate theological signposts must usher our people toward the elimination of the gaps between preaching one thing and practicing another, between heavenly myth and earthly reality.

7. Worship is of cardinal importance to the spirituality of the Black Story. Any theology which cannot be grounded in the authentic worshiping experience of Christian people, and which cannot be in service of that very experience, automatically disqualifies itself. This is of elemental importance to the meaning and use of the Bible in Christian worship, to the place of word and song and liturgical expression, and to the proclamation of the Word of God in terms that are not only loud and clear but also simple and sweet. This is why "Sunday-morning" theology takes precedence over all other types.

8. The major testimony of the Bible is that God is always making new things out of the old. God's power is manifested chiefly in a series of new beginnings, which seem to bring the future into the present. This is the eschatological grid that informs the Black Story as a whole. Without it, there would have been no hope for our people in the prison of an utterly hopeless situation. Consequently, we must look toward the future in the Black Story and interpret human advancement—both material and spiritual—in terms of divine fulfillment. The Black Story cannot wrest the future out of God's hands.

9. The theology must essentially be a provisional one, since it is engaging an essentially pilgrim people, a people on the move. Every stage it reaches must constitute the starting point for a new and more vigorous surge forward. As the Black Story unfolds itself, the theological task is more deeply enlisted in the service of our people, enabling them to respond more faithfully to that which God would have them do and become.

On the basis of the foregoing considerations, it is not only possible but positively desirable that a theologically illuminating method of interpretation for the Black Story should be constructed. This method would need to express quite amply the basic Christian concerns about God, Christ, the world, the family, the church, poverty, racism, power, death.[2] These concerns radically affect the lives of our people and therefore require appropriate attention as the constructs of any relevant theological perspective. Out of such an imaginative and creative method of theological exploration the determinants for a process of intercultural theological reflection could inevitably emerge.

THEOLOGY AND NARRATIVE

One of the many sayings of Jesus which the earliest Christians remembered and passed on to us in the Christian story goes like this: "Wisdom is justified by all her children" (Luke 7:35). I take this to mean that the human intellect is so versatile that it can rationalize and defend any contradictions in human behavior. Theological discourse has within the past fifty years become complex, cold, and calculated; science and philosophy have taken hold of the theological pens to such an extent that it is now possible to restate that saying of Jesus: "Wisdom is frustrated by some of her children." Theologians are reacting so strongly to the nontheological ingredients of modern theology itself, with all the excursions it has made into alien and arid territory, that a new wave of the theological quest has emerged. This quest has been centered on the renewed zeal for divine truth—truth that is expressed not by definition but by description, not by statement but by story, not by doctrine but by testimony. The importance of the narrative has again taken hold of some theologians. Gabriel Fackre, for example, in his imaginative work *The Christian Story*, expressed concern about the "variety of experimentation in perspective," which tended to domesticate the Christian faith "in the categories of the time, rendering it incapable of doing the critical work it must do vis-à-vis that time."[3] In espousing the narrative framework for theological reflection and discourse, therefore, Fackre placed great value on the "*art of perspective*," which was "to learn to *relate* but not to *capitulate* to the culture out of which that perspective grows."[4]

The literature on the virtues of narrative theology is rapidly expanding. The power of the story is more widely acknowledged today than ever before, among theologians other than Old Testament scholars. These Old Testament scholars long ago recognized the power and message of the Story in the Bible, but they generally restricted themselves to the call for treating the Bible as literature. They chided the church and the seminary for reading the Bible as Scripture, while the university and the world were reading it as literature, as if such a distinction had become institutionalized. Their claim was that, in reading the Bible as literature, the church could more powerfully hear it as Scripture. Old Testament characters such as Jonah, David, and Esther could come alive with a deeper religious meaning in their respective stories through the art of the storytellers. Whether through story or poem, the Old Testament as literature is said to possess such a mode of communication that it can evoke from us the capacity to be more creative, it can as a text leap the time gap of its own accord, and it can create worlds alternative to our own present reality.[5]

New Testament scholarship has pointed out that the Christian story is more than just the story of Jesus. It also includes early Christian modes of interpretation and redaction, as well as early Christian political and mythological structures. Thus, the pattern of theological reflection and discourse has moved away from the propositional axis and toward a more narrative framework. This relatively new approach inevitably has its detractors, since it is not as easy to control narrative as it is to define and control propositions. Theological imperialism is one of the most demonic forms of power to be exercised in any generation. The question is surely not who controls the course of theologically acceptable debate but whether the group or person who is telling the Christian story, in any generation, can be acknowledged as a part of the church—and no other single group or person has the power of veto.

Those concerned with the promotion of narrative theology have so far confined their efforts mainly to literary forms and sources. But the overwhelming majority of Christians in the world are sustained and nurtured by theological sources and methods that are essentially oral and visual. For millions of people who are full-fledged members of the community of faith, and who are no less eligible for reaching that city whose builder and maker is God, Christian theology has to sound good, it has to look good, and it has to produce good looks. Many of them cannot read, but they are more literate in the Word of God than many an erudite scholar and theologian. Many of them have little form and less comeliness—by standards unrelated to the Kingdom of God—but they share in a beauty of religious experience and response that transcends the art of literature. Most of the people who share in the world of the Black Story—whites and blacks—are numbered among them. How can we proceed in the light of these realities?

We cannot reap the full benefits of our electronic technology in our secular story and yet behave as if the printed word is paramount material for the record of our sacred story. Audiovisual resources are far more effective and efficacious for religious communication today. They incorporate so many more people into the action. Oral literature is older, more valuable, and more durable than the written species. Furthermore, human history has repeatedly demonstrated that, where the letter kills, the spirit gives life. We need to begin an earnest and systematic search for an intercultural theological process that places primary emphasis on oral theology and pays full deference to the fact of the oral tradition within the framework of the Black Story.

Narrative theology can broaden the cultural sources useful for constructive theological reflection. Since it places a heavy emphasis on the importance of the imagination, it thereby joins the religious imagination to the literary and the scientific.[6] The oral culture of the community of faith provides the broadest possible historical and situational framework for the emergence of an intercultural theology.

Those who have studied oral traditions in many cultures tell us that these traditions usually are preserved in two ways: by *improvisation*, which is the normal form, and by *memorization*, which is exceptional.[7] Whereas written composition may go through several drafts before the final version, oral composition usually is conducted by improvisation before an audience — so that composition and transmission are closely related, and transmission itself is often accomplished by continual recomposition. In this way, the work is created anew each time it is presented. Oral tradition therefore allows for creativity, and the members of the audience play an important part, not only as censors — thus making the speaker sensitive to the standards and needs of the audience — but also as guarantors of the continued existence of the tradition by reason of its acceptance. The transmission of the Black Story through improvisation is alive and well. The Black Story conveys the spiritual and social vitality of much of our church life and witness throughout the Western world. Theology as a science has a tremendous task of catching up with a large sector of its own constituency.

The narrative consciousness of those who share in the experience of the Black Story, therefore, does not impel a desire to repeat and present theories and propositions about the Christian faith that have been chronicled for generations and transmitted as sacred and classical. It rather impels the existential response to what is concrete and meaningful in the present, in the light of what the Gospel has been authentically identified with in the past, and in anticipation of what is the call of God toward a more wholesome and emancipatory future. Such an existential response cannot be ghettoized in any race, class, culture, or country. The Black Story touches far too many people for that. Those who have grown fat on the fruits of the Black Story throughout the world cannot dare to exclude themselves today from the possibilities for real growth and human renewal to which God in Christ is summoning us. There is no American dollar, no French franc, no British pound, no South African rand today that cannot be assessed in some measure by the meaning of the Black Story. Anyone who takes the ancient story of the Jews and makes it his own sacred story, but then rejects the modern Black Story as alien, is not fit for the Kingdom of God as we experience it today. Divine logos takes human flesh, and we acknowledge that glory in the fullness of grace and truth, but only through the optic of the poor, oppressed, and marginalized in history.

The Black Story establishes *continuity*, not only with many stories throughout the Western world but also with the Christian story itself. The Black Story creates a *conviction* arising out of a radical transformation in the relationships of fellow believers in the Gospel. The Black Story demands that there be *consequential* action from those who hear the call of God in Christ to work for justice and reconciliation in the light of their faith. The Black Story creates a new understanding of *community*, which liberates its sharers from the crushing weight of self-centered love and culture-bound conceit. It radiates the light of Pentecost and not the heat and gloom of Babel. These four criteria of continuity, conviction, consequence, and community are best pursued within the narrative framework of theological reflection and discourse — not confined to the books and their writers but encompassing all those who have something to tell because God has touched their hearts. Intercultural theology is the handmaid of this process.

INTERCULTURAL THEOLOGY

No theology is culture free. The history of the Christian church in Africa and the study of educational developments in that noble continent attest overwhelmingly to this fact. Political and economic factors have always determined which cultures will predominate in the scenario of Christendom. How could God dare to consider "himself" other than an Englishman with some American connections, it was thought. When the predominant literature refers to the "church," it almost always denotes a global community with a metropolitan North Atlantic center and a plethora of peripheral communities which reflect the results of metropolitan missionary effort. When the idea of "theology" is concretized, the centers of its production are metropolitan, but it is expected to be consumed and absorbed by the global community. On the other hand, theologies produced in non-metropolitan centers are seldom granted acceptance or respect by metropolitan minds. Can anything worthwhile come from the South? This is the underlying question in Northern minds. And yet we still contend that theology is the handmaid of the church, the Body of Christ, the Son of a God who is understood to be no respecter of persons. Theology, although it is not culture free, still has the task of expressing, in a multiplicity of cultures and languages, the eternal myths and religious symbols which signify that innate relationship between God, Christ, and the world. We need to struggle together in the search for an authentic theological approach which will contribute to the body of Christ as a whole, without assuming that any particular theology is the most important or the most academically significant of all.

Intercultural theology is theology reaching beyond itself. It is the theological attempt to eliminate any need to rationalize any of our cultural biases, by striving relentlessly to reflect the sacramental dimension and the universal character of the Christian faith while it is still conditioned by historical realities. It is not a flight from human reality, but it is a disciplined attempt to theologize in any culture without treating that culture as absolute. Such a process would first demand that Christian thinkers from differing cultures should focus attention on a common theme that would evoke in them a narrative affirmation of their faith. It is my contention that, for most of us, the Black Story can provide that common theme.

What conceivable benefits could our several cultural contexts, our communities of faith, our common fellowship of belief and practice derive from such a process? Several possible consequences are self-evident. First, we could experience a renewal of a sense of ritual in our common life, in the face of the drab, dull monotony of technological ascendancy. Second, theology itself could demonstrate to us new areas of emancipation because it would itself have been emancipated. Third, the ecumenical agenda of our time could be richly enhanced and moved upward beyond the realm of game playing and ecclesiastical strategizing, for there is a "passional dimension of ecumenism" about which Daniel Martensen so rightly speaks. Martensen suggests that "images rather than ideas, stories rather than concepts" communicate something of this dimension, which involves passional trust and passional hope.[8] Fourth, the greatest sin of our time—racism—could be assaulted from a far more serious and concerted theological frontline than heretofore. Fifth, the theological importance of the actual story of our own people—living and departed—could be more authentically related to the story of the Bible people. Sixth, theology could provide for us a more enlightened, integrated, and compelling motivation for mutual cooperation and human solidarity. Seventh, we could guarantee a greater sense of continuity between theological reflection and action from one generation to another. Eighth, our efforts to conduct a dialogue with men and women of other faiths would become less pretentious and accommodating and more positively stimulating and mutually enriching.

EMANCIPATORY CONNECTIONS

The Black Story is thus a most powerful framework through which Caribbeans and Americans, especially those of African descent, can move forward in an intercultural theological process in the struggle for Christian solidarity and the search for more concrete expressions of human freedom. We can contribute to each other's freedom by the collective engagement in the common discovery of our rich heritage. Most of the tensions that have historically tended to exist between Afro-Caribbeans and African-Americans have resulted from a lack of knowledge about each other—from our reluctance to understand each other's historical and cultural struggles and from our insensitivity in communicating with each other.

These tensions have been more in evidence on the North American mainland than in the Caribbean, for hundreds of thousands of Caribbean people have migrated to North America to seek their fortune and to provide sustenance for their relatives in the home region. Most of them have managed to thrive well in the United States. As with all other immigrant groups, Caribbean people in the United States have generally acquitted themselves industriously and have tended to make full use of their educational and economic opportunities. Such success has not always been accompanied by a readiness to establish fertile and mutually constructive linkages with their brothers and sisters of African descent who are native to the United States. Furthermore, several of the African-Americans who have achieved high social or political status have been of Caribbean descent. Shirley Chisholm in the Congress, Colin Powell as chairman of the Joint Chiefs of Staff, Sydney Poitier and Cicely Tyson in Hollywood films, Patrick Ewing in basketball—all come readily to mind.

North American history would have been somewhat different without the participation of Marcus Garvey, Stokely Carmichael, and Louis Farrakan in the sociopolitical process of the United States. All had Caribbean origins, and Martin Luther King, Jr., frequently recognized the inspiration that he himself had gained from the efforts of Marcus Garvey in promoting black dignity and black freedom. The common experience of oppression and slavery, the common struggle for full humanity and economic self-reliance, and the common fight against racism and other forms of social and systemic injustice are all too compelling to engender tensions of mistrust and hostility between Afro-Caribbeans and African-Americans. For wherever there are the linkages of bondage, there also the emancipatory linkages are indicated. The intercultural theological process must therefore become a tool for eliminating mutual ignorance and mistrust and constructing strong bridges of human solidarity and Christian fortitude. The Black Story, which we share, makes such solidarity theologically possible.

In Chapters Four and Seven, we pointed to the African soul, which we share as descendants of Africa, and also to the importance of praise as an inescapable dimension of our emancipatory religious experience. These are undoubtedly among our emancipatory connections in the Black Story; but other meaningful possibilities also demand our serious attention.

First, there is the area of *storytelling*. This is a very basic cultural method of communication within our two contexts. Caribbean storytelling has been a major channel of communicating values, myths, lessons, and folk wisdom for generations. Some stories are based on historical fact, while others are based on animal heroes and heroines dating back to Africa. African-Americans also have their wealth of stories. Caribbean people tell of their Brer Anancy, while African-Americans tell of their Brer Rabbit. There is much character and cunning behind these *dramatis personae*. The stories inherited from the slave societies of both contexts often bear many similarities, for they focus particular attention on the way in which slaves had to use every skill and strength to survive, as well as to get even with their masters. The emancipatory elements of these stories are immeasurable, and they can be easily shared in an intercultural narrative process for their theological significance.

The second area deals with *religious songs*. Here again, the linkages are already in place, for Afro-American freedom songs, Negro spirituals, and the other types of African-American music have long been the staple of the Afro-Caribbean repertoire. Most of the time, these songs tell their own stories about life, dreams, hopes, fears, and experiences. They point to a depth of culture and community that depicts fairly accurately how African-Americans feel about themselves. Afro-Caribbeans have often adopted these musical scores without much modification and have attempted to find their own soul and feelings as they use them. Further, the vast world of jazz has encompassed many Caribbean groups, and the singing of the blues has often enraptured thousands of Caribbean people over the years. In these musical traditions they have shared, Caribbean people have been at one with their African-American counterparts. However, Caribbean musical traditions have not generally been adopted by their North American counterparts; and many of the religious songs, the calypsos, and the reggae music have been kept alive in the United States by Caribbean people themselves.

Nonetheless, the emancipatory connections in mutual support of each other's musical traditions are quite obvious; for the offering of praise, or the interpretation of human feeling through the use of intercultural musicality, constitutes an important means of mutual understanding and affirmation. By embracing each other's means of communicating with God and with fellow human beings, we embrace each other. The Black Story consists in the cultural embrace of each other's musical story. It is a story that is constantly evolving, for much of the music reflects the struggles and expectations of the day.

Third, we should explore each other's *history*. The history of slavery on the plantations, or the history of the struggles for freedom from slavery, cannot have been vastly different in the Caribbean from that in the United States. Slave revolts were always being contemplated, and the masters were always being vigilant to avoid them. The fact that emancipation in the United States came some thirty years later than that in the Caribbean does not make all that much difference. Much the same type of racism existed in both places, even if the Negroes in the United States were a minority. The commonalities in history are far too important to be ignored, for they provide the intercultural theological process with a most important resource for the illumination of the emancipatory imperatives in the light of the Gospel for today and tomorrow. We must therefore explore each other's history, as well as embrace the implications for common witness which such a common history unmistakably suggests.

Fourth, we need to acknowledge each other's *heroes and heroines*. Apart from Malcolm X and Martin Luther King, Jr., very few Afro-American heroes are known to people in the Caribbean; and more portraits of John F. Kennedy adorn the homes of Caribbean families than of Martin Luther King, Jr. Fannie Lou Hamer, Mary McCleod Bethune, and other heroines are not heard about. From the Caribbean side, no heroes and heroines ever seem to appear on the horizon, especially since Caribbean heroes usually are cricket players, and cricket is neither played nor understood in the United States to any great extent. Political heroes in the Caribbean tend to be localized, so that their capacity to inspire large sectors of people across the seas is minimal. Clearly, we need to affirm the Black Story and its intercultural connections in a much more popular and demonstrable way. Our heroes and heroines embody who we really are and how we wish to be known. They provide historical inspiration for the tasks that lie ahead. We therefore need to lift them up more intentionally, especially in the context of our religious history, for the story of God's emancipation of oppressed peoples is a continuing saga.

Finally, there is an obvious need for *cultural exchanges* between both contexts, especially in the field of theological education and formation. Although African-Americans have a vague acquaintance with the theological initiatives, most of the theological connections tend to take place between the white American theologians and the Caribbean. The black church in the United States has not contributed much in the way of development assistance or theological explorations abroad; and Caribbean churches and church-related institutions have not generally been able to afford such exchanges. Such is the nature of the poverty on both sides. Yet an enormous amount of travel is undertaken by both groups; some of this travel could well be intentionally arranged for the mutual learning of each other's ecclesial and theological life. In any event, the systematic introduction of Caribbean materials into the African-American programs of learning, and vice versa, would generate greater interest and knowledge within both contexts. It is surely in this area that much of the intercultural theological work could be collectively undertaken, and a substantial amount of emancipation from ignorance about each other could be realized.

In conclusion, all that we have been discussing here may well be considered as nothing more than a contemporary representation of the Joseph story. Joseph was Jacob's dreaming son. Nevertheless, his own experience of hurt by his brothers resulted in his own salvation and that of his brothers. Egypt was for them the place of liberation from hunger, as well as the place of bondage. The Black Story is a continuing experience of Egypt—and the eternal religious truth is this: If you do not know your Egypt, you cannot know your Exodus. The methodology for the intercultural theological process cannot be defined by one person or one group of persons; but, at the very least, one group can inspire the initiative. The narrative framework provides some exciting possibilities, and the results can be mutually rewarding for all who would seek to put their theology to work in the historical realities of their context. The way may be long, but it need not be hard.

In the meantime, we can reinforce our emancipatory contextual connections by basking in the dawning radiance of this theological dream, and as Caribbean and African-American people we can still be inspired by the words of an illustrious character in the Black Story, Benjamin E. Mays:

It must be borne in mind that the tragedy in life doesn't lie in not reaching your goal. The tragedy lies in having no goal to reach. It isn't a calamity to die with dreams unfulfilled, but it is a calamity not to dream. It is not a disaster to be unable to capture your ideal, but it is a disaster to have no ideal to capture. It is not a disgrace not to reach the stars, but it is a disgrace to have no stars to reach for. Not failure, but low aim is sin.[9]

CHAPTER NINE

WHEN GOD EMANCIPATES ...

The central question for emancipatory theology is this: Can the Gospel of Jesus Christ be so interpreted, proclaimed, and practiced by Christians that they can experience the true meaning of human freedom in the context of continuing poverty, dependence, and marginalization? Such a question suggests that not only *religious* consciousness but also *historical* consciousness should be subject to reconstruction. The search for emancipation takes many forms in different contexts, particularly in the Third World. Christians struggle for new ways of discerning how the liberating hand of God the Emancipator can be felt and announced in their own sociohistorical context. Indian Christians struggle with pluralism, caste, and economic bondage. African Christians struggle with traditionalism, neocolonialism, and political instability.

In Africa, for example, we find Archbishop Ilunga of Zaire wrestling with the implications of liberation for the emergence of the new country. He suggests that liberation has to take place in many areas. Religion, he says, has to be liberated from its divisive and enslaving tendencies, so that it becomes a force for authentic human freedom. Truth itself has to be liberated by the courage of self-criticism: "The liberation of truth is ... a prior condition for any progress of emancipation. Ideological constructions, erroneous frames of interpretation, empty slogans and discourses, and tall tales all have one thing in common: they are ways of fleeing the real tasks."[1] The free society cannot be built in Zaire, he says, unless the prevalent chain of corruption in his country is broken. Ilunga speaks for the entire Third World.

There is corruption and bondage in the Third World, just as there was in the biblical land of Egypt. When God the Emancipator visits Egypt again to set oppressed people free, the armies of Pharaoh ready themselves to challenge such a force, but their pursuits are deluged in the rushing waters of false security and self-delusion. When God emancipates, every context becomes Egypt all of its own, particularly in the Caribbean.

Slavery was abolished in the Caribbean at different points of the nineteenth century. The British government took the lead in 1834, and was followed by Sweden in 1846, by France in 1848, and by Holland in 1863. The Spanish were somewhat reluctant; and so slaves in Puerto Rico gained

130

their freedom in 1873, and the Cubans seven years later. In 1863, Abraham Lincoln had issued the Emancipation Proclamation, freeing the slaves in states that were rebelling against the Union. Everywhere, then, throughout the Americas, new dimensions of human dignity were being acknowledged, for the emancipation of slaves inevitably carried with it the emancipation of slave owners as well. But the way in which the former slave owners in the West Indies interpreted their own emancipation differed quite naturally from the way in which the slaves interpreted theirs.

The late Eric Williams, the great Trinidadian historian and political leader, made a distinction between emancipation "from above" and emancipation "from below." Because there was widespread unrest among the slave population at the turn of the nineteenth century, for the abolitionists in Europe had stirred up new hopes and expectations in the hearts of the slaves, the planters had to choose one form of emancipation or the other. They therefore chose emancipation "from above" as the lesser of two evils. Williams cites the famous speech of Sir Thomas Buxton in the British Parliament on March 19, 1833:

> He was convinced that it was absolutely indispensable that this question should be settled, and further, that if it was not settled in that House, it would be settled elsewhere, in another and more disastrous manner.[2]

Emancipation from above did not mean, however, that the planters were about to lose control in any way; it only meant the cessation of free labor. It therefore carried with it a very high price. The plantocracy, or "Massa," was not about to go under. Williams comments thus:

> That was why, when slavery was abolished in 1833, and Massa was afraid that the emancipated slaves would no longer accept the drudgery and exploitation of the slave plantation but would work for themselves on small plots, Massa in Barbados and Massa in British Guiana destroyed the gardens and food plots which the slaves had been permitted to cultivate during slavery in order to force them, out of the threat of starvation, to accept starvation wages on the plantations.[3]

The plantocracy preferred an uneducated, docile, and self-contemptuous laboring class, which could be controlled by "barbarous ideas and practices of racial domination." There is lingering evidence in the Caribbean to suggest that, after a century and a half of evolution and reluctant change, these preferences have not entirely disappeared. One famous political leader in St. Vincent in this century was heard to exclaim at a public meeting one evening: "Comrades, dey talkin' 'bout education; what all you want education for? To gi' we trouble?" Williams's retort to that would have been: "To educate is to emancipate."

Because emancipation from above has not delivered the goods of free-dom, Caribbean people have been pursuing emancipation from below. Var-ious movements have emerged among, and on behalf of, the people to realize this highest of all goals in human existence. To be fully human is to be fully emancipated, and no one can properly grant such a condition from the outside. Thus, Caribbean history is replete with twentieth-century attempts to discover what emancipation from below entails concretely. The names of Marcus Garvey, Uriah Butler, Robert Bradshaw, Albert Marry-show, Norman Manley, Fidel Castro, Maurice Bishop, Walter Rodney, Errol Barrow, Grantley Adams, and Vere Cornwall Bird must find a place among others in the long list of Caribbean practitioners of emancipation. They have tried—each in his own way—to work out historically what it all means. Early in this century, for example, we find Marcus Garvey calling for a second emancipation, an emancipation of the mind.

But there are also those millions of unsung mothers and grandmothers who have nurtured the hopes and aspirations of their offspring, and fed them with the milk of expectation, by means of deep faith and strong religious fervor. For they have known all along that the real emancipation comes alive when the real Emancipator, the God of Jesus Christ, is acknowl-edged from below. No theological statement from a Caribbean woman has yet been able to match that which greeted me from the lips of a poor old woman sitting at the door of her humble home one day: "God is a good man!" Her sense of feminine dignity did not appear to be under assault, nor was she saying what she thought I wanted to hear. Rather, she was expressing her own experiences of suffering and poverty—experiences that had failed to mute her praise of the loving God whom she had known throughout.

The sandlike nature of the Caribbean condition has been reinforced by too heavy a reliance on the promise of emancipation from above. The more things change in the region, the more they appear to remain the same, however often the *dramatis personae* make their many exits and entrances. Promises of new beginnings and fresh hopes are often frustrated by the attractiveness of initiatives from the outside. Messianic pretensions prolif-erate in the region, for somehow Caribbean people manage to maintain the capacity to survive even the next possibility of failure. So they hold fast to the sayings, "Nothing beats a trial but a failure" and "What doesn't kill can only fatten." There are many false trials and many failures; and yet the Caribbean survives. There were many who hailed the American invasion (intervention?) of Grenada in 1983 as God's answer to prayer, for in the wake of American guns and armed forces there would be miraculous pros-perity through American investment. The national wounds of that historic episode are still being licked by the Grenadians, but the prosperity hoped for is still to be realized. Some Grenadians who sowed in joy are now reaping in tears, for the American economic liberation has not yet arrived, and the prospects grow dim with every passing day. Grenada no longer constitutes a "threat" to American security or to the safety of America's citizens. One Grenadian journalist has offered the following lament:

Constantly having their moral pride insensitively, cynically, and unscrupulously tampered with, engulfed by a money cult in which the values most recognised are money values, Grenadians now live in a society where such themes as "the maintenance of national dignity and pride," "striving for independence," "cultural sovereignty" have become alien concepts. No wonder that recently they have been witnessing an unprecedented moral decline especially among certain sections of the society."[4]

Yet Caribbean political leaders are not all convinced that emancipation from above is useless or uncertain. One of the grave issues in the region — an issue that continues to pit leader against leader and nation against nation — is how to deal with the United States of America. Maurice Bishop, prime minister of Grenada, traded unbecoming insults with Tom Adams, prime minister of Barbados, on the occasion of Ronald Reagan's election victory to the White House in 1980. The entire Caribbean was saddened that within a few short years, and long before Reagan left office, both leaders were taken from us by sudden death. Neither had lived to witness any appreciable change to their two countries as a result of their own political positions. In the meantime, another distinguished prime minister, Eugenia Charles of Dominica, holds fast to the wisdom of matching emancipation from above with the hope of bread for her people. She has made the following statement in Washington, D.C., America's capital:

We in the Caribbean, who see ourselves as allies of the Americas, wish to maintain that tradition and uphold the Monroe Doctrine as it has developed through the ages. And these are important. It is difficult to maintain freedoms on empty stomachs. It is difficult to maintain one's zeal when the resources are lacking to encourage our people in a firm commitment to democracy. With one side offering tempting solutions you are apt to look to the other side for assistance to resist the temptation.

The United States has always moved towards assisting under-privileged countries. Unfortunately, there are so many of these and the need so great that the resources do not seem extensive enough to play a meaningful part. But it is recognised that political freedom must be accompanied by social change brought about by our people with assistance from the larger countries.[5]

It is not feasible at this stage to draw out the many implications of the foregoing statement of a prominent Caribbean leader, but it is impossible to ignore the thrust of what it seeks to convey. When she claims that empty stomachs and freedom are hardly compatible, one is tempted to ask her what she considers to be the real price of freedom in the Caribbean. Caribbean folk wisdom carries a proverb that says: "Wha' sweet a' mout' sometime hot a' belly" (What is sweet at the mouth sometimes hurts the belly). That the poor and hungry people of the Caribbean should sacrifice their freedom for the lure of limited material gain, short-lived, expensive, and even demeaning, is too much to contemplate in the Caribbean sandscape. But short-term solutions are often the most attractive to short-sighted persons in the face of long-term problems. Unfortunately, many in the region hold to the view that the future of the Caribbean lies with the increased Americanization of the region. Many more, however, remain convinced that the freedom which Caribbean ancestors have struggled so hard to grasp should not be mortgaged for a morsel of bread.

Can the poor ever truly be free? If so, at what price? Is poverty the hallmark of unfreedom? If so, why are the rich often enchained by their own sense of materialism? Materialism also is manifested in countries, organizations, and churches that measure their worth and power in terms of paternalistic relationships with the poor. But the immortal words of Oscar Romero still ring out:

> The world of the poor teaches us that liberation will arrive only when the poor are not simply on the receiving end of handouts from governments or from the church, but when they themselves are the masters of, and protagonists in, their own struggle and liberation, thereby unmasking the root of false paternalism, including ecclesiastical paternalism.[6]

Although poverty is a serious form of bondage, it is not the worst possible form, and the poor of the world have always had to struggle not only for bread but also for justice, dignity, and freedom. The poor know that they cannot live by bread alone; but it is not always clear that the rich and powerful sections of the world understand this.

The transfer of a few resources from the rich to the poor may serve to relieve the consciences of the rich, but it does not contribute to a radical transformation of the structures that have reinforced the poor in their poverty and unfreedom. The history of rich/poor relations has constantly shown that emancipation from above usually benefits the strong and the powerful, while the poor and the weak remain in an unaltered condition. Bondage gives way to new forms of bondage, colonialism makes way for neocolonialism, patterns of domination change, but never the domination itself. Formal independence in India has not basically altered the social conditions of the "Untouchables." The people of Zaire now have constitutional power in their own hands, but constitutional opportunity has not ushered in patterns of social refinement and efficiency in that postcolonial society. A new nation has been born, but a new people has not yet emerged.

Emancipation from above does not by itself enjoy a rich heritage of guaranteeing the freedom of enslaved people. The Caribbean story is indeed a living testimony of this reality. We need to look the other way for possibilities of greater freedom.

EMANCIPATION FROM BELOW

We have had occasion earlier in this book to examine some areas of crisis that require consolidated attention on the part of all sectors of the Caribbean. These areas are poverty, alienation, dependence, fragmentation, migration, and drugs. We also must bear in mind the ongoing realities of racism, classism, social pluralism, and the cultural assaults that the Caribbean sustains from the strong blasts of external communications and tourism. While it is inappropriate to categorize all these characteristics as forms of bondage in themselves, they nevertheless point us to some critical areas in which the sense of historical enslavement and Caribbean anomie continue to find fertile ground. They stand in the way of authentic freedom, even if they do not actually constitute chains of unfreedom.

Clive Thomas has rightly stated that "oppression and liberation are dialectically related, and the strategy developed in the fight for liberation must be guided by the nature of the oppression of the vast majority of the population."[7] It is not always clear in the Caribbean that the nature of the oppression or the forms of common bondage are generally agreed on. Caribbean people actually agree with the common wisdom that "What is joke for one is death for another"; but they do not always agree on the nature of the "joke," for they are sometimes capable of laughing at themselves as a means of escaping the real task. The editor of *Caribbean Contact* suggests that "Caribbean peoples must recognize that whatever they do they must do with their own best interest in mind, not in a cynical and selfish manner but in a manner which exemplifies their concern for self-discipline and self-respect."[8] It takes a substantial amount of self-discipline and self-respect to identify the deeply embedded forms of oppression, for they often lie hidden within the social psyche of a people. Emancipation from below consists in the freeing of the mind from forms of bondage that cannot be removed by emancipation from above.

In Caribbean and African-American history, emancipation from below started long before emancipation from above. Our slave ancestors never regarded themselves as fully enslaved persons. They worked under the harsh whips of their masters, but they fought against those whips in whatever way they could. They sometimes amputated limbs of their offspring so that they would not grow up to put those limbs at the servile disposal of the slave owners. They maintained their own communities of persons as best they could. They dressed well on the days when they were allowed to. They sang their songs and praised their God with all their heart and soul. They created stories, and mimed their experiences, and affirmed each other, and planned their escape, and challenged their masters' rights, and they survived. All this was emancipation from below, already on the way long before the other form was eventually decreed. The persistence of the African soul in Caribbean religion is therefore a concrete testimony to the reality of emancipation from below.

Emancipation from above places high emphasis on the need for Caribbean countries to establish and maintain fertile relationships with the richer and more powerful countries of the world, particularly the United States, Europe, and Japan. Correspondingly, emancipation from below requires fruitful relationships with the poorer peoples and countries of the world. The linkages with other parts of the Third World always leave much to be desired, for the lines of communication seem inevitably to be joined through the agency of the rich Western countries. The Caribbean community should establish and sustain more programs of exchange and commerce, programs of mutual sharing and learning, programs of joint research and development, and programs of cultural reinforcement and discovery.

The Caribbean context itself will never be enriched if it is unable to account for the great treasures of wisdom and culture which are beyond the purchasing power or political control of the rich countries, and which alone can trigger a much deeper appreciation of its own cultural heritage, through mutual affirmation and common esteem. Caribbean regional integration must be augmented by interregional integration throughout the Third World, without the prior sanction of the First or Second World countries. In this connection, the simple embrace of Haiti, Cuba, Suriname, and the Netherlands Antilles within the CARICOM framework would be a way forward in earnest. The great goal of cultural emancipation in the Caribbean cannot effectively be pursued in isolation from those who share so much of the great cultural history with the rest of the region.

Cultural emancipation also involves the matter of popular language. Caribbean history is full of examples of those who exploited the masses of the people because of their persuasive speech or charismatic flair. To have an "English tongue in your head" and to be able to use it effectively was traditionally considered a passport to social privilege of some kind or other. The presumed inability on the part of the lower classes to "speak properly" incessantly redounded to their own frustration and social rejection, and certainly barred them from assuming many rights and privileges which "better" speech afforded. Mervin Alleyne contends that "while the masses were quiescent and accepted their low socioeconomic status and the low status of their culture and language, the communicative gap facilitated socioeconomic exploitation and political manipulation."[9] But times have changed, and emancipation from below is being more potently recognized in the more widespread use of creole languages without any sense of social inferiority. Alleyne speaks with positive certainty on this point:

> The use of creole languages, the mass vernaculars of the Caribbean, is now a vital factor in the democratization of national life and insti-

tutions and in the accessibility of these institutions to the mass of the population. Only in this way will the region be able to exploit the full potential of its human resources, and break down traditional elite structures, and remove the alienation which exists in the region.[10]

Emancipation from below also involves a constant determination to educate the people of the Caribbean not for domestication but for freedom and development. It involves the pursuit of human rights at all levels, especially the rights of women, workers, minorities, and other marginalized persons in our societies. The right to be human is inalienable for all, and it is to the credit of the Caribbean that such a provision is constitutionally enshrined. The rub comes when implementation of such a provision is suspended or called into question. In a historical context where people have had their basic claim to be human systematically denied for so long, the vigilance of every sector of the Caribbean community is crucial for the emancipatory task.

This brings us inevitably to the question of race. The history of racism in the Caribbean is well documented and needs no further explication. That the Caribbean still retains some vestiges of that racism is perhaps not debatable either, although overt forms may be less frequent than the endemic subtleties of the system. Yet racial prejudice and racial discrimination still abound, and there is no country in the region from which racism has been entirely removed. Many years ago, the Guyanese scholar Walter Rodney asserted that "so long as there are people who deny our humanity as blacks then for so long must we proclaim and assert our humanity as blacks."[11] The self-affirmation of their humanity by blacks, however, should not be at the expense of offending the racial heritage of other ethnic groups in the region. There are also Caribbean people of European, Hispanic, Asian, Indian, and Middle Eastern descent. They may as a body be more prosperous and self-sustaining than the broad masses of the Afro-Caribbean majority; nevertheless, the struggle for emancipation from below enjoins that the claims of all ethnic groupings be fully recognized, and their rights respected.

Racism in reverse is just another form of bondage, and Caribbean people cannot afford to repeat the mistakes of their history by turning the tables on each other, on the same grounds by which they were themselves oppressed. Racial integration may not be easy to accomplish, but racial harmony and mutuality are not beyond the capacity of an enlightened and emancipated Caribbean populace. It is through the search for racial harmony at all levels of social activity that the creative energies of Caribbean people in sports, the arts, industry, commerce, politics, religion, and social reconstruction can best be appropriated collectively. This may sound a little naive, given the current realities of power relations in the region; but it serves to remind us that the full emancipatory development of the Caribbean cannot be entrusted to one sector of the populace, to the exclusion or diminishing of the others. Participatory democracy involves more than electoral polling; it also involves taking emancipatory risks toward full human development. Matters of race cannot be left only for radicals to deal with.

Emancipation from below cannot escape the economic factors that led to the institution of Caribbean slavery and, ultimately, to emancipation from above. We have argued in this book that the Caribbean still lives in the shadow of the plantation, although tourism and manufacturing may have overtaken agriculture as the main dollar earners. The Caribbean is a poor region, and is more than likely to remain so, chiefly because it is lacking in major natural or mineral resources. The concept of the "product" (or the "crop") in the Caribbean will continue to undergo several permutations as the industrial base of the region changes. The Caribbean will always be good for something, economically, but it will not be the same thing all the time. Sugar, for example, is no longer king. Tourism is a volatile and fickle industry, and the time may soon be near when even the Caribbean will have priced itself out of the market, even with its overabundance of what is unfortunately referred to as "cheap labor."

The most fundamental Caribbean economic project is no different from the fundamental political one. It is the radical transformation of the whole Caribbean from the old plantation to the new society. The surge forward from poverty to relatively less poverty will in itself be emancipatory for the Caribbean if questions of ownership and control of the Caribbean continue to be debated openly; if the realities of political sovereignty are held closely to the struggle for economic sovereignty; if the productive energies of the broad masses of the people can be motivated for their dignified and remunerative exploitation; and if values, tastes, and expectations are defined from within rather than from without. Innovative ways of creative self-employment, better management and more equitable distribution of the public resources, and greater levels of social responsibility in private enterprise will contribute to the struggle for economic emancipation from below. The challenges for the future have been well stated by the president of the Caribbean Development Bank, Neville Nicholls. He sees the general goal as fourfold:

> The rapid improvement of the quality of life of our people, i.e. maintaining a healthy population with long life expectancy; ensuring the growth and as equitable a distribution of the material goods and services as is practical and optimal; preserving our cultural values and identity; [and] most importantly, having a society with spiritual values and upright and wholesome principles."[12]

As this leading representative of Caribbean economic activity clearly recognizes, material concerns must be integrated with spiritual concerns. The word is that Caribbean people cannot live by bread alone; they also need the Word of God. It is only in this way that the "upright and whole-some principles" of which Nicholls speaks can be interpreted. But the president's words beckon us further still. They suggest that neither emancipation from above nor emancipation from below is efficacious enough in the great struggle for human freedom in the Caribbean—or anywhere else, for that matter. Not even their combined force is sufficient. Emancipatory theology asserts, therefore, that when—out of the actual historical context—God is responded to in concrete faith, as the source from which all emancipation ultimately springs, then authentic emancipa-tion is infinitely greater than the sum of all other shades of emancipation that may be conceived. What, then, is involved contextually when God emancipates? What are the practical and theological underpinnings of this basic understanding of the Caribbean human struggle? Our concluding discussion will offer some reflections on several dimensions of this impor-tant issue.

EMANCIPATION STILL COMIN' . . .

The first dimension deals with the eschatological interpretation of God's emancipatory work in the Caribbean. Such an interpretation must convey two major truths. It must first demonstrate that the traditional conspiracies, which have historically attempted to keep the Caribbean in bondage and abject dependence on external sources for its survival, will never succeed. Those who have given up on the Caribbean as a hopeless case, including some of its own citizens, must be doomed to total frustration with such dreams. After Europe withdrew from the region, these people believed that its demise was inevitable. Caribbean people have often been treated as if they were living on borrowed time, since their survival period was expected to run out long ago. It is the power of the divine emancipatory presence in the Caribbean that has ensured continued existence. Second, this eschat-ological interpretation must demonstrate the meaning of faith not only as an existence in total receptivity and response but also as liberating assur-ance in a trustworthy God, who has disclosed in historical circumstances the promise of emancipation, as well as its fulfillment.

For the people who trust unconditionally in the sovereign free God, then, every experience of Egypt is followed by a miraculous exodus and a cove-nantal relationship that beckons them toward the edges of the wilderness. For that God, no genuine gift of faithful human existence is devoid of either creative suffering, threatening death, or radically transformed existence through resurrection. To hope in an utterly hopeless situation, and to inspire confidence in the value of a humanity whose claim to authenticity is systematically denied, is to live out the rejection of emptiness and mean-inglessness as an option for practical faith. Caribbean faith lives toward the future, and the eschatological dimension of that faith has been historically tried through all the phases of domination and dependence in its story.

Caribbean emancipatory eschatology does not permit any retreat in the face of negative scientific predictions, or in the wake of the hurricanes of despair. Human knowledge and advanced technology may relegate the Caribbean to obscurity and dubious political value, but when God emancipates Caribbean people even the Western angels of light lose their wings in flight. It is not pious escapism to assert in faith that the emancipatory future of the Caribbean belongs to God. To some it may appear to be wishful thinking, but for those who ground their faith in the concrete experience of the emancipating God, given the harsh realities of the Caribbean context, such an assertion is nothing short of identifying the transforming truth. In keeping with the tradition of the Fourth Gospel, Caribbean people of faith continue to affirm that it is this very truth that sets them free. It is an eschatological imperative in the Caribbean, therefore, that the vision of emancipation must be kept alive and passed on to generations yet to come; for this vision has kept hope alive in the crush of numbing hopelessness.

Such an emancipatory eschatology must be fully grounded on the consciousness of liberation as the most powerful generative theme among the Caribbean people. Our people must be made conscious of liberation through popular dialogue and effective communication, through collective solidarity and organization, and through the action of cultural synthesis, about which the eminent Brazilian scholar Paulo Freire has written so eloquently. Only through an active eschatological praxis can Caribbean oppressed peoples be empowered to work concretely, not merely for their social liberation but, more radically, for the transformation of the unjust reality with which they are encumbered. Only in this way can their constant prayer for heaven to come on earth be given historical expression. Yet none of this will be possible without actual leaders, who can incarnate in a very real way the practical implications of emancipatory leadership. In the words of Freire: "Joining the oppressed requires going to them and communicating with them. The people must find themselves in the emerging leaders, and the latter must find themselves in the people."[13]

Our second dimension deals with the meaning of the church as the people of God, the community of faith, the sign of the Kingdom, the sacramental movement of divine freedom in human history, and the body of the Spirit in Christ in the Caribbean historical experience. If these ecclesiological images are to make sense, their emancipatory significance must become paramount. The church, which God has given to the Caribbean, is to be a major sign of the liberating work of the God of Jesus Christ, as well as the guarantee that the gates of bondage (Hell) will not prevail. It should utterly reject any inclinations to reductionism—that is, reducing the imperatives of the Gospel of justice, bread, freedom, and peace, to accommodate absolutizing tendencies toward injustice, poverty, mediocrity, and alienation. It should resolutely reject all forms of discrimination against women, whether in the leadership of the church or in the sanctuary of the home and family. It calls for enlightened and progressive policies in the recruitment and formation of ministers, both clerical and lay; and it challenges the whole church to be fully responsible and relevant in the Caribbean theological enterprise. The slavish adaptation of foreign formulations must be abandoned, and the emancipatory and patient critical reflection on Caribbean existence in the light of the Gospel must become its primary focus in its liturgy and proclamation. In short, if the church is to consider itself the chief agency of God's emancipatory design in the Caribbean, it must at the very least be the historical community in which the meaning of that emancipation readily finds its authentic expression.

Caribbean spirituality is indeed a spirituality for freedom. There is a constant reaching out in prayer and praise to the sovereign free God, and there is a relentless yearning for the empowering sense of a relational presence that is liberating, emancipatory, and affirming. Much more needs to be made of the daily spirituality that enables Caribbean people to cope with the pressures of life; and these spiritual forces must find their formal expressions in culturally relevant liturgies and hymnodies which characterize regional worship. Further, Caribbean theodicy has made faith stronger rather than weaker, and the church owes it to the broad spectrum of its membership to reflect more faithfully the tremendous depths of trust, hope, and courage which Caribbean spirituality generates. In any case, the proclamation, prayers, and praxis of the Caribbean church must be culturally liberating and socially transforming.

Mention of the CCC and its programs brings us to the third dimension of the theological understanding of God's emancipatory work. This dimension has to do not only with the development of human dignity and the renewal of the church but also with the ecumenical imperatives of Caribbean historical existence. The Roman Catholic bishops in the region, in a major statement in 1988, affirmed very faithfully the vision of unity for the Caribbean in a most significant manner. Their spokesman (Bishop Dickson of Barbados) said this:

> We feel strongly that the unity of Caribbean people is part of God's overall plan for the unity of the entire human family. Jesus Christ has revealed that God is a community of Three Persons, Father, Son and Holy Spirit. In creating the human race, it was God's intention that all men and women would form a human community which would reflect the Divine Community. . . . Our history has been one of fragmentation and isolation, much of which has been imposed upon us by powers outside the region, but some of which we ourselves have perpetuated. The Catholic Church promotes and supports efforts to overcome the fragmentation and isolation of our Caribbean peoples and to bring about that unity of peoples which is God's plan for us.[14]

Caribbean ecumenism is a challenging call toward the frontiers of creating the new Caribbean society, in the power of God's emancipatory activity. Such emancipation dissolves all unnecessary divisions in the social order. It generates a new solidarity in education for human development; in religious cooperation between estranged groups, whether of African or European heritage; in the promotion of effective channels of communication and information; and, above all, in faithful pursuit of God's concern for the poor through solidarity with them. The most significant contribution that Caribbean emancipatory theology can make to Third World theology as a whole lies in the faithful orthopraxis of ecumenical solidarity with the poor and oppressed. It is chiefly in the faces and lives of the Caribbean's poor that God's free and emancipating gift of life finds its most powerful expression. When God emancipates, the poor of the region are those who know it first; for their vision of that new creation brings enlivening hope and radiating joy.

There are certainly no quick answers for change in the region, and the various approaches to Caribbean development may often run at cross-purposes with one another. Yet there can be no dissension about the importance of the younger generations in the region for its future emancipation. Here is where Caribbean ecumenism must make its most significant and formative moves. The young people of the Caribbean need to be taken far more seriously; and ecumenical endeavors, which founder on ideological and political issues, can in no way afford to ignore the crucial importance of creating a new generation of mature adults out of the minds and hearts of the young. Patterns of family life education, pedagogies of social formation in schools and other places of learning, curricular designs and other educational programs—all must have the future of the Caribbean in mind.

The youth of the region must be inspired to develop increasing levels of self-esteem, deepening patterns of commitment to regional integration and emancipation, and a sense of responsibility for leading the Caribbean into concrete experiences of cultural, political, and economic self-determination. They must produce that which can be exported from the region to the rest of the world, for the Caribbean cannot survive unless it produces and exports; but the quality of productive values, and the quantities of worthwhile exports, must be such that the Caribbean no longer mortgages its soul in the brokerage of alien powers. The emancipation of the Caribbean and the proper nurture of the young are inseparable. The future of the region is in their hands, and the current generation of leaders must do all in their power to help their successors. They must know when to hand over power to the next generation, and they must not thwart the march of emancipatory progress for God's people in the region.

The ecological dimension of God's emancipatory design is our fourth and final category. The Caribbean is advertised throughout the world as a haven for foreign tourists, a place of perpetual sand, sea, sun, and fun. It is offered to the world as a place where almost anything goes, for the chief intention is to deliver the best possible product for the visitors. "Best" always seems to mean whatever the tourists desire. Cultural distortions, ecological pollution, social dislocations, and human depravity, continue to threaten the entire region. With this constant and pervasive threat in the region, the nurture and edification of the youth suffer severe strains; weak family patterns are further eroded; levels of social responsibility, especially among males, are lowered; and the basic social institutions are assaulted by the rise of questionable values. Human ecology is threatened whenever cultural sovereignty is compromised. The theological task is therefore urgent and monumental, chiefly because questions of bread and butter are involved. Nevertheless, the famous challenge of Jesus of Nazareth still rings loud in the Caribbean situation: "What shall it profit the Caribbean to gain the whole world and lose its own soul?" We might thus be well served by endeavoring to discover once again that emancipated spirit which empowered the Jamaican poet Evan Jones to pen these words:

> So when you see dese ol' clothes brown wid stain,
> An' soaked right through wid de Portlan' rain,
> Don't cas' your eye, nor turn your nose,
> Don't judge a man by his patchy clothes,
> I'm a strong man, a proud man, an' I'm free,
> Free as dese mountains, free as dis sea,
> I know myself, an' I know m' ways
> An' will sing wid pride till de end o' m' days,
>
> Praise God an' m' big right han'
> I will live an' die a banana man.[15]

The Caribbean has been a historically dependent region, born out of the need to provide for the welfare of other countries, first Europe and then North America. Yet the Caribbean has always yearned to be free and to serve its own best interests. The struggles out of slavery and colonialism have made it a region that will never cease to yearn for full humanity and total emancipation. Many years ago, the late C. L. R. James wrote these significant words:

> Britain will hold us down as long as she wishes. Her cruisers and aeroplanes will ensure it. But a people like ours should be free to make its own failures and successes, free to gain that political wisdom and political experience which come only from the practice of political affairs. Otherwise, led as we are by a string, we remain without credit abroad and without self-respect at home, a bastard, feckless conglomeration of individuals, inspired by no common purpose, moving to no common end.[16]

Political freedom has indeed reached the former British territories for the most part, but the project of total emancipation is still to be realized.

Caribbean people as a whole have come to realize that, from beginning to end, their history is bound up not with the edicts of Britain, nor yet with the might of the United States, but chiefly with the ongoing emancipatory activity of the God who is the sovereign Lord of all creation.

When God emancipates, the strength, the dignity, the promise, and the beauty of the Caribbean right hand become the most powerful sign of human freedom. That hand is the symbol of God's own right hand. That is why Caribbean people will continue to affirm God's gift of freedom in the words of their own song:

> The right hand of God is writing in our land,
> Writing with power and with love.
> Our conflicts and our fears, our triumphs and our tears
> Are recorded by the right hand of God. . . .
>
> The right hand of God is planting in our land,
> Planting seeds of freedom, hope and love.
> In these Caribbean lands
> Let God's people all join hands,
> And be one with the right hand of God.[17]

NOTES

CHAPTER ONE

1. See Eric Williams, *From Columbus to Castro: The History of the Caribbean, 1492–1969.* (London: André Deutsch, 1978), p. 31.
2. Ibid.
3. Robert C. Neville, *The Cosmology of Freedom* (New Haven, Conn.: Yale University Press, 1974), p. 5.
4. Howard Thurman, *Deep Is the Hunger* (Richmond, Ind.: Friends United Press, 1973), p. 52.
5. Neville, *Cosmology*, pp. 6–7.
6. Ibid.
7. Ibid., p. 193.
8. Ibid., p. 13.

CHAPTER TWO

1. See Catherine A. Sunshine, *The Caribbean: Survival, Struggle and Sovereignty*. (Ecumenical Program for Interamerican Communication and Action, Washington, D.C., 1985), p. 151.
2. See *Caribbean Contact* 15, no. 4 (Sept. 1987): 8.
3. *Caribbean Contact* 16, no. 2 (July 1988): 3.
4. Anthony P. Maingot, "The Haitian Solution," *Caribbean Affairs* 1, no. 2 (1988): 23–24.
5. Susan Craig, "Sociological Theorizing in the English-Speaking Caribbean: A Review," in Susan Craig, ed., *Contemporary Caribbean: A Sociological Reader* (Trinidad and Tobago: Craig, 1982), 2:150.
6. Ibid., p. 170.
7. C. L. R. James, "The Birth of a Nation," in Craig, *Contemporary Caribbean*, 1:19.
8. Clive Y. Thomas, *The Rise of the Authoritarian State in Peripheral Societies* (New York: Monthly Review Press, 1984), p. 95.
9. See *Caribbean Contact* 11, no. 11 (Apr. 1984): 8.
10. Yussuff Haniff, ed., *Speeches by Errol Barrow* (London: Hansib, 1987), p. 178.
11. Clive Y. Thomas, *The Poor and the Powerless* (New York: Monthly Review Press, 1987), p. 194.
12. Paget Henry, "De-colonization, Tourism and Class/Race Structure in Antigua," in Craig, *Contemporary Caribbean*, 1:260.
13. Mervyn C. Alleyne, "A Linguistic Perspective on the Caribbean," in *Focus Caribbean* (Washington, D.C.: Woodrow Wilson International Center, 1985), p. 6.

14. Thomas, *The Poor and the Powerless*, p. 72.

15. Michael Manley, *Up the Down Escalator* (Washington, D.C.: Howard University Press, 1987), pp. 268–69.

CHAPTER THREE

1. Edward Brathwaite, *The Arrivants* (London: Oxford University Press, 1973), pp. 212–13.

2. Thomas, *The Poor and the Powerless*, p. 62.

3. Dawn Marshall, "Haitian Migration to the Bahamas," in Craig, *Contemporary Caribbean*, 123.

4. DeLisle Worrell, *The Caribbean Economy in the Nineties: Challenge and Response* (Barbados: Bridgetown Central Bank of Barbados, 1986), pp. 17–18.

5. George Beckford, *Persistent Poverty* (London: Oxford University Press, 1972), p. 206.

6. Kortright Davis, *Mission for Caribbean Change* (Frankfurt: Peter Lang, 1982), p. 25.

7. Thomas, *The Poor and the Powerless*, p. 324.

8. Gordon K. Lewis, *The Growth of the Modern West Indies* (New York: Monthly Review Press, 1968), p. 372.

9. See *Caribbean Contact*, Vol 15 (Feb., 1988): 16.

10. The Hon. Erskine Sandiford, remarks at Miami Conference on the Caribbean, Dec. 2, 1988 (mimeo), p. 3.

11. Williams, *From Columbus to Castro*, p. 503.

12. Dolores Yonker, "Rara In Haiti" (pp. 147–55) in John W. Nunley and Judith Bettelheim, eds., *Caribbean Festival Arts* (Seattle: University of Washington Press, 1988), p. 148.

13. Rex Nettleford, "Implications For Caribbean Development" pp. 183–197.

14. Ibid., p. 185.

15. Ibid., p. 196.

16. Kenneth M. Bilby, *The Caribbean as a Musical Region* (Washington, D.C.: Woodrow Wilson International Center, 1985), pp. 21–22.

17. Ibid., p. 24.

18. Keith Warner is currently professor of Romance languages at George Mason University in Virginia. These insights were shared with me in a private conversation.

19. C. L. R. James, "The Mighty Sparrow," in David Lowenthal and Lambros Comitas, eds., *The Aftermath of Sovereignty* (New York: Doubleday/Anchor Books, 1973), p. 375.

20. See Kortright Davis, *Mission for Caribbean Change*, p. 198.

CHAPTER FOUR

1. George Eaton Simpson, *Black Religions in the New World* (New York: Columbia University Press, 1978), p. 14.

2. I derived this name from the thousands of Caribbean persons who retain their allegiance to the basic principles of the Christian religion but who prefer not to be associated with any particular denomination. They call themselves "nowherians"; they belong to nowhere.

3. Daniel J. Crowley, "Plural and Differential Acculturation in Trinidad," *American Anthropologist* 59 (1957): 823.

4. Roger Bastide, *African Civilizations in the New World* (New York: Harper & Row, 1971), p. 171.

5. W. E. B. DuBois, *The Souls of Black Folk* (New York: Fawcett, 1961), p. 151.

6. George Eaton Simpson, "Afro-American Religions and Religious Behavior," *Caribbean Studies* 12, no. 2 (1972): 23.

7. *The Afro-Canadian*, Sept. 1988, p. 7.

8. Ibid.

9. Ibid., p. 10.

10. John S. Pobee, *Toward an African Theology* (Nashville: Abingdon Press, 1979), p. 43.

11. Quoted by Luke Mbefo, "Theology and Inculturation: The Nigerian Experience," *Crosscurrents* 37, no. 4. (Winter 1987–8): 395.

12. Ali A. Mazrui, *World Culture and the Black Experience* (Seattle: University of Washington Press, 1974), pp. 85–86.

13. Ibid., p. 104.

14. Mbefo, "Theology and Inculturation," p. 401.

15. E. Bolaji Idowu, *African Traditional Religion* (London: SCM Press, 1977), p. 207.

16. See Graham W. Irwin, *Africans Abroad* (New York: Columbia University Press, 1977), p. 195.

17. Ibid., p. 218.

18. Society for the Propagation of the Gospel S.P.G. Report, London 1889, p. 135.

19. Charles J. Branch, unpublished diary, St. Johns (Antigua), p. 194.

20. See Kortright Davis, *Cross and Crown in Barbados* (Frankfurt: Peter Lang, 1983).

21. Charles J. Branch, "Random Readings on the West Indies," unpublished article, St. Johns (Antigua), pp. 19–20.

22. John Mitchinson, *Can the Dry Bones Live?* (London: SPG, Society for the Propagation of the Gospel, 1883), p. 11.

23. Ibid., p. 13.

24. John Gilmore, *The Toiler of the Sees* (Barbados: Bridgetown Barbados National Trust, 1987).

25. See Kenneth J. King, "Some Notes on Arnold J. Ford and New World Black Attitudes to Ethopia," in R. K. Burkett and R. Newman, eds., *Black Apostles* (Boston: G. K. Hall, 1978), p. 51.

CHAPTER FIVE

1. WARC [World Alliance of Reformed Churches] *Newsletter* (Geneva) 4, (Feb. 1985): 6.

2. Gustavo Gutiérrez and Richard Shaull, *Liberation and Change* (Atlanta: John Knox Press, 1977), p. 69.

3. Ibid., p. 83.

4. Ibid., p. 86.

5. Henri J. M. Nouwen, *Gracias* (San Francisco: Harper & Row, 1983), p. 159.

6. See Robert J. Schreiter, *Constructing Local Theologies* (Maryknoll, N.Y.: Orbis Books, 1984).

7. "To steal from a thief makes God laugh." There are counterpart proverbs to be found in other slave societies.

CHAPTER SIX

1. Edmund Davis, *Roots and Blossoms* (Barbados: Bridgetown CEDAR Press, 1977), p. 115.

2. Ibid.

3. Edmund Davis, *Courage and Commitment* (Kingston, Jamaica: UWI Publishers Association, 1988), p. 9.

4. Burchell K. Taylor, "Caribbean Theology," *Caribbean Journal of Religious Studies* 3, no. 2 (Sept. 1980): 17.

5. Ibid., p. 19.

6. Ibid., p. 27.

7. Idris Hamid, "Caribbean Theological Perspectives," *Caribbean Group for Social and Religious Studies* 1, (1983): 4.

8. Ibid., p. 6.

9. *Towards a Caribbean Theology* (Trinidad: San Fernando Caribbean Ecumenical Programme, 1981), p. 30.

10. Ibid.

11. George Mulrain, "Is There a Calypso Exegesis?" *Caribbean Group for Social and Religious Studies* 1 (1983).

12. Caribbean Conference of Churches, *Peace: A Challenge to the Caribbean* (Barbados: Bridgetown CEDAR Press, 1982), p. 30.

13. Ibid.

14. Caribbean Conference of Churches, *Report of the Third Biennial Localisation Meeting, Grenada—May, 1981* (Bridgetown, Barbados: Caribbean Conference of Churches, 1981), pp. 2–3.

15. Kortright Davis, "Caribbean Liturgical Integration: Some Preliminary Perspectives," *Caribbean Group for Social and Religious Studies* 1 (1983).

16. Caribbean Conference of Churches, *Fashion Me a People* (Kingston, Jamaica: Caribbean Conference of Churches, 1981), introduction.

17. Ibid., preface.

18. William Watty, *From Shore to Shore* (Kingston, Jamaica: 1981), p. 4.

19. *Minutes of the Twelfth Annual Conference of the Methodist Church in the Caribbean and the Americas, May, 1978* (Antigua: Methodist Church in the Caribbean and the Americas, 1979), p. 159.

20. See *Sunday Advocate-News* (Barbados), Mar. 27, 1983.

CHAPTER SEVEN

1. Quoted in Walter Kasper, *Jesus the Christ* (New York: Paulist Press, 1977), p. 43.

2. Gail Bowman, "Foundations of Emancipatory Theology," unpublished essay, mimeo, 1985.

3. James M. Washington, ed., *A Testament of Hope* (San Francisco: Harper & Row, 1986), p. 246.

4. Kasper, *Jesus the Christ*, pp. 42–43.

5. Washington, *Testament of Hope*, p. 487.

6. Desmond Tutu, *Hope and Suffering* (Grand Rapids, Mich.: Eerdmans, 1984), p. 61.

7. *Weavings* 2, no. 6 (1987): 28–29.

8. Howard Thurman, Statement on the occasion of the death of John F. Kennedy, 1963. (Taken from a plaque in Howard Thurman Chapel, Howard University School of Divinity, Washington, D.C.).

9. Henry James Young, ed., *God and Human Freedom* (Richmond, Ind.: Friends United Press, 1983), p. 14.

10. Benjamin E. Mays, *Disturbed about Man* (Richmond, Va.: John Knox Press, 1969), p. 59.

11. Howard Thurman, *Deep River* (Richmond, Ind.: Friends United Press, 1975), pp. 57–58.

12. Howard Thurman, *The Negro Spiritual Speaks of Life and Death* (Richmond, Ind.: Friends United Press, 1975), p. 38.

13. DuBois, *Souls of Black Folk*, p. 206.

14. Washington, *Testament of Hope*, p. 247.

15. Mays, *Disturbed about Man*, p. 38.

16. Ibid., p. 139.

17. Tutu, *Hope and Suffering*, p. 117.

18. Benjamin E. Mays, *Lord, the People Have Driven Me On* (New York: Vantage Press, 1981), p. 71.

19. Washington, *Testament of Hope*, p. 508.

20. Ibid., p. 286.

21. Oscar Romero, *Voice of the Voiceless: The Four Pastoral Letters and Other Statements* (Maryknoll, N.Y.: Orbis Books, 1985), p. 51.

22. Cedric Mayson, *A Certain Sound: The Struggle for Liberation in Southern Africa* (Maryknoll, N.Y.: Orbis Books, 1985), p. 69.

23. Howard Thurman, *Meditations of the Heart* (Richmond, Ind.: Friends United Press, 1976), p. 206.

24. Washington, *Testament of Hope*, p. 226.

25. Thurman, *Deep Is the Hunger*, p. 95.

26. Langston Hughes and Arna Bontemps, eds., *The Book of Negro Folklore* (New York: Dodd, Mead, 1983), pp. 537–38.

CHAPTER EIGHT

1. *Washington Post*, Feb. 19, 1989.

2. For a discussion on some of these themes from a Caribbean theological perspective, see my *Mission for Caribbean Change*.

3. Gabriel Fackre, *The Christian Story* (Grand Rapids, Mich.: Eerdmans, 1978), p. 28.

4. Ibid.

5. See David J. S. Clines, "Story and Poem: The Old Testament as Literature and as Scripture," *Interpretation* (Richmond, Virginia: Union Theological Seminary), Apr. 1980, pp. 115–127.

6. See Lonnie D. Kliever, *The Shattered Spectrum* (Atlanta: John Knox Press, 1981), p. 182.

7. See a relevant essay by R. C. Culley in *Vetus Testamentum* 13, no. 2 (1963).

8. Daniel F. Martensen, "Lutheranism and the Ecumenical Challenge," *Lutheran Theological Seminary Bulletin* 63, no. 1, (1983): 53.

9. See *Ebony* 33, no. 2 (Dec. 1977): 76.

CHAPTER NINE

1. Bakole Wa Ilunga, *Paths of Liberation: A Third World Spirituality* (Maryknoll, N.Y.: Orbis Books, 1984), p. 140.

2. Williams, *From Columbus to Castro*, p. 325.

3. Eric Williams, "Massa Day Done," in Lowenthal and Comitas, *Aftermath of Sovereignty*, p. 9. This was the speech delivered by Williams in Port-of-Spain, Trinidad, in 1961, to assert the political implications of sovereignty and emancipation for Caribbean people in general and Trinidadians in particular. It remains a masterpiece of emancipatory oratory in the annals of Caribbean history.

4. See *Caribbean Contact*, Vol. 16, no. 6 (Nov. 1988): 2.

5. Eugenia Charles, "Isolationism vs One-ness: The Continuing Validity of the Monroe Doctrine," *Caribbean Affairs* 1, no. 2 (Apr.–June, 1988): 154.

6. Romero, *Voice of the Voiceless*, p. 184.

7. Thomas, *Rise of the Authoritarian State*, p. 136.

8. See *Caribbean Contact*, Vol. 16, no. 5 (Oct. 1988): 3.

9. Alleyne, "A Linguistic Perspective," p. 21.

10. Ibid.

11. Walter Rodney, *The Groundings with My Brothers* (London: Bogle-L'Ouverture, 1971), p. 39.

12. Neville V. Nicholls, "A Time of Hope, a Period of Change: The Challenge of the Future," Address to Second General Conference of the Caribbean Association of Media Workers, Barbados, Dec. 3, 1988. Mimeo.

13. Paulo Freire, *Pedagogy of the Oppressed*, trans. Myra Bergman Ramos (London: Penguin Books, 1970), p. 131.

14. See *Caribbean Contact*, Vol. 15, no. 8 (Jan. 1988): 8.

15. Evan Jones, "The Song of the Banana Man," in Howard Sergeant, ed., *New Voices of the Commonwealth* (London: Evans Brothers, 1968), p. 74.

16. C.L.R. James, "The Case for West-Indian Self-Government," in *The Future and the Present: Selected Writings of C.L.R. James* (London: Allison & Busby, 1980), p. 40.

17. These are words from the hymn of the CCC, "The Right Hand of God." For the full version, see Kortright Davis, *Mission for Caribbean Change*, p. 204.

A SELECT BIBLIOGRAPHY

BOOKS AND ARTICLES

Abrahams, Roger D., ed. *Afro-American Folk Tales*. New York: Pantheon Books, 1985.

Alleyne, Mervyn C. "A Lingustic Perspective on the Caribbean." In *Focus Caribbean*. Washington, D.C.: Woodrow Wilson International Center, 1985.

Appiah, Peggy. *The Children of Ananse*. London: Evans Brothers, 1978.

Augier, F. R. and Shirley Gordon. *Sources of West Indian History*. London: Longmans, 1960.

Augier, F. R., Shirley Gordon, Douglas Hall, and Mary Reckord. *The Making of the West Indies*. London: Longmans, 1960.

Augustus, Earl. *The Spiritual Quest of Antillean Man*. Trinidad: Scope Caribbean, 1977.

Ayearst, Morley. *The British West Indies: The Search for Self-Government*. New York: New York University Press, 1960.

Barrett, Leonard E. *The Rastafarians: A Study in Messianic Cultism in Jamaica*. Rio Piedras: Institute of Caribbean Studies, University of Puerto Rico, 1968.

Barrett, Leonard E. *Soul Force: African Heritage In Afro-American Religion*. New York: Doubleday (Anchor Press), 1974.

Barry, T., B. Wood, and D. Preusch. *The Other Side of Paradise: Foreign Control in the Caribbean*. New York: Grove Press, 1984.

Bascom, William R. *Shango in the New World*. Austin: African and Afro-American Research Institute, University of Texas, 1972.

Bastide, Roger. *African Civilizations in the New World*. New York: Harper & Row, 1971.

Beckford, George. *Persistent Poverty*. London: Oxford University Press, 1972.

Bilby, Kenneth M. *The Caribbean as a Musical Region*. Washington, D.C.: Woodrow Wilson International Center, 1985.

Brathwaite, Edward. *The Development of Creole Society in Jamaica 1770-1820*. London: Oxford University Press, 1971.

Brathwaite, Edward. *The Arrivants*. London: Oxford University Press, 1973.

Brathwaite, Edward. *Our Ancestral Heritage: A Bibliography of the Roots of Culture in the English Speaking Caribbean*. Kingston, Jamaica: Carifesta Committee, 1976.

Brathwaite, Joan, ed. *Handbook of the Churches in the Caribbean*. Bridgetown, Barbados: Christian Action for Development in the Caribbean, 1973.

Brown, Aggrey and Carl Stone. *Essays on Power and Change in Jamaica*. Kingston: Jamaica Publishing House, 1977.

Burkett, R. K. and R. Newman, eds., *Black Apostles*. Boston: G. K. Hall, 1978.

CADEC. *Called To Be*. Barbados: Christian Action for Development in the Caribbean, 1972.

Callender, Jean A. *African Survivals in Caribbean Religion: A Select Bibliography.* Cave Hill, Barbados: University of the West Indies, 1986.

Caribbean Conference of Churches. *Christians in Dialogue and Joint Action.* Bridgetown: Barbados, Caribbean Conference of Churches, 1976.

Caribbean Conference of Churches. *Theological Education in a New Caribbean.* Barbados: CEDAR Press, 1976.

Caribbean Conference of Churches. *Fashion Me a People.* Kingston, Jamaica: Caribbean Conference of Churches 1981.

Caribbean Conference of Churches. *Peace: A Challenge to the Caribbean.* Barbados: CEDAR Press, 1982.

Comitas, Lambros. *The Complete Caribbeana, 1900-1975.* Millwood, N. Y.: K.T.O. Press, 1977.

Cone, James H. *God of the Oppressed.* London: Society for the Promotion of Christian Knowledge, 1977.

Coupland, Reginald. *The British Anti-Slavery Movement.* London: Frank Cass, 1964.

Courlander, Harold. *The Drum and the Hoe: Life and Lore of the Haitian People.* Berkeley: University of California Press, 1960.

Courlander, Harold and Remy Bastien. *Religion and Politics in Haiti.* Washington, D.C.: Institute for Cross-Cultural Research, 1966.

Crahan, Margaret E., and Franklin W. Knight, eds., *Africa and the Caribbean: The Legacies of a Link.* Baltimore: Johns Hopkins University Press, 1979.

Craig, Susan, ed. *Contemporary Caribbean: A Sociological Reader* (vols. I and II). Trinidad & Tobago: Port-of-Spain, 1981, 1982.

Cronon, Edmund David. *Black Moses: The Story of Marcus Garvey and the Universal Negro Improvement Association.* Madison: University of Wisconsin Press, 1964.

Cross, Malcolm, ed. *West Indian Social Problems.* Trinidad: Columbus Publishers, 1976.

Cuthbert, Robert W. M. *Ecumenism and Development.* Bridgetown, Barbados: Caribbean Conference of Churches, 1986.

Da Breo D. Sinclair. *The Grenada Revolution.* St. Lucia: Management Advertising and Publicity Services, 1979.

Dathorne, O. R., ed. *Caribbean Narrative.* London: Hiennemann, 1966.

Davis, David Brion. *Slavery and Human Progress.* New York: Oxford University Press, 1984.

Davis, Edmund. *Roots and Blossoms.* Barbados: CEDAR Press, 1977.

Davis, Edmund. *Courage and Commitment.* Kingston, Jamaica: UWI Publishers Association, 1988.

Davis, Kortright, ed. *Moving into Freedom.* Barbados: CEDAR Press, 1977.

Davis, Kortright. *Mission for Caribbean Change.* Frankfurt: Peter Lang, 1982.

Davis, Kortright. *Cross and Crown in Barbados.* Frankfurt: Peter Lang, 1983.

Dubois, W. E. B. *The Souls of Black Folk.* New York: Fawcett, 1961.

Erisman, M., ed. *The Caribbean Challenge: US Policy in a Volatile Region.* Boulder, Colo.: Westview Press, 1984.

Erskine, Noel Leo. *Decolonizing Theology: A Caribbean Perspective.* Maryknoll, N.Y.: Orbis Books, 1981.

Fabella, Virginia, and Sergio Torres, eds. *Irruption of the Third World: Challenge to Theology.* Maryknoll, N.Y.: Orbis Books, 1983.

Fabella, Virginia, and Sergio Torres, eds., *Doing Theology in a Divided World.* Maryknoll, N.Y.: Orbis Books, 1985.

Fackre, Gabriel. *The Christian Story.* Grand Rapids, Michigan: Eerdmans, 1978.

Figueroa, John, ed. *Caribbean Voices.* London: Evans Brothers, 1971.

Freire, Paulo. *Pedagogy of the Oppressed*, trans. Myra Bergman Ramos. London: Penguin Books, 1972.

Freire, Paulo. *Cultural Action for Freedom.* London: Penguin Books, 1970.

Gates, Brian, ed. *Afro-Caribbean Religions.* London: Ward Lock Educational, 1980.

Gilmore, John. *The Toiler of the Sees.* Barbados: Barbados National Trust, 1987.

Girvan, N. *Corporate Imperialism, Conflict and Expropriation.* New York: Monthly Review Press, 1976.

Girvan, N., and Owen Jefferson, eds. *Readings in the Political Economy of the Caribbean.* Trinidad: New World Group, 1971.

Glazier, Stephen D., ed. *Perspectives on Pentecostalism: Case Studies from the Caribbean and Latin America.* Washington, D.C.: University Press of America, 1980.

Glazier, Stephen D. *Marchin' the Pilgrims Home: Leadership and Decision-Making in an Afro-Caribbean Faith.* Westport, Conn.: Greenwood Press, 1983.

Goveia, Elsa. *Slave Society in the British Leeward Islands at the End of the 18th Century.* New Haven, Conn.: Yale University Press, 1965.

Hamid, Idris, ed. *Troubling of the Waters.* Trinidad: San Fernando, 1973.

Hamid, Idris, ed. *Out of the Depths.* Trinidad: St. Andrew's Theological College, 1977.

Hamid, Idris. *A History of the Presbyterian Church in Trinidad, 1868-1968.* Trinidad: St. Andrew's Theological College, 1980.

Haniff, Yussuff, ed. *Speeches by Errol Barrow*, London: Hansib, 1987.

Hawkins, Irene. *The Changing Face of the Caribbean.* Barbados: CEDAR Press, 1976.

Haynes, Lilith M., ed. *Fambli.* New York: Planned Parenthood Program, Church World Service, 1972.

Henney, Jeannette H. *"Mourning": A Religious Ritual among the Spiritual Baptists of St. Vincent: An Experience in Sensory Deprivation.* Columbus: Department of Anthropolgy, Ohio State University, 1968.

Henry, Paget. *Peripheral Capitalism and Underdevelopment in Antigua.* New Brunswick, New Jersey: Transaction Books, 1985.

Herskovits, Frances S., ed. *The New World Negro: Selected Papers in Afro-American Studies.* Bloomington: Indiana University Press, 1966.

Herskovits, Melville J. *The Myth of the Negro Past.* Boston: Beacon Press, 1958.

Herskovits, Melville J. *Life in a Haitian Valley.* New York: Doubleday, 1971.

Hill, Clifford. *Black Churches: West Indian and African Sects in Britain.* London: British Council of Churches, 1971.

Horowitz, Michael M., ed. *Peoples and Cultures of the Caribbean: an Anthropological Reader.* New York: Natural History Press, 1971.

Hughes, Langston, and Arna Bontemps, eds. *The Book of Negro Folklore.* New York: Dodd, Mead, 1983.

Idowu, E. Bolaji. *African Traditional Religion.* London: SCM Press, 1977.

Illich, Ivan D. *Celebration of Awareness.* London: Penguin Books, 1973.

Ilunga, Bakole Wa. *Paths of Liberation: A Third World Spirituality*. Maryknoll, N.Y.: Orbis Books, 1984.

Irwin, Graham W. *Africans Abroad*. New York: Columbia University Press, 1977.

James, C. L. R. *Beyond a Boundary*. London: Hutchinson, 1963.

James, C. L. R. *The Black Jacobins* (2nd ed.). New York: Vintage Books, 1963.

James, C. L. R. *The Future and the Present: Selected Writings of C. L. R. James*. London: Allison and Busby, 1980.

Jones, S. B. *Annals of Anguilla, 1650-1923*. Belfast: Christian Journals Ltd., 1976.

Kasper, Walter. *Jesus the Christ*. New York: Paulist Press, 1977.

Kliever, Lonnie D. *The Shattered Spectrum*. Altanta: John Knox Press, 1981.

Lamming, G. *Natives of My Person*. London: Pan Books, 1974.

Lamming, G., ed. *Reader in Caribbean Development*. Kingston, Jamaica: Department of Economics, University West Indies, 1987.

Lewis, Gordon K. *The Growth of the Modern West Indies*. New York: Monthly Review Press, 1968.

Lewis, Gordon K. *Main Currents in Caribbean Thought*. Baltimore: Johns Hopkins University Press, 1983.

Lewis, Kingsley. *The Moravian Mission in Barbados, 1816-1886*. Frankfurt: Peter Lang, 1985.

Lowenthal, David. *West Indian Societies*. London: Oxford University Press, 1972.

Lowenthal, David, and Lambros Comitas, eds. Volumes subtitled *West Indian Perspectives Work and Family Life; Slaves, Free Men, Citizens; Consequences of Class and Color; The Aftermath of Sovereignty*. New York: Doubleday (Anchor Books), 1973.

MacPherson, John. *Caribbean Lands: A Geography of the West Indies*. London: Longmans, 1963.

Manickam, S. *Slavery in the Tamil Country*. Madras: Christian Literature Society, 1982.

Manley, Michael. *The Politics of Change: A Jamaican Testament*. London: Andre Deutsch, 1974.

Manley, Michael. *Jamaica: Struggle in the Periphery*. London: Third World Media, 1982.

Manley, Michael. *Up the Down Escalator*. Washington, D.C.: Howard University Press, 1987.

Marcus, B., and M. Taber, eds. *Maurice Bishop Speaks: The Grenada Revolution, 1979-1983*. New York: Pathfinder Press, 1983.

Mason, Philip. *Patterns of Dominance*. London: Oxford University Press, 1970.

Matthews, Dom Basil. *Crisis Of The West Indian Family: A Sample Study*. Jamaica: University College of the West Indies, 1953.

Mays, Benjamin E. *Disturbed about Man*. Richmond, Virginia: John Knox Press, 1969.

Mays, Benjamin E. *Born To Rebel: An Autobiography*. Athens: University of Georgia Press, 1987.

Mayson, Cedric. *A Certain Sound: The Struggle for Liberation in Southern Africa*. Maryknoll, N.Y.: Orbis Books, 1985.

Mazrui, Ali A. *World Culture and the Black Experience*. Seattle: University of Washington Press, 1974.

Mazrui, Ali A. *The Africans: A Triple Heritage*. Boston: Little, Brown, 1986.

Metraux, Alfred. *Haiti: Black Peasants and Voodoo*, trans. Peter Lengyel. New York: Universe Books, 1960.

Metraux, Alfred. *Voodoo in Haiti*, trans. Hugo Charteris. New York: Schocken Books, 1972.

Michner, James. *The Caribbean*. New York: Random House, 1989.

Mintz, Sidney. *Caribbean Transformation*. Chicago: Aldine, 1974.

Mitchell, David, ed. *With Eyes Wide Open*. Bridgetown, Barbados: Christian Action for Development in the Caribbean, 1973.

Mitchell, David, ed. *New Mission for a New People*. New York: Friendship Press, 1977.

Mitchinson, John. *Can the Dry Bones Live?* London: Society For the Propagation of the Gospel, 1883.

Mulrain, George. *Theology in Folk Culture: The Theological Significance of Haitian Folk Religion*. Frankfurt: Peter Lang, 1984.

Naipaul, V. S. *The Middle Passage*. London: Andre Deutsch, 1962.

Naipaul, V. S. *Mimic Men*. London: Andre Deutsch, 1967.

Nettleford, Rex M. *Identity, Race and Protest in Jamaica*. New York: Morrow, 1972.

Neymeyer, Robert. *Bibliography of the English-Speaking Caribbean*, Vol. 1. Parkersburg, Iowa: 1979.

Nodal, Roberto. *A Tentative Bibliography of Caribbean Folklore*. Milwaukee: University Of Wisconsin, Department of Afro-American Studies, 1975.

Nunley, John W., and Judith Bettelheim, eds. *Caribbean Festival Arts*. Seattle: University of Washington Press, 1988.

Ortiz, Fernandez Fernando. *Los Bailes y el teatro de los negros en el folklore de Cuba*. Havana: Ministerio de Educacion, Direccion de Cultura, 1951.

Ortiz, Fernandez Fernando. *Historia de una pelea cubana contra los demonios*. Havana: Editorial de Ciencias Sociales, 1975.

Owens, Joseph. *Dread: The Rastafarians of Jamaica*. Kingston, Jamaica: Sangster, 1976.

Palmer, Ransford W. *Caribbean Dependence on the United States Economy*. New York: Praeger, 1979.

Parry, J. H. and P. Sherlock. *A Short History of the West Indies*. London: Macmillan, 1971.

Patterson, Orlando. *The Children of Sisyphus*. London: New Authors, 1964

Patterson, Orlando. *An Absence of Ruins*. London: Hutchinson, 1967.

Patterson, Orlando. *The Sociology of Slavery*. London: McGibbon and Kee, 1967.

Payne, Ernest A. *Freedom in Jamaica: Some Chapters in the Story of the Baptist Missionary Society* (2nd ed.). London: Carey Press, 1946.

Pobee, John S. *Toward an African Theology*. Nashville: Abingdon Press, 1979.

Price-Mars, Jean. *So Spoke the Uncle*, trans. and intro. Magdaline W. Shannon. Washington, D.C.: Three Continents Press, 1983.

Robinson, Gnana, and Dhyanchand Carr. *Solidarity of the Oppressed*. Madurai, India: TTS Publications, 1981.

Rodney, Walter. *The Groundings with My Brothers*. London: Bogle-L'Ouverture, 1971.

Rodney, Walter. *A History of the Guyanese Working People, 1881-1905*. London: Heinemann Educational Books, 1981.

Romero, Oscar. *Voice of the Voiceless: The Four Pastoral Letters and Other Statements*. Maryknoll, N.Y.: Orbis Books, 1985.

Salkey, Andrew. *Caribbean Essays*. London: Evans Brothers, 1973.

Salkey, Andrew, ed. *West Indian Stories*. London: Faber & Faber, 1979.

Salkey, Andrew. *Caribbean Folk Tales and Legends*. London: Bogle-L'Ouverture, 1980.

Sergeant, Howard, ed. *New Voices of the Commonwealth*. London: Evans Brothers, 1968.

Sernett, Milton, ed. *Afro-American Religious History: A Documentary Witness*. Duham, N.C.: Duke University Press, 1985.

Seymour, A. J., ed. *New Writing in the Caribbean*. Guyana: Guyana Lithographic Co., 1972.

Sherlock, Philip M. *West Indian Folk Tales*. London: Oxford University Press, 1966.

Simpson, George Eaton. *Religious Cults of the Caribbean: Trinidad, Jamaica, and Haiti*. Rio Piedras: University of Puerto Rico, 1970.

Simpson, George Eaton. *Black Religions in the New World*. New York: Columbia University Press, 1978.

Sitkoff, Harvard. *The Struggle for Black Equality, 1954-1980*. New York: Hill & Wang, 1982.

Smith, Ashley. *Real Roots and Potted Plants*. Mandeville, Jamaica: Eureka Press, 1984.

Smith, M. G. *The Plural Society in the British West Indies*. Berkeley: University of California Press, 1965.

Smith, R. T. *The Negro Family in British Guiana*. London: Routledge & Kegan Paul, 1956.

Stroup, George W. *The Promise of Narrative Theology*. Atlanta: John Knox Press, 1981.

Sunshine, Catherine A. *The Caribbean Survival, Struggle and Sovereignty*. Washington, D.C.: Ecumenical Program for Interamerican Communication and Action, 1985.

Thomas, Clive Y. *Dependence and Transformation*. New York: Monthly Review Press, 1974.

Thomas, Clive Y. *Plantation, Peasants and State*. Los Angeles: University of California, 1984.

Thomas, Clive Y. *The Rise of the Authoritarian State in Peripheral Societies*. New York: Monthly Review Press, 1984.

Thomas, Clive Y. *The Poor and the Powerless*. New York: Monthly Review Press, 1987.

Thome, James A., and J. Horace Kimball. *Emancipation in the West Indies*. New York: American Anti-Slavery Society, 1838.

Thurman, Howard. *Deep Is the Hunger*. Richmond, Ind.: Friends United Press, 1973.

Thurman, Howard. *Deep River*. Richmond, Ind.: Friends United Press, 1975.

Thurman, Howard. *The Negro Spiritual Speaks of Life and Death*. Richmond, Ind.: Friends United Press, 1975.

Thurman, Howard. *Meditations of the Heart*. Richmond, Ind.: Friends United Press, 1976.

Torres, Sergio, and Virginia Fabella, eds. *The Emergent Gospel: Theology from the*

A SELECT BIBLIOGRAPHY   157

Underside of History. Maryknoll, N.Y: Orbis Books, 1978.

Trompf, G. W., ed. *The Gospel Is not Western: Black Theologies from the South Pacific.* Maryknoll, N.Y.: Orbis Books, 1987.

Tutu, Desmond. *Hope and Suffering.* Grand Rapids, Mich.: Eerdmans, 1984.

Wallace, Elizabeth. *The British Caribbean from the Decline of Colonialism to the End of Federation.* Toronto: University of Toronto Press, 1977.

Washington, James M., ed. *A Testament of Hope.* San Francisco: Harper & Row, 1986.

Watty, William. *From Shore to Shore.* Kingston, Jamaica: 1981.

Williams, Eric. *Capitalism and Slavery.* Chapel Hill: University of North Carolina Press, 1944.

Williams, Eric. *The Negro in the Caribbean.* New York: Haskell House, 1970.

Williams, Eric. *British Historians and the West Indies.* London: Andre Deutsch, 1972.

Williams, Eric. *From Columbus to Castro: The History of the Caribbean, 1492-1969.* London: Andre Deutsch, 1978.

Wilmore, Gayraud S. *Black Religion and Black Radicalism: An Interpretation of the Religious History of Afro-American People* (2nd Ed.). Maryknoll, N.Y.: Orbis Books, 1983.

Wilmore, Gayraud S., and James H. Cone, eds. *Black Theology: A Documentary History, 1966-1979.* Maryknoll, N.Y.: Orbis Books, 1979.

Witvliet, Theo. *A Place in the Sun: An Introduction to Liberation Theology in the Third World.* Maryknoll, N.Y.: Orbis Books, 1985.

Worrell, Delisle. *Caribbean Economy in the Nineties: Challenge and Response.* Bridgetown, Barbados: Central Bank of Barbados, 1986.

Young, Henry James, ed. *God and Human Freedom.* Richmond, Ind.: Friends United Press, 1983.

JOURNALS AND SPECIAL REPORTS

Caribbean Affairs, Imprint Caribbean Ltd., Trinidad

Caribbean Conference of Churches, Bridgetown, Barbados (various reports and studies on regional issues)

Caribbean Contact, Caribbean Conference of Churches, Bridgetown, Barbados

Caribbean Development Bank, Bridgetown, Barbados (annual presidential statements)

Caribbean Group for Social and Religious Studies, Codrington College, Barbados

Caribbean Journal of Religious Studies, Kingston, Jamaica

Caribbean Quarterly, University of the West Indies, Kingston, Jamaica

Caribbean Studies, Institute of Caribbean Studies, University of Puerto Rico, Rio Piedras

Social and Economic Studies, University of the West Indies, Kingston, Jamaica

INDEX

Absenteeism, 3, 4
Adams, Grantley, 27, 132
Adams, Tom, 133
Africa: effects of slave trade on, 57-58
African Association Conference, the, 63
African consciousness, 56
African soul, the, 50-67; Caribbean emancipation and, 63-67; Caribbean religion and, 62-67; communalism, 59; concepts of, 58-59; definition of, 51; E. Bolaji Idowu on, 58; time and, 59
African spirituality: W.E.B. Du Bois on, 55
Afro-Caribbean, the, 7
Agriculture: tourism and, 20-21
Alienation, cultural. *See* Cultural alienation
Alleyne, Mervin: on language, 136-37
Anglican Church, Caribbean, 1
Anglo-Caribbean, the, 7
Anguilla: independence and, 19
Antigua, x; European attempts to settle, 5; Henry Paget on, 26; tourism and, 26 Antilles Episcopal Conference of the Roman Catholic Church: Bishops' pastoral letter, *Justice and Peace in the Caribbean*, 100; *True Freedom and Development in the Caribbean*, 100
Arawaks, the, 5
Bahamas: the Arawaks and, 5
Barbados, x, 1
Barrett, Leonard, 52
Barrow, Errol, 132; on Caribbean-US ties, 19-20
Bascom, William, 52
Bastide, Roger, 52; on Caribbean religion, 54

Beckford, George, 18; on dependence, 36
Belize, 3
Bertley, Leo: on the Ooni of Ife, 56-57
Best, Lloyd, 18
Bethune, Mary McCloud, 128
Bible, the, 96
Biblical tradition, 110
Bilby, Kenneth: *The Caribbean as a Musical Region*, 43
Bird, Vere Cornwall, 27, 132
Bishop, Maurice, 132, 133
Black Power movement, the, 63
Black Story, the, 117-29; cultural exchanges and, 129; emancipatory connections and, 126-29; heroes and, 128-29; history and, 128; religious songs and, 127-28; storytelling and, 127; theological framework of, 120-21; theology, 119-21
Black theology, 105
Blyden, Edward Wilmot: on blacks, 62-63
Bowman, Gail, 106
Bradshaw, Robert, 132
Brain drain: emigration and, 34
Branch, Bishop: on African religions, 61
Brathwaite, Edward, 18, 63
Bree, Bishop: on black religions, 60-61
Britain: land ownership and, 3
British Virgin Islands, 19
Butler, Uriah, 132
Buxton, Sir Thomas: on emancipation, 131
Callendar, Jean, 52
Calypso, 43; "calypso mentality," 22; Keith Warner on, 45; origins of, 44; social function of, 45

Canada: Caribbean affairs and, 19

Caribbean as a Musical Region, The (Bilby), 43

Caribbean Christian Living Series, The, 101

Caribbean Conference of Churches, the, 15-16, 96, 141; constitution of, 47; on development, 99-100; ecumenism and, 101; *Fashion Me a People,* 101; major goals, 48; on peace, 98-99; *Peace: A Challenge to the Caribbean,* 99; social change and, 47-48; theological education and, 92; theological reflection and, 98; "Theological Reflection and Conscientization," 102

Caribbean Contact, 98, 135

Caribbean context, ix, x, xi

Caribbean emancipation, ix-x

Caribbean emancipatory theology, xi

Caribbean faith, x

Caribbean people, 5-7; ability to thrive, ix; hope, ix; struggle for emancipation, 6; struggle for power, 6

"Caribbean religion," 51

Caribbean social history, 17-21

"Caribbean theology," 94-95

Caribbean transition, x

Caribs, the, 5

CARICOM, 136

Carmichael, Stokely, 127

Carnival, 40-45; benefits of, 41-42; music of, 42-43

Carr, Andrew, 52

Castro, Fidel, 132

Change, Caribbean, 12-28; revolutionary approaches to, 37-38; signals for, 92-94; social, 45-49; theological priorities for, 10

Charles, Eugenia, 133

Charles, Sydney: on development, 99-100

Chevannes, Barry, 52

Chisholm, Shirley, 126

Christian Action for Development in the Caribbean, 99

Christian Church. *See* Church, Christian

Christian education: Caribbean theo-

logical praxis and, 101-102

Christianity, Caribbean: African religions and, 60-62; discrimination and, 61; history of, 53-54

Christian Story, The (Fackre), 122

Christmas Masquerade, 41

Christology, Caribbean, 82

Chrysostom, John: on the body, 108

Church, Christian: ecumenical movements and, 47; emancipation and, 140-41; emancipatory theology and, 103-106, 110; history of, 45-49, 72-73; lower classes and, 46; mission of, 88; sociocultural revolution and, 46-47

Churches, Haitian, 15

Claguaramas, Trinidad, 47

Classism, Caribbean, 25-26

Clergy, Caribbean: education of, 92

Codrington, Christopher, 1

Codrington College, 1

Colonialism: Caribbean, 17; effects on Africa, 57-58; internal, 37; racism and, 24

Colonization: and the plantation, 18-19

Columbus, Christopher: on the Caribs, 5

Communalism: the African soul and, 59

Communication, modern, 21

Community, spirit of, 83-84

Community of the Resurrection, the, 1

Confederation of African Associations of Trinidad and Tobago, the, 56

Congregational nurture, 91

Consistency, moral, 82

Context, Caribbean, ix, x, xi, 2

Contextual priorities for freedom, 9

Corruption, political, 39, 97

Courage, 82-83

Courage and Commitment (Davis), 94

Courlander, Harold, 52

Craig, Susan: on Caribbean society, 17-18

Creole language, 21

"Creole Society" theory, 18

Creolization, Caribbean, 6, 21, 23

Crises, Caribbean, 30-40

Crises, European, 30-31

Crop-Over, 41